Reading, Writing & Language

INSIDE

LANGUAGE · LITERACY · CONTENT

PROGRAM AUTHORS

Deborah J. Short

Josefina Villamil Tinajero

NATIONAL GEOGRAPHIC LEARNING | CENGAGE Learning

Acknowledgments

Grateful acknowledgment is given to the authors, artists, photographers, museums, publishers, and agents for permission to reprint copyrighted material. Every effort has been made to secure the appropriate permission. If any omissions have been made or if corrections are required, please contact the Publisher.

Photographic Credits

Cover (front): Leafcutter Bee on Fishhook Barrel Cactus Blossom, Sonoran Desert, Arizona, USA, John Cancalosi. Photograph © John Cancalosi/Peter Arnold/Getty Images. **Cover (back):** Fishhook Barrel Cactus, Sonoran Desert, Arizona, USA, Gerald C. Kelley. Photograph © Gerald C. Kelley/Science Source.

Acknowledgments continue on page 367.

For product information and technology assistance, contact us at **Cengage Learning Customer & Sales Support, 888-915-3276**

For permission to use material from this text or product, submit all requests online at **www.cengage.com/permissions** Further permissions questions can be emailed to **permissionrequest@cengage.com**

National Geographic Learning | Cengage Learning
1 Lower Ragsdale Drive
Building 1, Suite 200
Monterey, CA 93940

Cengage Learning is a leading provider of customized learning solutions with office locations around the globe, including Singapore, the United Kingdom, Australia, Mexico, Brazil, and Japan. Locate your local office at **www.cengage.com/global**.

Visit National Geographic Learning online at **ngl.cengage.com**
Visit our corporate website at **www.cengage.com**

Printer: RR Donnelley, Willard, OH

ISBN: 9781285439426

Printed in the United States of America

14 15 16 17 18 19 20 21 22

10 9 8 7 6 5 4 3 2

Contents at a Glance

Unit	Vocabulary	Language & Grammar		Reading		Writing
		Function	**Grammar**	**Phonics/Decoding**	**Comprehension**	
1	Personal Information Communication Words	Exchange Greetings and Good-byes Give Information Use the Telephone	Pronouns Present Tense Verbs (*am, are, is*) Statements and Exclamations	Short *a*, Short *o*	Sequence	E-mail
2	Colors, Shapes, and Sizes Foods	Express Likes Describe	Action Verbs Negative Sentences	Short *i*, Short *u*, *ch*, and *tch*	Steps in a Process Classify	How-To Card
3	Tools and Careers	Give Information Ask and Answer Questions	Present Tense Verbs Yes-or-No Questions *Who? What? Where?* and *When?* Questions	Short *e*, *sh*, *ck*, and Double Consonants	Details	Interview
4	Cardinal Numbers Ordinal Numbers	Ask Questions Give Information Express Needs	Negative Sentences Contractions with *Not*	Blends and Digraphs	Problems and Solutions Details	Fact Sheet
5	Location Words Neighborhood Words	Ask for and Give Information	Regular Past Tense Verbs Statements with *There is* and *There are* Contractions	Word Patterns and Multisyllabic Words	Details	Journal Page
6	Family Rooms in a House Household Objects	Give Information Ask and Answer Questions	Present Tense Verbs (*have* and *has*) Plural Nouns	Long Vowels (*a, i, o, u*)	Main Idea and Details	Family Description
7	Landforms and Transportation Weather and Clothing	Give and Carry Out Commands Describe Places Give Information	Verbs: *Can* Capitalization: Proper Nouns	Long Vowels (*ai, ay; ee, ea; oa, ow*)	Classify	Travel Guide
8	Feelings	Describe Actions Express Feelings	Past Tense Verbs: *Was* and *Were* Negative Sentences Contractions with *Not* Possessive Nouns	Verb Ending (*-ed*)	Cause and Effect	Memory Story
9	Country Words	Ask and Answer Questions Describe People	Present Progressive Verbs Phrases with *Like to* and *Want to*	Verb Ending (*-ing*)	Classify	Blog

Reviewers

We gratefully acknowledge the many contributions of the following dedicated educators in creating a program that is not only pedagogically sound, but also appealing to and motivating for middle school students.

Teacher Reviewers

Idalia Apodaca
English Language Development Teacher
Shaw Middle School
Spokane, WA

Pat E. Baggett-Hopkins
Area Reading Coach
Chicago Public Schools
Chicago, IL

Judy Chin
ESOL Teacher
Arvida Middle School
Miami, FL

Sonia Flores
Teacher Supporter
Los Angeles Unified School District
Los Angeles, CA

Brenda Garcia
ESL Teacher
Crockett Middle School
Irving, TX

Kristine Hoffman
Teacher on Special Assignment
Newport-Mesa Unified School District
Costa Mesa, CA

Dr. Margaret R. Keefe
ELL Contact and Secondary Advocate
Martin County School District
Stuart, FL

Julianne Kosareff
Curriculum Specialist
Paramount Unified School District
Paramount, CA

Lore Levene
Coordinator of Language Arts
Community Consolidated School District 59
Arlington Heights, IL

Natalie M. Mangini
Teacher/ELD Coordinator
Serrano Intermediate School
Lake Forest, CA

Laurie Manikowski
Teacher/Trainer
Lee Mathson Middle School
San Jose, CA

Patsy Mills
Supervisor, Bilingual-ESL
Houston Independent School District
Houston, TX

Juliane M. Prager-Nored
High Point Expert
Los Angeles Unified School District
Los Angeles, CA

Patricia Previdi
ESOL Teacher
Patapsco Middle School
Ellicott City, MD

Dr. Louisa Rogers
Middle School Team Leader
Broward County Public Schools
Fort Lauderdale, FL

Rebecca Varner
ESL Teacher
Copley-Fairlawn Middle School
Copley, OH

Hailey F. Wade
ESL Teacher/Instructional Specialist
Lake Highlands Junior High
Richardson, TX

Cassandra Yorke
ESOL Coordinator
Palm Beach School District
West Palm Beach, FL

Program Authors

Deborah J. Short, Ph.D.

Dr. Deborah Short is a co-developer of the research-validated SIOP Model for sheltered instruction. She has directed quasi-experimental and experimental studies on English language learners funded by the Carnegie Corporation of New York, the Rockefeller Foundation, and the U.S. Dept. of Education. She recently chaired an expert panel on adolescent ELL literacy and coauthored a policy report: *Double the Work: Challenges and Solutions to Acquiring Language and Academic Literacy for Adolescent English Language Learners*. She has also conducted extensive research on secondary level newcomer programs. Her research articles have appeared in the *TESOL Quarterly*, the *Journal of Educational Research*, *Educational Leadership*, *Education and Urban Society*, *TESOL Journal*, *Social Education*, and *Journal of Research in Education*.

Josefina Villamil Tinajero, Ph.D.

Dr. Josefina Villamil Tinajero specializes in staff development and school-university partnership programs, and consulted with school districts in the U.S. to design ESL, bilingual, literacy, and biliteracy programs. She has served on state and national advisory committees for standards development, including the English as a New Language Advisory Panel of the National Board of Professional Teaching Standards. She is currently Professor of Education and Associate Dean at the University of Texas at El Paso, and was President of the National Association for Bilingual Education, 1997–2000.

Unit 1

Glad to Meet You!

Unit Launch 2

Language Development

Language: **Exchange Greetings and Good-byes** 4

Grammar: **Pronouns** 5

Grammar: **Present Tense Verbs** 6

Language and Vocabulary: **Give Information/Personal Information** 8

Language and Vocabulary: **Use the Telephone/Communication** 9

REALISTIC FICTION **Good News** 10

Comprehension: **Sequence**. 11

Language and Literacy

High Frequency Words. 12

Reading and Spelling: **Short a, Short o** 14

REALISTIC FICTION **New at School** 16

Comprehension: **Sequence**. 17

Written Conventions: **Statements and Exclamations** 18

Language and Content

Success in Mathematics: **Basic Operations** 19

Build Background 20

Key Vocabulary 21

PHOTO ESSAY **Many People to Meet** 22

Comprehension: **Sequence**. 30

Writing Project

E-mail 31

THEME BOOK

Unit 2

Set the Table

Unit Launch 34

Language Development

Language: **Express Likes; Describe** 36
Vocabulary: **Colors, Shapes, and Sizes** 37
Language and Vocabulary: **Describe/Foods**. 38
Grammar: **Action Verbs**. 39

CAREER
SKETCH **I Make Pictures Move!** 40
Comprehension: **Steps in a Process** 41

THEME BOOK

Language and Literacy

High Frequency Words. 42
Reading and Spelling: **Short *i*, Short *u*, *ch*, and *tch*** 44

REALISTIC
FICTION **Something Good for Lunch** 46
Comprehension: **Steps in a Process** 47
Grammar: **Negative Sentences** 48

Language and Content

Success in Science: **Classification** 49
Build Background 50
Key Vocabulary 51

FACT
BOOK **U.S. Tour of Food** 52
Comprehension: **Classify**. 60

Writing Project ✎

How-To Card. 61

Unit 3

ON THE JOB

Unit Launch 64

Language Development

Language: **Give Information**	66
Grammar: **Present Tense Verbs**	67
Grammar: **Yes-Or-No Questions**	68
Language and Vocabulary: **Ask and Answer Questions/Tools and Careers**	69
FANTASY **What Is It?**	70
Comprehension: **Details**	71

THEME BOOK

Language and Literacy

High Frequency Words	72
Reading and Spelling: **Short *e*, *sh*, *ck*, and Double Consonants**	74
REALISTIC FICTION **Let Ben Take It**	76
Comprehension: **Details**	77
Language: **Questions with *Who?*, *What?*, *Where?*, and *When?***	78

Language and Content

Success in Science and Mathematics: **Observation Log**	79
Build Background	80
Key Vocabulary	81
INFORMATIONAL TEXT **Geologists: Rock Scientists**	82
Comprehension: **Details**	90

Writing Project

Interview	91

Unit 4

NUMBERS COUNT

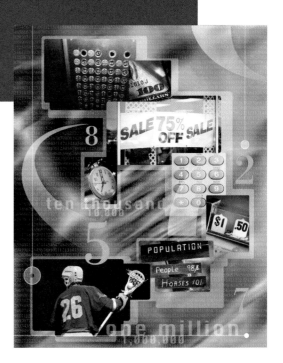

Unit Launch 94

Language Development

Language: **Ask Questions** 96

Language and Vocabulary: **Give Information/Cardinal Numbers** 97

Grammar: **Negative Sentences** 98

Language and Vocabulary: **Express Needs/Ordinal Numbers** 99

HISTORICAL FICTION   **A Year Without Rain** 100

Comprehension: **Problem and Solution** 101

Language and Literacy

High Frequency Words 102

Reading and Spelling: **Blends and Digraphs** 104

REALISTIC FICTION   **Rush!** 106

Comprehension: **Details** 107

Grammar: **Contractions with** *not* 108

Language and Content

Success in Social Science: **Tables** 109

Build Background 110

Key Vocabulary 111

PERSONAL NARRATIVE   **The Mighty Maya** 112

Comprehension: **Details** 120

Writing Project

Fact Sheet 121

THEME BOOK

Unit 5

Unit Launch **124**

Language Development	

Language: **Ask for and Give Information** 126

Language and Vocabulary: **Ask for and Give Information/Neighborhood** . . . 127

Grammar: **Regular Past Tense Verbs** 129

Grammar: Statements with *There is* and *There are* 131

REALISTIC FICTION   **More Than a Meal** 132

Comprehension: **Details** 133

Language and Literacy	

High Frequency Words 134

Reading and Spelling: **Word Patterns and Multisyllabic Words** 136

NEWSPAPER ARTICLE   **Meet Jo** 138

Comprehension: **Details** 139

Grammar: **Pronoun-Verb Contractions** 140

Language and Content	

Success in Social Science: **Maps** 141

Build Background 142

Key Vocabulary 143

TRAVEL ARTICLE   **San Francisco** 144

Comprehension: **Details** 152

Writing Project ✎	

Journal Page 153

THEME BOOK

Unit 6

Welcome Home!

Unit Launch 156

Language Development

Language: **Give Information** 158
Vocabulary: **Present Tense Verbs:** *Have* and *Has* 159
Language and Vocabulary: **Give Information/Rooms in a House** 160
Language and Vocabulary: **Ask and Answer Questions/Household Objects** . . . 161
PHOTO ESSAY **Families** 162
Comprehension: **Main Idea and Details** 163

Language and Literacy

High Frequency Words 164
Reading and Spelling: **Long Vowels:** *a, i, o, u* 166
PERSONAL NARRATIVE **When We Came to Wisconsin** 168
Comprehension: **Supporting Details** 169
Grammar: **Plural Nouns** 170

Language and Content

Success in Mathematics: **Fractions, Decimals, and Percents** 171
Build Background 172
Key Vocabulary 173
PERSONAL NARRATIVE **The Family Reunion** 174
Comprehension: **Main Idea and Details** 182

Writing Project

Description 183

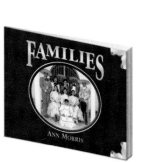

THEME BOOK

Unit 7

PACK YOUR BAGS

Unit Launch 186

Language Development

Language: **Give and Carry Out Commands** 188

Language and Vocabulary: **Describe Places/Landforms and Transportation** . . 189

Language and Vocabulary: **Give Information/Weather and Clothing**. 190

Verbs: *Can* 191

PHOTO ESSAY **Explore!** 192

Comprehension: **Classify**. 193

THEME BOOK

Language and Literacy

High Frequency Words. 194

Reading and Spelling: **Long Vowels:** *ai, ay; ee, ea; oa, ow* 196

SCIENCE ARTICLE **Explore a Wetland** 198

Comprehension: **Classify**. 199

Written Conventions: **Capitalization of Proper Nouns** 200

Language and Content

Success in Science: **Diagrams**. 201

Build Background 202

Key Vocabulary 203

EXPOSITORY NONFICTION **The Water Planet** 204

Comprehension: **Classify**. 212

Writing Project

Travel Guide 213

Unit 8

Friend to Friend

Unit Launch **216**

Language Development

Language: **Describe Actions** 218

Language and Vocabulary: **Express Feelings/Feeling Words** 219

Grammar: **Irregular Past Tense Verbs:** *Was* **and** *Were* 220

Grammar: **Negative Sentences and Contractions with** *Not* 221

JOURNAL **Friends Are Like That** 222

Comprehension: **Cause and Effect** 223

Language and Literacy

High Frequency Words. 224

Reading and Spelling: **Verb Ending:** *–ed* 226

REALISTIC FICTION **Eva's Lesson** 228

Comprehension: **Cause and Effect** 229

Written Conventions: **Apostrophes in Possessive Nouns** 230

Language and Content

Success in Mathematics: **Bar Graphs** 231

Build Background 232

Key Vocabulary 233

MAGAZINE ARTICLE **Hand in Hand** 234

Comprehension: **Cause and Effect** 242

Writing Project

Memory Story 243

THEME BOOK

Unit 9

Let's Celebrate!

Unit Launch **246**

Language Development

Language: **Ask and Answer Questions** 248

Grammar: **Present Progressive Verbs** 249

Language and Vocabulary: **Describe People/Country Words** 250

Grammar: **Phrases with** *Like To* **and** *Want To* 251

PHOTO ESSAY **Let's Dance!** 252

Comprehension: **Classify** 253

Language and Literacy

High Frequency Words 254

Reading and Spelling: **Verb Ending** *–ing* 256

INFORMATIONAL TEXT **Dance to Celebrate!** 258

Comprehension: **Details** 260

Language and Content

Success in Social Studies: **Maps** 261

Build Background 262

Key Vocabulary 263

MAGAZINE ARTICLE **Kite Festival** 264

Comprehension: **Classify** 272

Writing Project

Blog 273

THEME BOOK

Resources

Handbook

Strategies for Learning Language 278

Grammar 280–305
   Sentences 280
   Punctuation Marks 283
   Capital Letters 286
   Nouns 289
   Pronouns 294
   Adjectives 296
   Verbs 301

Handwriting 306–313
   Manuscript Hints 306
   Cursive Hints 307
   Manuscript Alphabet, Numbers, and Punctuation Marks 308
   Writing Manuscript Letters 309
   Writing Manuscript Words and Sentences 310
   Cursive Alphabet 311
   Writing Cursive Letters 312
   Writing Cursive Words and Sentences 313

The Writing Process 314–319
   Prewrite 314
   Draft and Revise 316
   Edit and Proofread 318
   Publish 319

Using Information Resources 320–333
   How to Find Information 320
   Dictionary 322
   Thesaurus 324
   Parts of a Book 326
   Atlas: Maps 328
   Globe 329
   Internet 330

Decodable Passages 334–356

Key Vocabulary Glossary 357–362

Index of Skills 363

Acknowledgments 367

Common Core State Standards Correlations . . . . CCSS 1

Genres at a Glance

LITERATURE

Fantasy
What Is It? 70

Fictional Journal
Friends Are Like That 222

Historical Fiction
A Year Without Rain 100

Realistic Fiction
Good News 10
New at School 16
Something Good for Lunch 46
Let Ben Take It 76
Rush! 106
More Than a Meal 132
Eva's Lesson 228

INFORMATIONAL TEXTS

Career Sketch
I Make Pictures Move! 40

Fact Book
U.S. Tour of Food 52

Expository Nonfiction
Geologists: Rock Scientists 82
The Water Planet 204
Dance to Celebrate! 258

Magazine Article
Hand in Hand 234
Kite Festival 264

Newspaper Article
Meet Jo 138

▲ San Francicsco is a great place to visit!

Personal Narrative
The Mighty Maya 112
When We Came to Wisconsin 168
The Family Reunion 174

Photo Essay
Many People to Meet 22
Families 162

Explore! 192
Let's Dance! 252

Science Article
Explore a Wetland 198

Travel Article
San Francisco 144

Everyone can make new friends at a new school.

I am Imran Khan.
I am from Pakistan.
I am 13 years old.
I go to Lakeside School.
I like dogs.
I also like music.

I am Lupe Valle.
I am from Nicaragua.
I am 14 years old.
I go to Lakeside School.
I like the band Loud Mouth.
I also like art.

Glad to Meet You!

Make a card about yourself.

Put your photo on one side.

Write about yourself on the other side.

Trade cards with a classmate.

Tell your class about the card.

In This Unit

▶ **Language Development**

▶ **Language and Literacy**

▶ **Language and Content**
   Mathematics

▶ **Writing Project**

Vocabulary
- Personal Information
- Communication
- Key Vocabulary

Language Functions
- Exchange Greetings and Good-byes
- Give Information
- Use the Telephone

Grammar
- Pronouns
- Present Tense Verbs

Reading
- Short *a*, Short *o*
- High Frequency Words
- Comprehension: Identify Sequence
- Text Features: Photos and Captions

Writing
- E-mail

Nice to Meet You

▶ **Language: Exchange Greetings and Good-byes**

Listen and chant. CD

Hello, Good-bye

Hello.
　Hi.
How are you?
　I am fine.
　And how are you?
I am fine.
　Are you fine, too?
　Then we are fine.
　Isn't that true?
Hey, okay!
Whatever you say!
　Good-bye.
So long.
　Have a nice day!

Pronouns

A pronoun is a word that can take the place of a noun in a sentence.

Use *I* to talk about yourself.

　I am fine.

Use *you* when you talk to someone else.

　Are you fine?

Use *we* to talk about yourself and someone else.

　We are fine.

EXPRESS YOURSELF ▶ EXCHANGE GREETINGS AND GOOD-BYES

<u>1.</u> **Work with a partner. Say the chant and act it out. Add your names to the first 2 lines.**

EXAMPLE **1.** Hello, Juan.
　　　　　 Hi, Nikolai.

<u>2.–4.</u> **Work with a partner. Take turns saying the sentences below. Fill in the blanks as you speak.**

EXAMPLE **2.** I am Nikolai.

2. I am _____.

3. You are _____.

4. We are _____.

They Are Friends

▶ **Pronouns**

> **When you talk about other people or things, use the correct pronoun.**

For a girl or a woman, use *she*. For a boy or man, use *he*.
> Today **she** is 14 years old.
> **He** is a great friend.

For a thing, use *it*.
> **It** is a birthday cake.

Use *they* to talk about more than one person or thing.
> **They** are ready to eat!

BUILD SENTENCES

Say each sentence. Add the correct pronoun.   EXAMPLE **1.** He is 12 years old.

1.

_____ is 12 years old.

2.

_____ is from Nicaragua.

3.

_____ are friends.

4.

They eat soup.
_____ is hot.

5.

They share a sandwich.
_____ is big.

6.

Here are 2 bottles of milk.
_____ are for the friends.

WRITE SENTENCES

7.–10. Write 4 sentences to tell about this picture.
Use *He is*, *She is*, *It is*, and *They are*.
EXAMPLE **7.** He is Imran.

We Are Friends

▶ Present Tense Verbs: *Am* and *Are*

Use the verbs *am* and *are* correctly.

Pronoun	Verb	Example
I	am	I **am** Ron.
you	are	You **are** Juan.
we	are	We **are** friends.

BUILD SENTENCES

Look at each picture below. Add the correct verb.
Say the new sentence.

EXAMPLE **1.** You are Anna.

1. You _____ Anna.

2. I _____ glad to meet you.

3. We _____ new to this school.

WRITE SENTENCES

4.–9. Work with a partner. Write 6 sentences.
Tell about yourself, your partner, and both
of you. Use *I am*, *You are*, and *We are*.

EXAMPLE **4.** I am 13 years old.

They Are Ready for Class

▶ **Present Tense Verbs:** *Is* and *Are*

| Use the verbs *is* and *are* correctly.

Pronoun	Verb	Example
he she it	is	He **is** on the steps. She **is** in front of the door. It **is** closed.
they	are	They **are** ready for class.

BUILD SENTENCES

Look at each sentence below. Add the correct verb.
Say the new sentence.

EXAMPLE **1.** Lupe is in P.E. class.

1. Lupe ＿＿＿ in P.E. class.
2. She wears sneakers. They ＿＿ white.
3. She wears a sweatshirt. It ＿＿ gray.

4. Now Lupe ＿＿ in the cafeteria.
5. Juan ＿＿ at the table.
6. They ＿＿ ready for lunch.

WRITE SENTENCES

<u>7.–9.</u> Where are your friends now? Write 3
sentences about them. Use *is* and *are*.

EXAMPLE **7.** Juan is in the gym.

Language Development

Fill In an Order Form

▶ **Vocabulary: Personal Information**
▶ **Language: Give Information**

Two people want to buy some things. Read each order form.

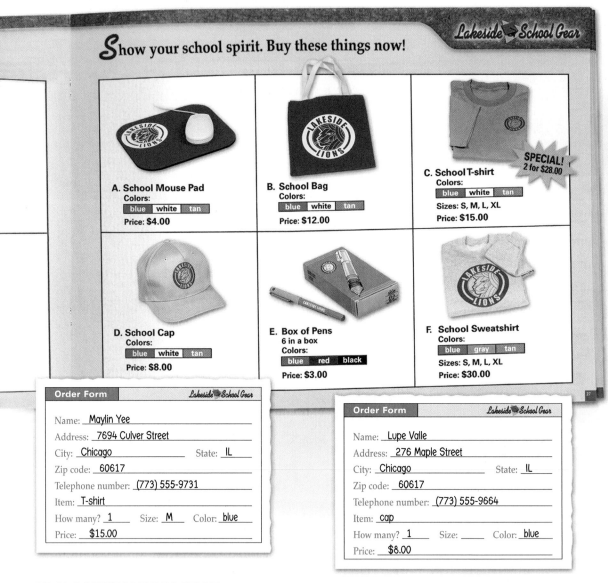

Show your school spirit. Buy these things now!

Lakeside School Gear

A. School Mouse Pad
Colors:
blue | white | tan
Price: $4.00

B. School Bag
Colors:
blue | white | tan
Price: $12.00

C. School T-shirt
Colors:
blue | white | tan
Sizes: S, M, L, XL
Price: $15.00

SPECIAL!
2 for $28.00

D. School Cap
Colors:
blue | white | tan
Price: $8.00

E. Box of Pens
6 in a box
Colors:
blue | red | black
Price: $3.00

F. School Sweatshirt
Colors:
blue | gray | tan
Sizes: S, M, L, XL
Price: $30.00

Order Form — Lakeside School Gear

Name: Maylin Yee
Address: 7694 Culver Street
City: Chicago   State: IL
Zip code: 60617
Telephone number: (773) 555-9731
Item: T-shirt
How many? 1   Size: M   Color: blue
Price: $15.00

Order Form — Lakeside School Gear

Name: Lupe Valle
Address: 276 Maple Street
City: Chicago   State: IL
Zip code: 60617
Telephone number: (773) 555-9664
Item: cap
How many? 1   Size: ___   Color: blue
Price: $8.00

ORAL LANGUAGE PRACTICE ▶ GIVE INFORMATION

<u>1.–2.</u> **Who's talking?** CD

Listen. Point to the correct order form. Tell the name of the person.

WRITTEN PRACTICE

<u>3.</u> **Choose an item from the catalog. Make an order form**
and write down your order. Tell a partner about the item you want.
Then have your partner tell about the item he or she wants.

How Can You Communicate?

▶ **Vocabulary: Communication**
▶ **Language: Use the Telephone**

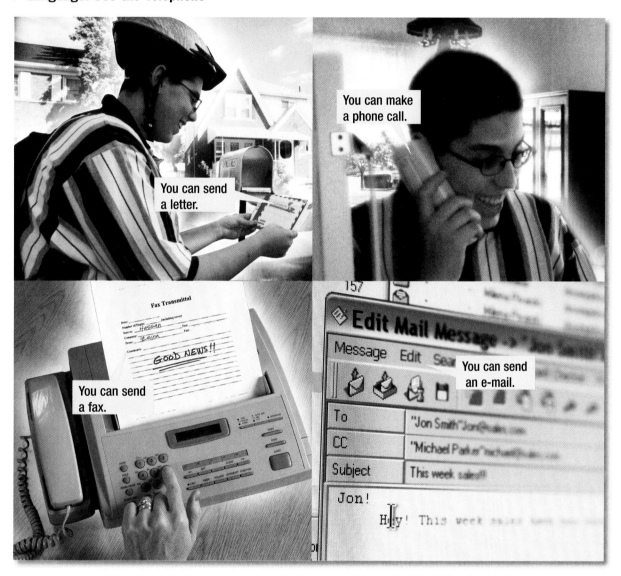

You can send a letter.

You can make a phone call.

You can send a fax.

You can send an e-mail.

ORAL LANGUAGE PRACTICE ▶ USE THE TELEPHONE

<u>1.</u> **You want to order a school T-shirt. How can you do it?**
Act out a phone call with a partner.

EXAMPLE **1.** **Euching:** Hello, Mariana. This is Euching.
Mariana: Hello, Euching.
Euching: How can I get a school T-shirt?
Mariana: Send a fax to the school.
Euching: I don't have a fax machine.
Mariana: Then just call on the phone.

Euching: How much is a school T-shirt?
Mariana: It is $15.00.
Euching: Thanks.
Mariana: You're welcome. Bye!
Euching: See you tomorrow.

Listen and Read Along

FOCUS ON GENRE

Realistic Fiction Realistic fiction is a story that is not true but could happen in real life. This story is about how people can communicate.

FOCUS ON VOCABULARY

Communication Words You have been learning words like the ones below. Use these words as you talk about *Good News*. Collect more words to put in the web.

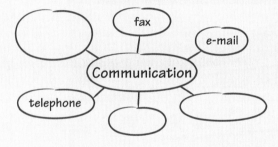

THEME BOOK

Read this realistic fiction about how people communicate.

Machines like the phone and the computer have made it easier to communicate with people who live far away.

Think About *Good News*

Make a sequence chain for *Good News.*
Follow these steps.

1 Think about the story. Who got the good news first? Draw a box and write the name.

> | Ali |
> |---|

2 How did he get the news? Write your answer in the box.

> | Ali – letter |
> |---|

3 Draw boxes to show who got the news next. Tell how the news came: by e-mail, fax, or phone.

> | Ali – letter |
> |---|
> ↓
> | |
> |---|
> ↓
> | |
> |---|
> ↓
> | |
> |---|

4 Use your sequence chain to tell the story to a friend.

High Frequency Words

▲ The girls eat lunch together.

REVIEW HIGH FREQUENCY WORDS

Read the words aloud. Which word goes in the sentence?

soon school	1. The girls are at _____.
The They	2. _____ eat lunch.
has help	3. She _____ a lot of food.

LEARN NEW WORDS

Study these words. Say them as whole words when you read.

from	I am **from** Russia.
home	My **home** is now in Detroit.
new	I have a **new** school, too.
go	I will **go** to school with my friend Rob.
there	My school schedule is **there** on the table.

PRACTICE

**Where does each new word fit in the chart?
Say the word and spell it.**

EXAMPLE **4.** from
f-r-o-m

What to Look For	Word
4. starts with **fr**	_ _ _ _
5. means "where you live"	_ _ _ _
6. starts with **th**	_ _ _ _ _
7. rhymes with **no**	_ _
8. is the opposite of **old**	_ _ _

**Write each new word on a card. Work with a
partner to put the words in alphabetical order.**

EXAMPLE

from   go

More High Frequency Words

How to Learn a New Word

- Look at the word.
- Listen to the word.
- Listen to the word in a sentence. What does it mean?
- Say the word.
- Spell the word.
- Say the word again.

REVIEW HIGH FREQUENCY WORDS

Read the words aloud. Which word goes in the sentence?

The	I
is	this
You	Here

1. _____ am going to school.
2. Where _____ my bag?
3. _____ it is!

LEARN NEW WORDS

Study these words. Say them as whole words when you read.

many	I have **many** different classes!
first	**First** I have English class.
next	**Next** I have science class.
then	**Then** I have lunch.
one	I have only **one** class with Rob—math.

PRACTICE

Where does each new word fit in the chart? Say the word and spell it.

EXAMPLE 4. *then*
t-h-e-n

What to Look For	Word
4. ends with **n**	_ _ _ _
5. ends with **y**	_ _ _ _
6. is the opposite of **last**	_ _ _ _ _
7. starts with **n**	_ _ _ _
8. means "1"	_ _ _

Write each new word on a card. Work with a partner to put the words in alphabetical order.

EXAMPLE

first   many

Reading and Spelling

▶ **Short _a_, Short _o_**

Listen and learn. CD

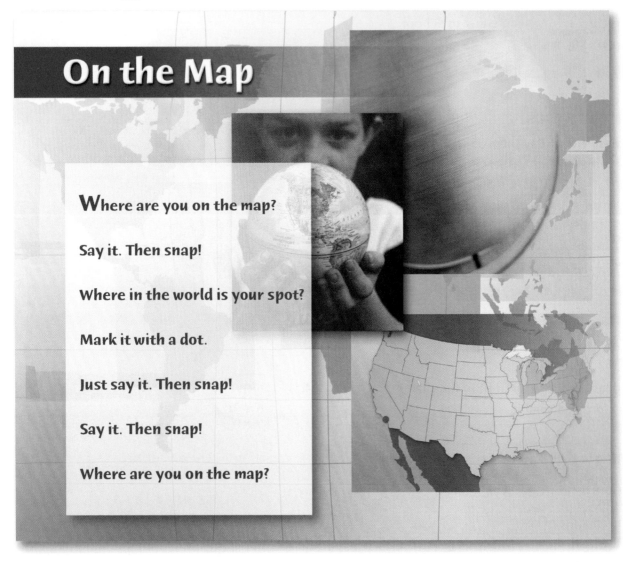

On the Map

Where are you on the map?

Say it. Then snap!

Where in the world is your spot?

Mark it with a dot.

Just say it. Then snap!

Say it. Then snap!

Where are you on the map?

CONNECT SOUNDS AND LETTERS

What sound does each letter make?

m<u>a</u>p

b<u>a</u>g

j<u>o</u>g

d<u>o</u>t

Follow these steps to read a word.

1 Point to the
first spelling.
Say the sound.

2 Point to the
second spelling.
Say the sound.

3 Point to the
last spelling.
Say the sound.

4 Now blend all the
sounds together
to say the word.
Say the word again.
What is it?

sad

sad

sad

s + a + d = sad

I blend 3 sounds
to say **sad**.

READING PRACTICE

Blend the sounds to read these words.

  1. job   **2.** at   **3.** gas   **4.** mom   **5.** mad   **6.** pot

Use what you learned to read the sentences.

  7. What a bad day!

  8. First I drop a new pot.

  9. Then my mom is mad at me.

10. Next the van has no gas.

11. I go to my job.

12. At last, I go home!

SPELLING PRACTICE

13.–16. **Now write the sentences that your teacher reads.**

WORD WORK

**Look at the first picture. Then read the word. Use letter cards to make a
new word for the next picture. Change just 1 letter each time.**

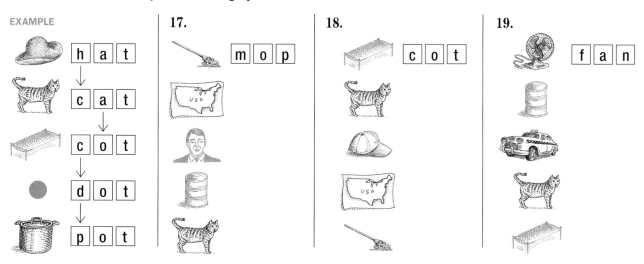

Read on Your Own

FOCUS ON GENRE

Realistic Fiction   Realistic fiction is a story that is not true. Events in the story could happen in real life, but they did not.

FOCUS ON WORDS

Short *a* and Short *o*   When you read and come to a word you don't know, blend the sounds together to read it. You just learned about words with short *a* and short *o*.

map   dot

High Frequency Words   Say these words as whole words when you read.

from	home
new	go
there	many
first	next
then	one

New at School

This is Lupe.

Lupe is new at Lakeside School.

First she has science lab with Pat and Ron.

Pat helps Lupe.

They have many things to do.

Next they have P.E. class.

They go from one class to the next.

Pat and Lupe go fast. Ron does not go fast.

He has a cold and has to stop!

Then Pat, Lupe, and Ron go to lunch.

They have a lot of hot soup there.

At last it is time to go home.

Lupe is glad to have 2 new friends!

Think About "New at School"

CHECK YOUR UNDERSTANDING

Tell the story to your partner. Use the words and pictures.

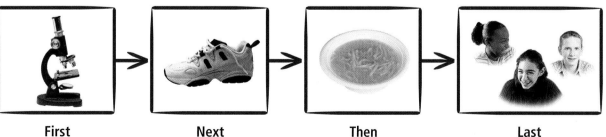

First   Next   Then   Last

She Likes School a Lot

▶ **Statements and Exclamations**

A statement tells something. It ends with a period. An exclamation shows strong feelings. It ends with an exclamation mark.

This sentence tells something. It ends with a period.

> Pizza is a new food for Lupe.

This sentence shows a strong feeling. It ends with an **exclamation mark.**

> She likes it a lot!

All sentences start with a **capital letter.**

> **S**he wants to eat pizza every day.

STUDY SENTENCES

Look at the story on pages 16–17. Answer these questions.

EXAMPLE **1.** The first sentence ends with a period.

1. What does the first sentence end with?
2. What does the last sentence end with?
3. How many words are in the fifth sentence?
4. How many words are in the sixth sentence?
5. Does each sentence start with a capital letter?

WRITE SENTENCES

Listen. CD **Write these sentences correctly.**

EXAMPLE **6.** Lupe likes science lab.

6. Lupe likes science lab
7. she likes to study
8. the class has a test tomorrow
9. Lupe will do well
10. she also likes P.E. class
11. her teacher is Ms. Sampson
12. they run a lot
13. Lupe is fast
14. she likes soccer and football
15. Lupe likes school a lot

Language and Content

Success in Mathematics

▶ **Learn About Math Problems**

Basic Operations

ADDITION

plus sign

$17 + 14 = 31$ sum

equals sign

▲ **Say:**
- Seventeen plus fourteen equals thirty-one.
- Seventeen and fourteen is thirty-one.

SUBTRACTION

minus sign

$$\begin{array}{r} 23 \\ -\ 9 \\ \hline 14 \end{array}$$ difference

▲ **Say:**
- Twenty-three minus nine is fourteen.
- The difference between nine and twenty-three is fourteen.

MULTIPLICATION

times sign or multiplication sign

$$\begin{array}{r} 25 \\ \times\ 3 \\ \hline 75 \end{array}$$ product

▲ **Say:**
- Twenty-five times three equals seventy-five.
- Twenty-five multiplied by three is seventy-five.

DIVISION

quotient

$39 \div 3 = 13$

division sign

$$3\overline{)39} \quad \begin{array}{r} 13 \\ \hline -3 \\ \hline 09 \\ -\ 9 \\ \hline 0 \end{array}$$

▲ **Say:**
- Thirty-nine divided by three is thirteen.
- Three into thirty-nine is thirteen.

Solve each problem. Then read it aloud.

Add, Subtract, Multiply, and Divide

EXAMPLE

$2 \times 3 = \underline{6}$

▲ **Say:**
Two times three equals six.

① $\begin{array}{r} 7 \\ +\ 8 \\ \hline \end{array}$

② $38 + 6 = \underline{\hspace{1cm}}$

③ $\begin{array}{r} 92 \\ -\ 49 \\ \hline \end{array}$

④ $88 - 29 = \underline{\hspace{1cm}}$

⑤ $\begin{array}{r} 7 \\ \times\ 6 \\ \hline \end{array}$

⑥ $12 \times 3 = \underline{\hspace{1cm}}$

⑦ $12\overline{)96}$

⑧ $99 \div 3 = \underline{\hspace{1cm}}$

Math in Action

☐ Write your age.
$\times\ 7$

☐ Find the product.
$\times\ 1443$

☐ Find the product. It is your age written 3 times.

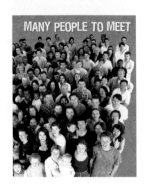

Build Background for "Many People to Meet"

COMMUNICATION

We meet many people each day. We communicate with the people we meet.

▲ Students talk to each other at lunchtime.

▲ This teacher greets the students.

Learn Key Vocabulary

Rate and Study the Words Rate how well you know each word. Then:

1. Pronounce the word. Say it aloud several times. Spell it.
2. Study the example.
3. Tell more about the word.
4. Practice it. Make the word your own.

Key Words

first (furst) *adverb*

Something that happens **first** comes before other things. This person gets to go **first**.

home (hōm) *noun*

A **home** is a place where people live. This is one kind of **home**.

meet (mēt) *verb*

When you **meet** a person, you see the person at a certain place. These students **meet** at school.

next (nekst) *adverb*

Something that happens **next** comes right after. This person gets to go **next**.

people (pē-pul) *noun*

The word **people** is the plural of person. There are many **people** to talk to in a neighborhood.

Practice the Words With a partner, make a Vocabulary Study Card for each Key Word.

Write the word.

front

> home

Tell what it means and use it in a sentence.

back

> where people live
>
> My <u>home</u> is in Chicago.

Use the cards to quiz your partner. Take turns answering.

Listen and Read Along

FOCUS ON GENRE

Photo Essay   A photo essay has a lot of pictures to tell about a topic. It is nonfiction. This photo essay tells about how many people we meet each day.

FOCUS ON COMPREHENSION

Sequence   Sequence is the order in which things happen. A sequence chain can help you put events in order.

When do we meet people?

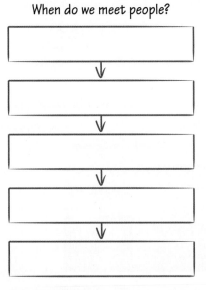

Sequence Chain

MANY PEOPLE TO MEET

Selection Recording

How many **people** do you **meet** each day?

First, you meet people when you go to school.

8 boys + 6 girls = 14 people

Key Vocabulary

people *n.*, human beings

meet *v.*, to see; to come upon

first *adv.*, before anything else

Next, you meet people at school.

4 students +
1 teacher = 5 people

Key Vocabulary
next *adv.*, following right
after

In Other Words
at when you are in

Before You Move On

1. **Viewing** Are there more boys than
girls in the photo on page 24?
2. **Analyze Information** How many
students are in the photo on
page 25?

Then you meet people at lunch.

3 students eating apples +
2 students eating plums = 5 students

Before You Move On

1. **Sequence** Do you eat lunch first or do you go to school first?
2. **Analyze Information** How many people are eating lunch in the photo on page 27?

Next you meet workers on your way home.

**And then you see
your family at home!**
22 workers +
7 family = 29 people

Key Vocabulary
   home *n.*, the place where
    you live

In Other Words
on your way when you go

28 **Unit 1** Glad to Meet You!

How many people did you meet today?

14 boys and girls + 5 students and teachers +
5 students at lunch + 29 workers and family = 53 people

Before You Move On

1. **Sequence** Did you go home first or go to school first?
2. **Analyze Information** How many people are counted in the selection?

Language and Content

Think About "Many People to Meet"

CHECK YOUR UNDERSTANDING

<u>1.–2.</u> **Work with a partner to complete each item.**

1. Identify Sequence Make a sequence chain like the one below. Show when the essay says that we meet people.

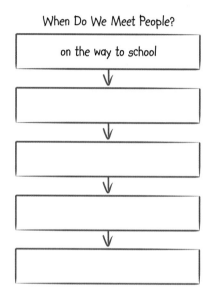

When Do We Meet People?

on the way to school

2. Sum It Up Use your sequence chain to retell "Many People to Meet." Tell what happened **first** and **next**. Tell about all the **people**.

REVIEW VOCABULARY

<u>3.–7.</u> **Read the paragraph aloud. Add the vocabulary words.**

This is how your day starts. ____, you ____ people as you go to school. ____, you meet ____at school. Then, you go ____.

Vocabulary
first
home
meet
next
people

WRITE ABOUT THE PEOPLE YOU MEET

<u>8.</u> **Write about other places where you meet people, such as at the park.**

Writing Project

E-mail

WHAT IS AN E-MAIL?

An e-mail is a message that you send to someone by computer. You can write about almost anything in an e-mail.

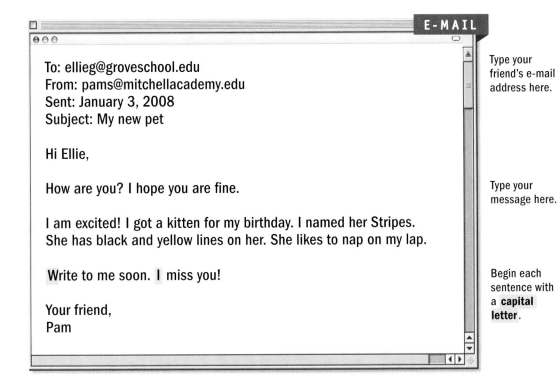

E-MAIL

To: ellieg@groveschool.edu
From: pams@mitchellacademy.edu
Sent: January 3, 2008
Subject: My new pet

Hi Ellie,

How are you? I hope you are fine.

I am excited! I got a kitten for my birthday. I named her Stripes. She has black and yellow lines on her. She likes to nap on my lap.

Write to me soon. I miss you!

Your friend,
Pam

Type your friend's e-mail address here.

Type your message here.

Begin each sentence with a **capital letter**.

Writing Project

Write an E-Mail

WRITING PROMPT What do you want to tell someone about your life? Write an e-mail about yourself. Send it to a friend or someone in your family.

Plan and Write

1 PLAN YOUR E-MAIL

Think about the person you will write to. What can you tell him or her? Here is Lupe's list.

My cousin	new friend at school
Grandma	what I do for fun
My friend	when my cousin came to visit

2 WRITE SENTENCES

Choose one idea. Write your e-mail. Here is part of Lupe's e-mail.

To: jaimeg@teenschool.edu
From: lupen@mitchellacademy.edu
Sent: May 10, 2008
Subject: My new friend

Hi Jaime,

How are you? I am fine.
I am going to a new school now. I have a new friend.

Sentence Frames
I am _____.
You are _____.
He is _____.
She is _____.
We are _____.

Check Your Work

Read more of Lupe's e-mail. She needs to make some changes.

- The first sentence needs a capital letter. To show the change, she put three lines under the letter: ≡.
- Lupe needs to add an exclamation point. To add it, she used this mark: ∧.

What other errors does she need to fix?

<u>h</u>er name is Pat I like her a lot̸she is the same age as i am.
<u>W</u>rite to me soon. I miss you

Your cousin,
Lupe

Look back at your e-mail. Read it aloud. Then ask yourself the questions in this checklist. Mark your changes.

Finish and Share

Use these steps to finish your e-mail.

1. Write the e-mail address correctly.
2. Write the subject of the e-mail.
3. Write the body of the e-mail correctly.

READ ALOUD

Take turns reading your e-mail to someone in your class. Use these tips.

Presenting Tips

If You Are the Speaker:	If You Are the Listener:
• Stay on topic.	• Think about your purpose for listening.
• Read loudly and clearly.	• Pay attention to the reader's voice.

Checklist

- ✓ Do my sentences start with a capital letter?
- ✓ Do my sentences end with the correct mark?
- ✓ Did I include enough details?

Reflect

- Did you tell about yourself?
- What did you like about writing an e-mail?

Do any of
these funny
foods look
tasty to you?

Set the Table

There are many things wrong with this picture! Tell your partner about them. Then draw a picture of another funny food. Ask the class to guess what is wrong with your picture.

In This Unit

▶ **Language Development**

▶ **Language and Literacy**

▶ **Language and Content**
   Science

▶ **Writing Project**

Vocabulary
- Colors, Shapes, and Sizes
- Foods and Food Groups
- Key Vocabulary

Language Functions
- Express Likes
- Describe

Grammar
- Action Verbs

Reading
- Short *u*, Short *i*
- High Frequency Words
- Comprehension: Identify Steps in a Process
- Text Features: Picture Charts

Writing
- How-To Card

Language Development

What Foods Do You Like?

▶ **Language: Express Likes; Describe**

Listen and chant. CD

little, red tomatoes

Tasty Salad

yellow corn

Lettuce, lettuce,
Fresh, green lettuce.
Carrots, carrots,
Long, orange carrots.
Onions, onions,
Large, round onions.
Salad, salad,
Tasty salad.
What a treat!

tiny, green peas

big, white cauliflower

long, orange carrot

purple cabbage

fresh, green lettuce

large, round onion

> **Adjectives**
> An **adjective** is a word that describes a noun. An adjective describes a person, place, or thing.
> **long, orange** carrots
> **large, round** onions

EXPRESS YOURSELF ▶ EXPRESS LIKES; DESCRIBE

1.–6. Work with a partner. Tell your partner about 6 foods you like. Have your partner tell you about 6 foods he or she likes. Use an adjective to describe each food.

EXAMPLE **1.** I like yellow corn.

7.–10. Draw 4 foods you like. Tell a partner about each food. Use adjectives to describe each food. Have your partner do the same.

EXAMPLE **7.**

big, round bagel

What Is Red and Round? A Tomato!

▶ Vocabulary: Colors, Shapes, and Sizes

Look at the picture. Read the words that name a color or shape.

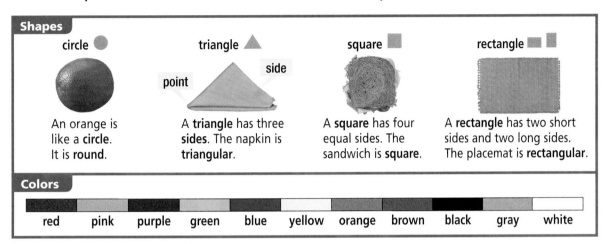

Shapes

circle — An orange is like a **circle**. It is **round**.

triangle — A **triangle** has three **sides**. The napkin is **triangular**.

square — A **square** has four equal sides. The sandwich is **square**.

rectangle — A **rectangle** has two short sides and two long sides. The placemat is **rectangular**.

Colors

red   pink   purple   green   blue   yellow   orange   brown   black   gray   white

BUILD SENTENCES

Read each sentence below. Add words to tell the color, size, or shape. Say the new sentence.

EXAMPLE **1.** A blueberry is round.
It is also small.

1.

A blueberry is ____.
It is also ____.

2.

A pickle is ____.
It is also ____.

3.

A tomato is ____.
It is also ____.

4.

The cheese is ____.
It is ____.

5.

The candy bar is ____. It is ____.

6.

The lettuce is ____.
It is also ____.

7.

The banana is ____.
It is also ____.

8.

The slice of bread is ____. It is also ____.

WRITE SENTENCES

9.–16. Write a sentence for each picture above. Tell about the shape of the food.

EXAMPLE **9.** A blueberry is like a circle.

Language Development

What's for Lunch?

▶ **Vocabulary: Foods**
▶ **Language: Describe**

Look at the picture. Say the name of each food.

ORAL LANGUAGE PRACTICE ▶ DESCRIBE

1.–3. Who's talking? CD

Listen to each person talk about the lunch.
Point to the correct lunch. Then describe it.

WRITTEN PRACTICE

4. What do you want for lunch? Write a list.
Draw a picture of each food. Use adjectives
to describe the food.

EXAMPLE **4.**

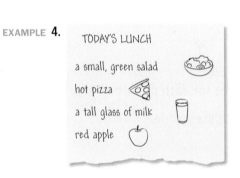

TODAY'S LUNCH

a small, green salad

hot pizza

a tall glass of milk

red apple

How Do You Make a Fruit Drink?

▶ **Action Verbs**

An action verb tells the action in a sentence. It tells what the noun in the sentence does.

I **make** great fruit drinks.

I **cut** bananas.

I **put** them in the blender.

I **add** ice.

BUILD SENTENCES

Tell how to make a fruit drink. Choose a verb from the box to complete each sentence. Say the new sentence.

Action Verbs

put   open   cut
get   push   wash

EXAMPLE **1.** I wash the strawberries.

1.

I _____ the strawberries.

2.

I _____ the strawberries.

3.

I _____ some ice.

4.

I _____ the yogurt.

5.

I _____ the yogurt in the blender.

6.

I _____ the button.

WRITE SENTENCES

<u>7.–10.</u> Write 4 sentences to tell how you make a sandwich. Write each sentence on a card. Mix up the cards. Have your partner do the same. Switch cards with your partner and put the sentences in order.

EXAMPLE **7.**

I put jam on the bread.

Language Development

Listen and Read Along

FOCUS ON GENRE

Career Sketch   A career sketch gives factual information about a career. A career sketch is nonfiction. This career sketch is about an artist.

FOCUS ON VOCABULARY

Food, Color, Shape, and Size Words   You have been learning words like the ones below. Use these words as you talk about *I Make Pictures Move!* Collect more words to put in the web. Make webs for color words, shape words, and size words, too.

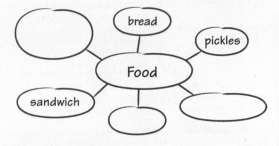

THEME BOOK

Read this career sketch about an artist.

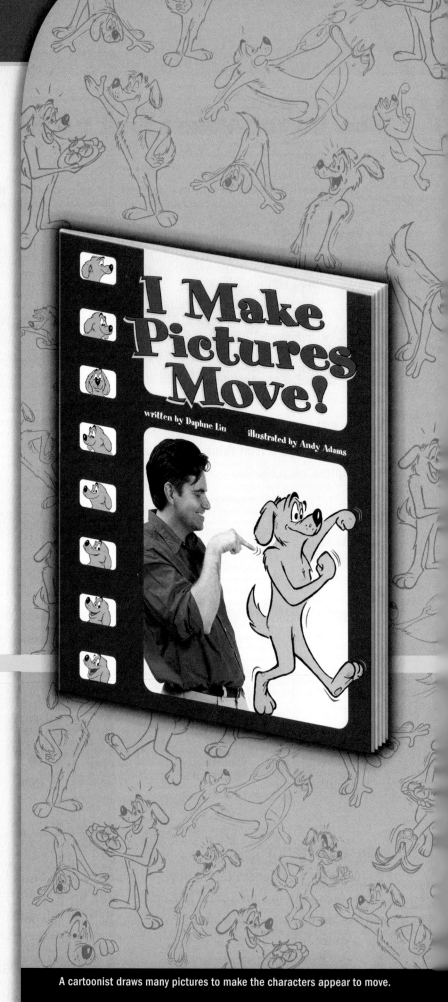

A cartoonist draws many pictures to make the characters appear to move.

Think About
I Make Pictures Move!

IDENTIFY STEPS IN A PROCESS

Make a sequence chain to tell about *I Make Pictures Move!* Follow these steps.

1 Think about how Andy makes his drawing. Draw a box. In it, write what Andy does first.

> Andy draws bread.

2 Draw 4 more boxes. Tell what else Andy does.

> Andy draws bread.
> ↓
> He draws tomatoes.
> ↓
>
> ↓
>
> ↓
>

3 Use your sequence chain to tell a partner how Andy makes his drawing. Then have your partner tell what Dingo does at the end of the story.

High Frequency Words

▲ These kids like their lunch.

REVIEW HIGH FREQUENCY WORDS

Read the words aloud. Which word goes in the sentence?

good	go
like	look
who	with

1. The lunch is _____ .
2. These kids _____ the food.
3. They eat _____ their hands.

LEARN NEW WORDS

Study these words. Say them as whole words when you read.

something	I want **something** to eat.
make	I can **make** spaghetti!
long	First, I get a box of **long** noodles.
large	I put them in a **large** pot of hot water.
move	I **move** the pot to the back of the stove.

PRACTICE

<u>4.–8.</u> **Draw a picture to show each new word. Write a sentence under the picture. Use the word in a sentence.**

EXAMPLE **4.**

I buy something at the store.

Write each new word on a card. Sort the cards into these groups:

EXAMPLE **9.**

long   large

long
large

9. These 2 words start with **l**.
10. This word has 2 syllables.
11. These 3 words end with an **e**.
12. These 4 words have 1 syllable.

Read the words in each group aloud. Then make up new groups with a partner.

More High Frequency Words

> ## How to Learn a New Word
> - Look at the word.
> - Listen to the word.
> - Listen to the word in a sentence. What does it mean?
> - Say the word.
> - Spell the word.
> - Say the word again.

REVIEW HIGH FREQUENCY WORDS

Read the words aloud. Which word goes in the sentence?

soon   school   **1.** We will make lunch _____.

has   help   **2.** I will _____ you.

The   They   **3.** _____ will like the food.

LEARN NEW WORDS

Study these words. Say them as whole words when you read.

different	Then, I use a **different** pot for the sauce.
small	I cut an onion into **small** pieces.
open	I **open** a can of tomatoes.
same	I cook the onions and tomatoes in the **same** pot.
eat	At last, I **eat** my pasta!

PRACTICE

<u>4.–8.</u> **Draw a picture to show each new word. Write a sentence under the picture. Use the word in the sentence.**

EXAMPLE **4.**

This ant is very small.

Write each new word on a card. Sort the cards into these groups:

EXAMPLE **9.**

small   same

  9. These 2 words start with **s.**

10. This word starts with an **e.**

11. This word means the opposite of "closed."

12. This word has 9 letters.

Read the words in each group aloud. Then make up new groups with a partner.

Reading and Spelling

▶ **Words with short _i_, short _u_, _ch_, and _tch_**

Listen and learn. CD

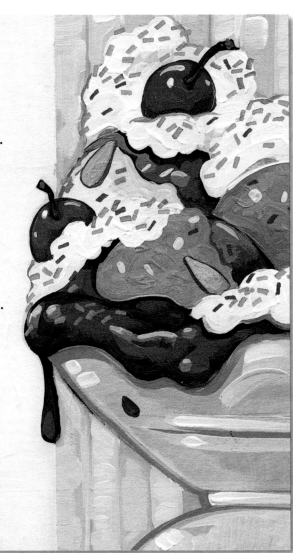

Ice Cream

Fill your cup with ice cream.

Fill it to the brim.

Catch the melted chocolate

Dripping down your chin.

Fill your cup with ice cream.

Add some nuts and then,

Catch the melted chocolate

Dripping down your chin!

CONNECT SOUNDS AND LETTERS

How many sounds does each word have?

c_u_p

n_u_t

li̱d

chi̱n

Follow these steps to read a word.

1 Point to the spelling **ch**. Say the sound.

ch<u>i</u>n

2 Point to the next spelling. Say the sound.

ch<u>i</u>n

3 Point to the last spelling. Say the sound.

chi<u>n</u>

4 Now blend all the sounds together to say the word. Say the word again. What is it?

ch + i + n = chin

The letters *ch* make one sound. I blend 3 sounds to say *chin*.

READING PRACTICE

Blend the sounds to read these words.

1. chin   **2.** cup   **3.** can   **4.** catch   **5.** jumps   **6.** bug

Use what you learned to read the sentences.

7. There is something in my cup.

8. I can see it move.

9. It is small and green.

10. It jumps up and lands on my hand.

11. Now the bug is on my chin!

12. Can I catch it? No!

SPELLING PRACTICE

13.–16. Now write the sentences that your teacher reads.

WORD WORK

Look at the first picture. Then read the word. Use letter cards to make a new word for the next picture.

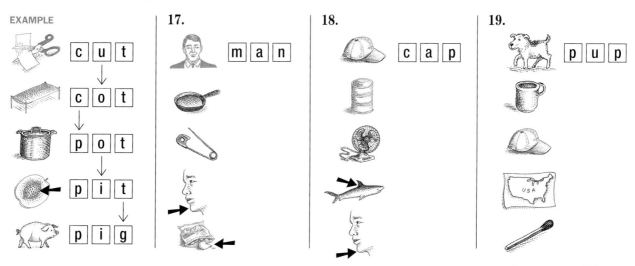

EXAMPLE

c u t → c o t → p o t → p i t → p i g

17. m a n

18. c a p

19. p u p

Read on Your Own

FOCUS ON GENRE

Realistic Fiction   Realistic fiction is a
story that did not happen. It is realistic,
which means that events in the story
could happen in real life. This story
is about a girl who makes lunch for a
friend.

FOCUS ON WORDS

**Words with Short *i*, Short *u*, *ch*,
and *tch***   When you read and come to a
word you don't know, blend the sounds
together to read it.

Remember that the letters *ch* and *tch*
make one sound. You just learned about
words with these spellings:

i   u   ch   tch

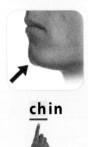

<u>ch</u> in

High Frequency Words   Say these
words as whole words when you read.

something	make
large	long
different	move
open	small
eat	same

Something **Good** for **Lunch**

Kim and Mitch eat lunch.

Kim wants something to eat.

Kim will make hot dogs for lunch.

She cooks a batch of long hot dogs in a big pot.

Next Kim chops some small onions.

She moves the onions to a different spot.

She opens a large bag of buns.

She fills the buns with hot dogs, mustard, and onions.

She opens a small bag of chips, too.

She pours a cup of punch.

This is too much food to eat!

Kim calls Mitch.

He wants the same lunch as Kim.

Then they sit and eat a great lunch!

Think About "Something Good for Lunch"

CHECK YOUR UNDERSTANDING

Tell the story to your partner. Use the words and pictures.

Kim makes hot dogs. → She adds chips and punch. → Kim calls Mitch. → They eat lunch!

I Am Not a Cook!

▶ **Negative Sentences**

A negative sentence has a negative word, such as *not*.

The cake is **not** right.

The cookies are **not** good.

The kitchen is **not** clean.

I am **not** happy.

BUILD SENTENCES

Look at each picture below. Add a verb and the word *not* to complete each sentence. Say the new sentence.

EXAMPLE **1.** The burrito is not green.

1.

The burrito
_____ _____ green.

2.

The limes
_____ _____ square.

3.

The watermelon
_____ _____ thin.

4.

The crackers
_____ _____ blue.

5.

The kiwi _____ _____
triangular.

6.

I _____ _____ a nurse.

WRITE SENTENCES

7.–12. Work with a partner. For each picture, take turns writing a new negative sentence. Use *is not* or *are not*.

EXAMPLE **7.** The burrito is not purple.

Success in Science

▶ **Learn About Food Groups**

Classification

When you **classify**, you put things in **categories**, or **groups**.

category	Vegetables
a list of foods in the category	1. peas
	2. carrots
	3. lettuce
	4. peppers
	5. mushrooms

Study the food pyramid. Then do the activity.

What Kinds of Foods Do You Eat?

You will need: a notebook and a pencil

ACTIVITY STEPS

1 Make a List
Write all the foods you ate yesterday.

2 Put the Foods in Groups
Classify the foods on your list. Use the 6 food groups you learned about.

3 Count the Servings
Draw the food pyramid. Next to each group, write the number of servings you ate.

THINK IT OVER

1. Look at the food pyramid you drew. From which food group did you eat the most servings?
2. Do you need to eat more from some groups? Which ones?
3. Do you need to eat less from some groups? Which ones?

FOOD PYRAMID

Grains	Vegetables	Fruits
6 oz. every day	$2\frac{1}{2}$ cups every day	2 cups every day
Fats and Oils	**Milk**	**Meat & Beans**
use sparingly	3 cups every day	$5\frac{1}{2}$ oz. every day

Language and Content

U.S. Tour of Food

Build Background for "U.S. Tour of Food"

FOODS AND FOOD GROUPS

Food is an important part of everyday life. There are many kinds of food.

bread

cheese

◀ To be healthy, eat foods from different food groups.

shrimp

limes

tomatoes

▲ Families enjoy sharing food together.

Learn Key Vocabulary

Rate and Study the Words Rate how well you know each word. Then:

1. Pronounce the word. Say it aloud several times. Spell it.
2. Study the example.
3. Tell more about the word.
4. Practice it. Make the word your own.

Key Words

color (kuh-ler) *noun*

A **color** is a shade like red, blue, or green. Vegetables can be many different **colors**.

foods (fōdz) *noun*

Foods are things that we can eat. There are many kinds of **foods** at a farmers' market.

shapes (shāps) *noun*

Circles, ovals, and squares are **shapes**. People make bread in different **shapes**.

sizes (sīz-ez) *noun*

When things are big and small, they are different **sizes**. Fruits can be many different **sizes**.

visit (vih-zit) *verb*

People **visit** a place when they stay for a short time. Family members **visit** each other often.

Practice the Words Work with a partner to take turns writing 4 sentences. Use at least 2 Key Words in each sentence.

> Foods come in many different shapes and sizes.

Listen and Read Along

FOCUS ON GENRE

Fact Book   A fact is something that is true. This selection is full of facts. It gives information about different kinds of food throughout the United States.

FOCUS ON COMPREHENSION

Classify   When you classify, or group, information, it is easier to remember what you read. Here are some groups:

Grains	Fruits & Vegetables
Dairy	Meat

West

tomatoes▽

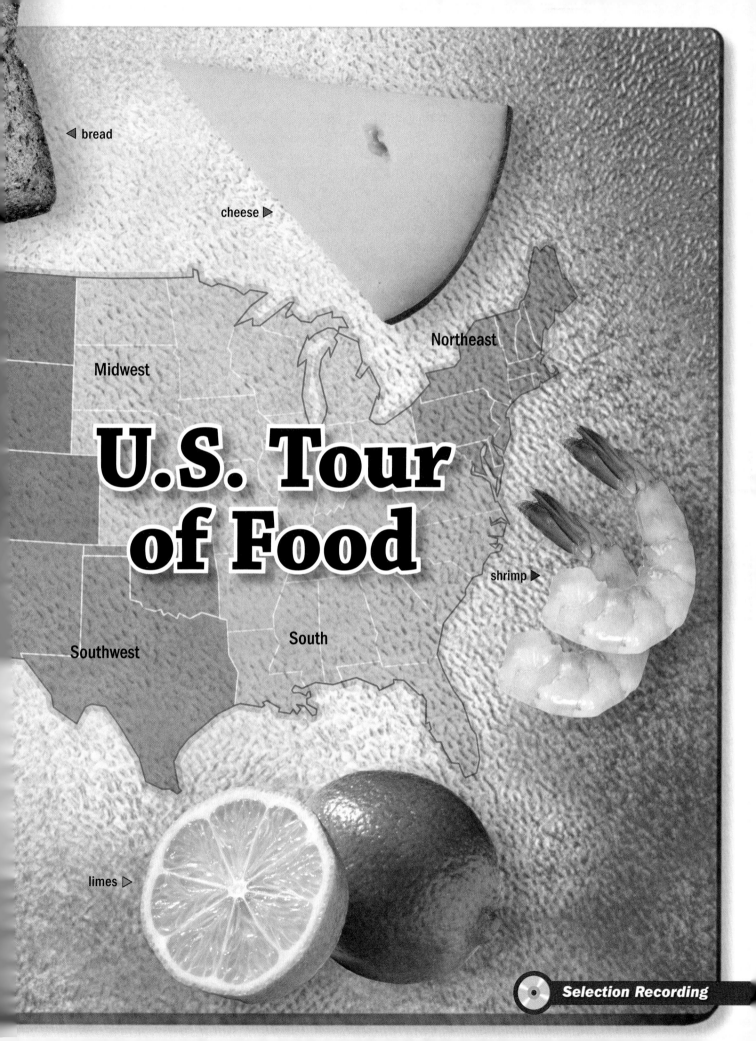

◁ bread

cheese ▷

Northeast

Midwest

U.S. Tour of Food

shrimp ▷

Southwest

South

limes ▷

Great Grains

All of these **foods** are grains.

wheat   pasta   rice   bread

Visit Iowa and you will see a lot of wheat. People make bread from wheat. Bread comes in many **shapes**.

Iowa

▲ A machine cuts wheat from a field in Iowa. Wheat is a kind of grain.

These are breads from around the world. ▼

Key Vocabulary

foods *n.*, things that you eat or drink

visit *v.*, to go somewhere and stay for a short time

shapes *n.*, forms, such as circles or squares

Say Cheese!

All of these are **dairy foods**.

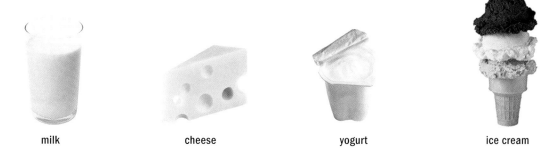

milk　　　　cheese　　　　yogurt　　　　ice cream

Visit Wisconsin and meet some cows. Cows make milk. Their milk is used to make cheese and other **dairy foods**.

Wisconsin

▲ hard cheese

▲ Dairy foods come from cows. Cows make milk.

▲ soft cheese

In Other Words
dairy foods foods made from milk

Before You Move On

1. **Analyze Information** What kind of **food** is wheat?
2. **Draw Conclusions** What is used to make ice cream?

Fruit Flavors

All of these foods are fruits. Fruits come in many **sizes**.

apple

bananas

watermelon

grapes

pineapple

Visit Florida and pick an orange. **Squeeze** it to make orange juice!

Florida

▲ Oranges grow on trees.

orange juice ▷

Key Vocabulary
sizes *n.*, how big or small objects are

In Other Words
Squeeze Push hard on

Vegetables on Your Table

All of these foods are vegetables. Vegetables come in many **colors**.

lettuce

cabbage

carrots

potatoes

onions

Visit California and you will find a lot of vegetables.

California

△ You can buy many different kinds of
vegetables at a farmers' market.

Key Vocabulary
   colors *n*., red, blue yellow,
    and any other shade

Before You Move On

1. **Viewing** Name the **colors** of some
   vegetables.
2. **Classify** Name some fruits.

Meats & Beans

These foods are meats and beans.

poultry

fish

eggs

navy beans

lentils

Meats come from animals of all sizes. Visit Maryland and you will see a lot of fish. Seafood is meat that can be found in the water.

Maryland

▲ Crabs are a kind of seafood called shellfish.

▽ Meats come from animals like chickens and pigs.

Food Brings People Together

The United States is a big place. Each part of the United States has its own foods. Some are **spicy**. Some are **sweet**. But food is an important part of life everywhere. Families and friends **share food**. What foods are from your area?

▽ Food brings people together.

Before You Move On

1. **Analyze Information** Where can you find fish?
2. **Classify** What kind of **food** is fish?

Language and Content

Think About "U.S. Tour of Food"

CHECK YOUR UNDERSTANDING

<u>1.–2.</u> **Work with a partner to complete each item.**

1. **Classify** Make a chart like the one below. Complete the chart by using what you learned about foods in the selection.

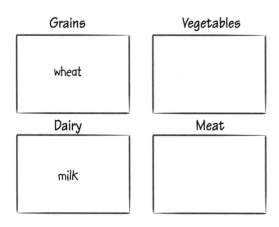

Grains

wheat

Vegetables

Dairy

milk

Meat

2. **Sum It Up** Use your chart to talk about groups of **food**. Tell about the **colors**, **sizes**, and **shapes** of foods.

REVIEW VOCABULARY

<u>3.–7.</u> **Read the paragraph aloud. Add the vocabulary words.**

You can _____ Iowa to see how people grow wheat. We use wheat to make a _____ called bread. Bread comes in many __ ___ like round and oval. In California, people grow vegetables that are yellow, green, and many other _____. The _____ of vegetables can be big or small.

Vocabulary
colors
food
shapes
sizes
visit

WRITE ABOUT FOOD

<u>8.</u> **Write about your favorite meal to eat with friends or family.**

How-To Card

WHAT IS A HOW-TO CARD?

A how-to card tells how to make something. It gives all the steps in the right order. Writers often number the steps on a how-to card.

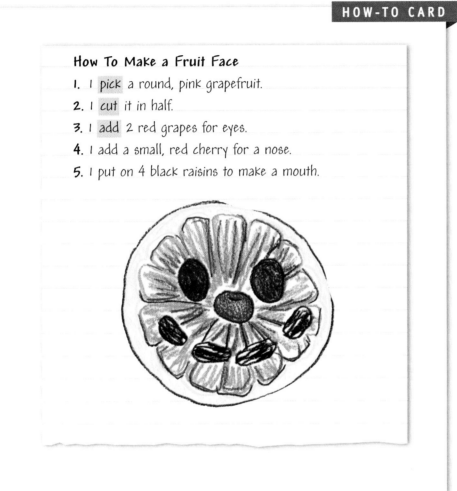

HOW-TO CARD

How To Make a Fruit Face

1. I pick a round, pink grapefruit.
2. I cut it in half.
3. I add 2 red grapes for eyes.
4. I add a small, red cherry for a nose.
5. I put on 4 black raisins to make a mouth.

Action verbs tell you what to do.

Begin each sentence with a **capital letter.**

Writing Project

Write a How-To Card

WRITING PROMPT   How can you turn food into art? Pick some food to make a piece of art. Write the steps that will tell how to make it.

Plan and Write

1 **PLAN YOUR HOW-TO CARD**

Think of art you can make with food. Draw pictures of what the food will look like. Here are Dan's ideas.

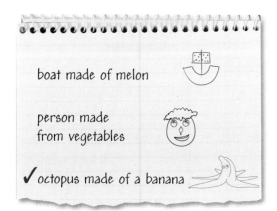

boat made of melon

person made
from vegetables

✓ octopus made of a banana

> **Foods**
> corn
> melon
> banana
> peas
> beans
> pasta
> bread

2 **PLAN THE STEPS**

Think about the food you will need. Plan each step.

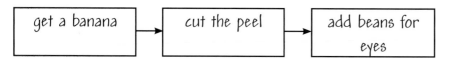

| get a banana | → | cut the peel | → | add beans for eyes |

3 **WRITE THE STEPS**

Turn your steps into sentences. Use adjectives.

1. I use a long, yellow banana.
2. I cut the peel into long, thin strips.

> **Adjectives**
> An **adjective** describes a person, place, or thing.
>
> **long, orange** carrots
> **large, round** onions

Check Your Work

Read more of Dan's how-to card. He needs to make some changes.

- The first sentence needs an action verb. To add it, he used this mark: ∧.

- Step 4 needs an adjective. To add it, Dan used this mark: ∧.

- Step 4 needs to start with a capital letter. He put three lines under the letter: ≡.

What other errors does Dan need to fix?

         add
3. I ∧ little black beans for eyes.
                 long
4. then I spread the ∧ strips out.
   ≡

Look back at your how-to card. Read it aloud. Then ask yourself the questions in the checklist. Mark your changes.

Finish and Share

Use these steps to finish your how-to card.

1. Copy the steps neatly and correctly.

2. Number the steps.

3. Add a title that tells what you are making.

4. Add a photo or drawing.

5. Trade cards with a partner. Follow the steps to make or draw the piece of art described on the card.

PRESENT

Take turns reading your how-to card aloud to the class. Use these tips.

Presenting Tips

If You Are the Speaker:	If You Are the Listener:
• Tell the steps in order.	• Pay attention to the reader's voice. • Follow the steps carefully.

Checklist

- ☑ Did I use action verbs?
- ☑ Did I include adjectives?
- ☑ Did I use a capital letter for the first word in a sentence?

Reflect

- Did you include all the steps?
- Did you use action verbs and adjectives in your steps?

People can do many
different kinds of jobs.

ON THE JOB

Work with a partner. Look at the picture.

What workers do you see?

Draw tools they use. Trade drawings.

Match the drawings to the correct workers.

In This Unit

▶ **Language Development**

▶ **Language and Literacy**

▶ **Language and Content**
  Science and Mathematics

▶ **Writing Project**

Vocabulary
- Actions
- Tools and Careers
- Key Vocabulary

Language Functions
- Give Information
- Ask and Answer Questions

Grammar
- Present Tense Verbs
- Yes-or-No Questions
- Questions with *Who?*, *What?*, *Where?*, and *When?*

Reading
- Short *e*, *sh*, *ck*, and Double Consonants
- High Frequency Words
- Comprehension: Identify Details
- Text Features: Callouts

Writing
- Interview

Language Development

What Is the Job for Me?

▶ **Language: Give Information**

Listen and sing. CD

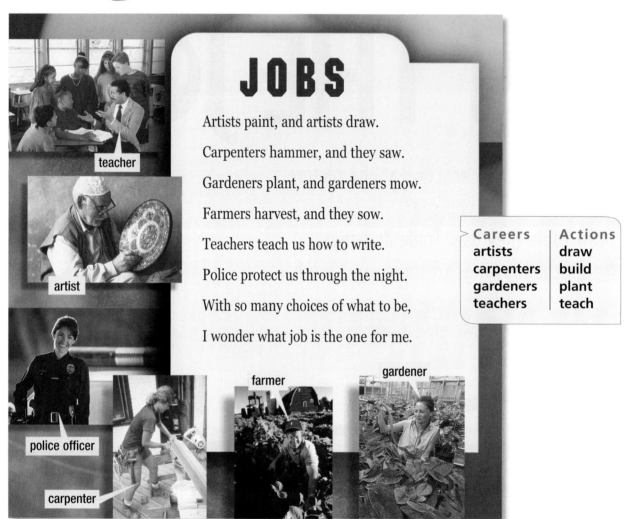

JOBS

Artists paint, and artists draw.

Carpenters hammer, and they saw.

Gardeners plant, and gardeners mow.

Farmers harvest, and they sow.

Teachers teach us how to write.

Police protect us through the night.

With so many choices of what to be,

I wonder what job is the one for me.

Careers	Actions
artists	draw
carpenters	build
gardeners	plant
teachers	teach

Labels: teacher, artist, police officer, carpenter, farmer, gardener

EXPRESS YOURSELF ▶ GIVE INFORMATION

<u>1.–3.</u> **Choose 3 different jobs. Say each job and tell what the workers do.**

EXAMPLE **1.** Artists paint and draw.

<u>4.</u> **Draw a picture of a worker. Tell a partner about the worker in the picture. Then listen as your partner tells you about his or her picture.**

EXAMPLE **4.** This is a cab driver. He drives a cab.

People in Action

▶ **Present Tense Verbs**

> To tell what another person or thing does, use a verb that ends in **-s**.

The carpenter **builds** a box.

He **uses** glue.

It **holds** the sides together.

His son **helps**.

BUILD SENTENCES

Say each sentence. Add the correct form of the action verb.　　EXAMPLE **1.** He mops the floor.

1.

He ＿＿ the floor. (**mop**)

2.

She ＿＿ the plants. (**water**)

3.

She ＿＿ newspapers. (**sell**)

4.

It ＿＿ the clothes. (**clean**)

5.

He ＿＿ . (**run**)

6.

She ＿＿ the news. (**report**)

WRITE SENTENCES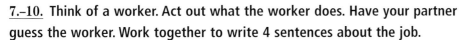

7.–10. Think of a worker. Act out what the worker does. Have your partner guess the worker. Work together to write 4 sentences about the job.

EXAMPLE **7.** The gardener pulls the weeds.

Language Development

Are They at Work?

▶ **Yes-Or-No Questions**

> A question asks for information. It ends with a **question mark.**

You can answer some questions with
yes or *no*.

> Is this the gym? Yes.

**When you tell more in your answer,
use the correct pronoun.**

> Is this the gym? Yes, **it** is.
>
> Are the girls alone? No, **they** are not.
>
> Can Rob play? Yes, **he** can.

ORAL LANGUAGE PRACTICE

Look at each picture below. Read the question.
Answer it.

EXAMPLE **1.** Yes, she can.

1.

Can the writer use
the computer?

2.

Is the photographer
in an office?

3.

Are Linda and Brian
carpenters?

4.

Are Dave and Wendy pilots?

5.

Can the architect draw?

6.

Are Julia and Miguel
dancers?

WRITTEN PRACTICE

<u>7.–12.</u> Write a new question for each picture above. Start each question
with *Is*, *Are*, or *Can*. Put a question mark at the end.

EXAMPLE **7.** Is she a writer?

Tools of the Trade

▶ **Vocabulary: Tools and Careers**
▶ **Language: Ask and Answer Questions**

Look at the pictures. Read the words.

The Beauty Shop

brush
scissors
stylist
hair dryer
customer

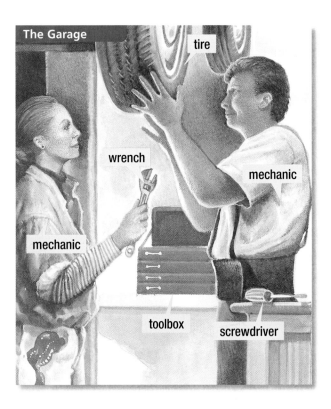

The Garage

tire
wrench
mechanic
mechanic
toolbox
screwdriver

ORAL LANGUAGE PRACTICE ▶ ASK AND ANSWER QUESTIONS

<u>1.–2.</u> Who's talking? CD
Listen. Point to the correct person.
Then act out the scene with a partner.
Ask and answer questions.

WRITTEN PRACTICE

Look at the pictures above. Ask a partner each
question. Write your partner's answer.

EXAMPLE **3.** Can the stylist cut hair?
Yes, she can.

In the Beauty Shop

3. Can the stylist cut hair?
4. Is a customer in the chair?
5. Is the hair dryer in her hand?
6. Are they in a cafeteria?

In the Garage

7. Are they in a garage?
8. Is she a teacher?
9. Is the wrench in the toolbox?
10. Can they fix the car?

Language Development

Listen and Read Along

FOCUS ON GENRE

Fantasy   A fantasy story is a fiction story that could not be true. The characters often do things that people could never do in real life. This story is about a visitor from another planet.

FOCUS ON VOCABULARY

Career Words   You have been learning words like the ones below. Use these words as you talk about *What Is It?* Collect more words to put in the web.

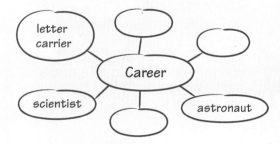

THEME BOOK

Read this fantasy about a visitor from space.

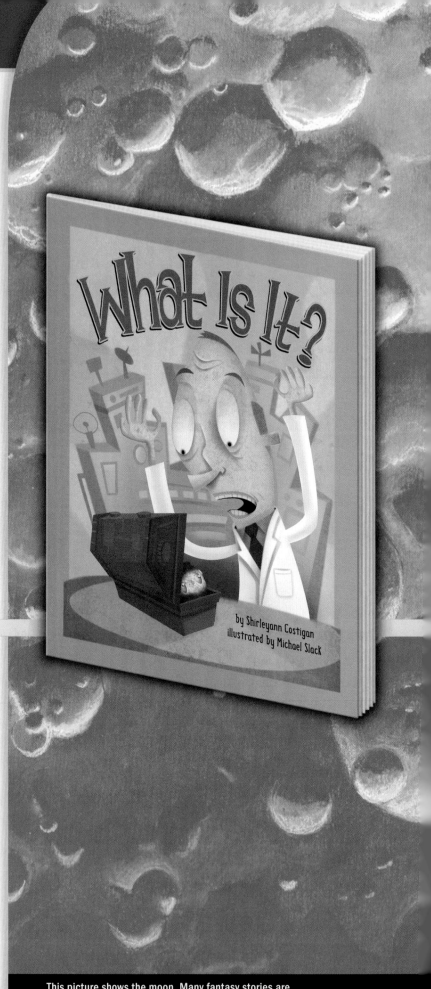

This picture shows the moon. Many fantasy stories are about life on the moon.

Think About *What Is It?*

IDENTIFY DETAILS

Make a concept web to tell about the people in *What Is It?* Follow these steps.

1 Think about the story. Who is in it?

> Who is in
> the story?

2 Who is the first person in the story? Write the name of her job.

astronaut

> Who is in
> the story?

3 Add the other people in the story to the web.

astronaut   scientist

> Who is in
> the story?

4 Finish the web. Use it to tell the story to a partner. Then have your partner tell the story to you.

High Frequency Words

▲ Photographers take pictures at a bicycle race.

REVIEW HIGH FREQUENCY WORDS

Read the words aloud. Which word goes in the sentence?

what	work
many	you
There	Then

1. The photographers _____ at the race.
2. They take _____ pictures.
3. _____ are 25 people in the race.

LEARN NEW WORDS

Study these words. Say them as whole words when you read.

study	I **study** photography in school.
learn	I **learn** how to use a camera.
carry	I **carry** a camera in my backpack.
find	I always **find** something to photograph.
use	I **use** a lot of film.

PRACTICE

4.–8. **Make a map for each new word. Write the word in the center. Complete the other boxes. Then use the word in a sentence of your own.**

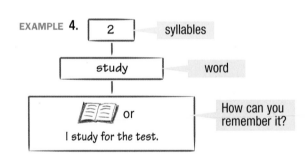

EXAMPLE **4.**

2 ← syllables

study ← word

📖 or
I study for the test.

How can you remember it?

9.–13. **Work with a partner. Write each new word on a card. Mix your cards together for the game. Turn them so the words are down. Then:**
- Turn over 2 cards.
- Spell the words. Are they the same?
- If so, keep them. If not, turn them over again.
- The player with more cards at the end wins.

EXAMPLE **9.**

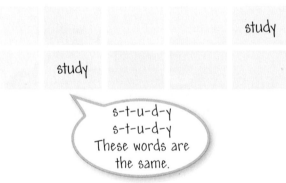

study

study

s-t-u-d-y
s-t-u-d-y
These words are the same.

More High Frequency Words

REVIEW HIGH FREQUENCY WORDS

Read the words aloud. Which word goes in the sentence?

soon school   1. Students go to _____ every day.

The They   2. _____ have a job to do in class.

when was   3. They work _____ they do homework.

> **How to Learn a New Word**
> • Look at the word.
> • Listen to the word.
> • Listen to the word in a sentence. What does it mean?
> • Say the word.
> • Spell the word.
> • Say the word again.

LEARN NEW WORDS

Study these words. Say them as whole words when you read.

love	I **love** to take pictures of my mom.
face	She always has a smile on her **face**.
when	My friends run **when** they see me.
want	They don't **want** to be photographed.
say	They **say**, "Don't take a picture of us!"

PRACTICE

4.–8. Make a map for each new word. Write the word in the center. Complete the other boxes. Then use the word in a sentence of your own.

EXAMPLE **4.**

| 1 | syllables |

| love | word |

| ♥ or / I love my family. | How can you remember it? |

9.–13. Work with a partner. Write each new word on a card. Mix your cards together for the game. Turn them so the words are down. Then:
• Turn over 2 cards.
• Spell the words. Are they the same?
• If so, keep them. If not, turn them over again.
• The player with more cards at the end wins.

EXAMPLE **9.**

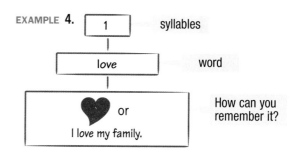

when

when

w–h–e–n
w–h–e–n
These words are the same.

Language and Literacy

Reading and Spelling

▶ **Short *e*, *sh*, *ck*, and Double Consonants**

Listen and learn. CD

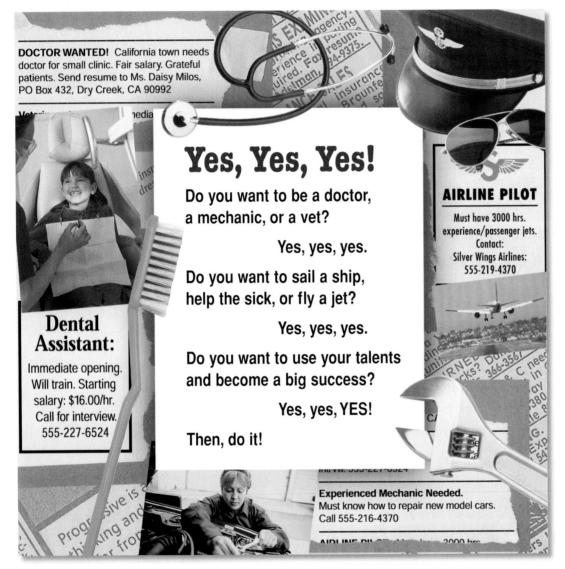

DOCTOR WANTED! California town needs doctor for small clinic. Fair salary. Grateful patients. Send resume to Ms. Daisy Milos, PO Box 432, Dry Creek, CA 90992

Dental Assistant:
Immediate opening. Will train. Starting salary: $16.00/hr. Call for interview. 555-227-6524

Yes, Yes, Yes!

Do you want to be a doctor,
a mechanic, or a vet?

Yes, yes, yes.

Do you want to sail a ship,
help the sick, or fly a jet?

Yes, yes, yes.

Do you want to use your talents
and become a big success?

Yes, yes, YES!

Then, do it!

AIRLINE PILOT
Must have 3000 hrs. experience/passenger jets.
Contact:
Silver Wings Airlines:
555-219-4370

Experienced Mechanic Needed.
Must know how to repair new model cars.
Call 555-216-4370

CONNECT SOUNDS AND LETTERS

How many sounds does each word have?

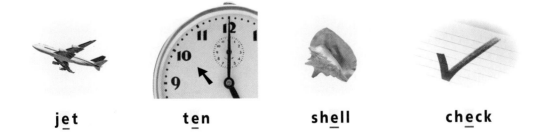

j**e**t   t**e**n   sh**e**ll   ch**e**ck

READING STRATEGY

Follow these steps to read a word.

1 Point to the first spelling. Say the sound.

2 Point to the second spelling. Say the sound.

3 Point to the last spelling. Say the sound.

4 Now blend all the sounds together to say the word. Say the word again. What is it?

b e l l

b e l l

b e l l

b + e + ll = bell

These two consonants are the same, so I say just one sound.

READING PRACTICE

Blend the sounds to read these words.

1. shot   2. neck   3. vet   4. black   5. kiss   6. ten

Use what you learned to read the sentences.

7. My cat, Fuzz, is sick.
8. I carry him to the vet.
9. I kiss him on the neck.
10. The vet gives my cat a shot.
11. He gives me ten black pills for my cat.
12. Then I tell Fuzz, "Let's go home."

SPELLING PRACTICE

13.–16. **Now write the sentences that your teacher reads.**

WORD WORK

Name each picture. What letters are missing from the names? Use letter cards to make the words.

EXAMPLE **17.** | j | e | t |

17. j _ t

18. h _ l l

19. r o _ _

20. b _ s

21. v _ n

22.  _ _ e l l

23. c h _ c k

24. f i _ _

25. c _ p

26. p _ t

27. **10** t _ n

28. c _ p

Read on Your Own

FOCUS ON GENRE

Realistic Fiction   Realistic fiction is a story that is not true, but could happen in real life. This story is about a person who works as a bike messenger.

FOCUS ON WORDS

Words with Short *e*, *sh*, *ck*, and Double Consonants   When you read and come to a word you don't know, blend the sounds together to read it.

Remember that the letters *sh* and *ck* make one sound. When you see two of the same consonants together, say just one sound. You just learned about words with these spellings:

e   sh   ck

check

High Frequency Words   Say these words as whole words when you read.

study	learn
carry	find
use	love
face	when
want	say

Let Ben Take It

Ben is a bike messenger.

Ben is a bike messenger.

Do you want to send something?

Ben can get it there fast.

Just say where it must go.

He gets his map.

He can study it to learn the best route.

He uses it to find a shop.

Then he hops on his bike and . . . zip!

He is off like a jet.

Ben can carry a lot of different things:

food, pictures, letters, flowers.

They fit in the big bag on his back.

Ben loves his job.

He has a smile on his face.

When you want to send something,

let Ben take it!

Think About "Let Ben Take It"

CHECK YOUR UNDERSTANDING

Make a web. Then tell a partner about Ben's job.

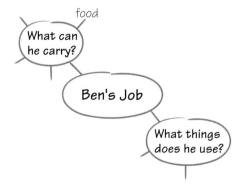

Questions About Work

▶ **Questions with *Who?*, *What?*, *Where?*, and *When?***

> You can use the words *Who, What, Where,* or *When* to start a question.

Use *Who* to ask about a person.
  Who are you?
Use *What* to ask about a thing.
  What is in your bag?
Use *Where* to ask about a place.
  Where is the shop?
Use *When* to ask about a time.
  When can you deliver the box?

MATCH QUESTIONS AND ANSWERS

Read each question. Find the sentence that answers it.
Take turns reading the questions and answers with a partner.

EXAMPLE **1.** Who is the bike messenger?
    E. Ben is the bike messenger.

Questions	Answers
1. Who is the bike messenger?	**A.** His helmet is on his head.
2. What is in his bag?	**B.** A box is in his bag.
3. Where is his helmet?	**C.** His next delivery is at 8:30.
4. When is his next delivery?	**D.** Ben is in the city.
5. Where is Ben?	**E.** Ben is the bike messenger.

WRITE QUESTIONS AND ANSWERS

Make a question to go with each answer.
Then write the question and answer.

EXAMPLE **6.** What is in the bag? A box of candy is in the bag.

 6. What _____? A box of candy is in the bag.
 7. What _____? It is a birthday present for Mr. Lee.
 8. Where _____? His office is in that tall building.
 9. When _____? His birthday is tomorrow.
10. Who _____? Ben can deliver the box.
11. Where _____? Ben is near the tall building.
12. When _____? Ben is ready to deliver the box now!

Success in Science and Mathematics

▶ **Learn About Measurement**

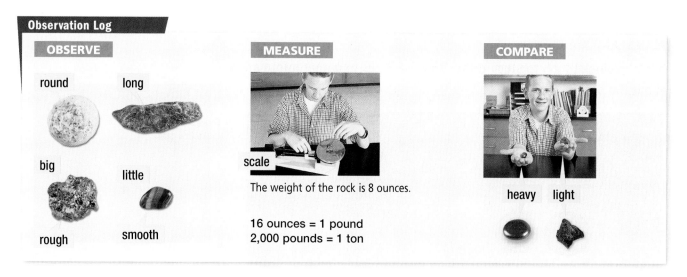

Observation Log

OBSERVE

round long

big little

rough smooth

MEASURE

scale

The weight of the rock is 8 ounces.

16 ounces = 1 pound
2,000 pounds = 1 ton

COMPARE

heavy light

Read the instructions. Then do the activity.

Be a Scientist: Study Rocks

• **You will need:** different kinds of rocks, a scale, a notebook, and a pencil

ACTIVITY STEPS

1 Observe
Make an observation log. Assign each rock a letter to identify it. Study the rocks. Take notes in the log about how each rock looks and feels.

2 Measure
Weigh each rock. Write the weights in your log.

3 Compare
How are the rocks alike? How are they different? Find out which rocks are the lightest. Find out which are the heaviest.

4 Sort
Put the rocks in groups, or categories. Is each rock heavy or light? Is it rough or smooth?

Observation Log

Rock	Color	Size	Shape	Weight
A	gray	big	round	10 oz.

THINK IT OVER

1. Is a big rock always heavier than a small one? Explain what you learned.
2. Where do you see different types of rocks in nature? How are they different?

GEOLOGISTS:
Rock Scientists

Build Background for "Geologists: Rock Scientists"

TOOLS AND CAREERS

It is a geologist's job to study rocks. They use rocks to gather information about the past.

◀ This geologist studies rocks in a cave.

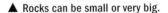

▲ Rocks can be small or very big.

Learn Key Vocabulary

Rate and Study the Words Rate how well you know each word. Then:

1. Pronounce the word. Say it aloud several times. Spell it.

2. Study the example.

3. Tell more about the word.

4. Practice it. Make the word your own.

Key Words

learn (lurn) *verb*

When people **learn**, they get information about a subject. These people **learn** about rocks.

rock (rok) *noun*

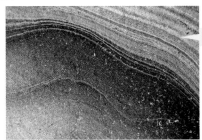

layer

A **rock** is made of little pieces of earth called minerals. Some **rocks** have layers.

scientist (sī-yun-tist) *noun*

A **scientist** studies the natural and physical world. A **scientist** who knows about rocks is a geologist.

study (stuh-dē) *verb*

People **study** to learn more about a subject. These people **study** by reading books.

use (yūz) *verb*

When people **use** a tool, they do something with it. Geologists **use** tools to take samples of rocks.

Practice the Words With a partner, make an Expanded Meaning Map for each Key Word. Take turns quizzing each other. For example, ask: "What is something that is like a rock?"

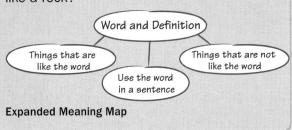

Word and Definition

Things that are like the word

Use the word in a sentence

Things that are not like the word

Expanded Meaning Map

Listen and Read Along

FOCUS ON GENRE

Informational Text   Informational text gives facts and details about a topic. It is nonfiction. This text explains how scientists use rocks to get information about the past.

FOCUS ON COMPREHENSION

Identify Details   When a writer gives information, he or she includes details about the topic. As you read this selection, look for details about rocks and how scientists use them.

GEOLOGISTS:
Rock Scientists

Scientists look at rocks to find out information about the past.

Smart Rocks

What can we **learn** from **rocks**? Rocks tell us about **the past**. Geologists are **scientists** who **study** rocks.

This cliff is made of rock. ▶

geologist

▲ A geologist studies rocks in this cave.

Key Vocabulary
learn *v.*, to gain knowledge
rocks *n.*, a stone of any size
scientists *n.*, an expert in science
study *n.*, to learn about

In Other Words
the past things that happened long ago

A Mountain of Layers

Some rocks are small. You can **pick them up**. Some rocks are big. These hills are really big rocks! They are made of many **layers**.

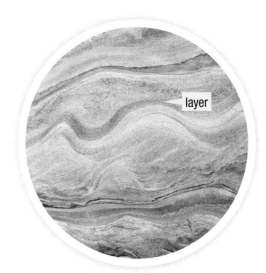

layer

▲ Compare the layers.

▼ These hills are made of a type of rock called sandstone.

In Other Words

pick them up hold them in your hand

layers flat parts that sit on top of one another

Before You Move On

1. **Analyze Information** What do geologists **study**?
2. **Details** Describe what a **rock** might look like.

Old Rocks, Young Rocks

The layers tell us when the rock was made. The **lower layers** of rock are older.

This rock in Utah formed many years ago. ▶

▼ Lower layers of rock are older than higher layers of rock.

Young Rock

Old Rock

In Other Words
lower layers layers on the bottom

▼ The rock layers of the Grand Canyon show changes over time.

Before You Move On

1. **Summary** Why do geologists look at the layers in **rock**?

2. **Details** Are the top layers of **rocks** older or younger than the bottom?

Fossils

Geologists **use** rocks to learn about plants and animals from the past. After they died, plants and animals left marks or parts in rocks. These are called fossils.

▲ A fish fossil

A plant fossil ▶

▼ This rock shows detail of an animal that lived long ago.

Key Vocabulary
use *v.*, to do something with

Think Like a Geologist

Now it is your turn. Find some rocks and look at them.
Write down what you see.

▼ Geologists look at fossils frozen in rock.

Before You Move On

1. **Details** What is a fossil?
2. **Draw Conclusions** Are fossils old or young? How do you know?

Think About "Geologists: Rock Scientists"

CHECK YOUR UNDERSTANDING

<u>1.–2.</u> Work with a partner to complete each item.

1. **Identify Details** Make a concept web like the one below. Put the topic in the middle. Then complete the web using details from the selection.

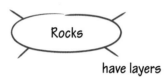

have layers

2. **Sum It Up** Use your concept web to tell about **rocks**. What did you **learn** about **scientists**?

REVIEW VOCABULARY

<u>3.–7.</u> Read the paragraph aloud. Add the vocabulary words.

> Geologists are _____ who look at _____ to find out about plants and animals. They _____ about plants and animals that lived long ago. Geologists _____ special tools to _____ fossils of plants and animals.

Vocabulary

rocks

learn

scientists

study

use

WRITE ABOUT JOBS

<u>8.</u> Write about a job that you might like to have when you are older. What makes the job interesting to you? What do you need to study to be good at the job?

Interview for a Job Handbook

WHAT IS AN INTERVIEW?

In an interview, one person asks questions. Another person gives answers.

Later, you can write the interview. Some written interviews use a **Q** before each question and an **A** before each answer.

INTERVIEW

Computer Specialist

Q: **Why do you work on computers?**

A: I like to know how they work. I like trying new things to see what computers can do.

Q: **What is the best part about your job?**

A: Every day is different. There are always new things to learn.

Q: **How can I get a job as a computer specialist?**

A: You take lots of classes about computers. When you finish school, you can look for a job.

Use a **question mark** when you write a question.

Use a **period** when you write a statement in the answer.

Writing Project

Write an Interview

WRITING PROMPT Interview a worker about his or her job. Take notes. Then write the interview for a class book. Give information about the person.

Plan and Write

❶ PLAN THE INTERVIEW

Think of a worker you want to interview. Make a list of what you want to know. What are the most important things? Put a check mark next to the things to focus on. Johanna chose to interview a teacher. Here is part of her list.

> **Interview with a Teacher**
> ✓ best part of the job
>   where you teach

Workers
artist
gardener
carpenter
teacher
mechanic
doctor
scientist

❷ WRITE QUESTIONS

Turn the ideas in your list into questions.

> **Interview with a Teacher**
> ✓best part of the job ⟶ **What is the best part of your job?**

❸ INTERVIEW THE WORKER

Plan a time you can talk with the person. Ask your questions and write the person's answers. Ask the person for a picture.

> **Q: What is your name?**
> **A:** My name is Mrs. Varela.
>
> **Q: What is your job?**
> **A:** I am a history teacher.

❹ WRITE THE INTERVIEW

Put the questions and answers in the order you like best.

Check Your Work

Read more of Johanna's interview. She needs to make some changes.

- The first question needs a question mark. To add it, she used this mark: ∧.
- The first answer needs to start with a capital letter. To show the change, she put three lines under the letter: ≡.

What other errors does she need to fix?

Q: What is the best part of your job?∧

A: <u>i</u> like working with my students.

Q: why do you teach history?

A: History was my favorite class in school

Look back at your interview. Read it aloud. Then ask yourself the questions in the checklist. Mark your changes.

Finish and Share

Use these steps to finish your interview.

1. Write the worker's job at the top of your page.
2. Write the questions and answers.
3. Add the picture.
4. Put all the pages together into a job handbook. Add a cover.

READ ALOUD

Take turns reading the interviews aloud. Use these tips.

Presenting Tips

If You Are the Speaker:	If You Are the Listener:
• Read loudly and clearly.	• Look at the pictures.
• Show the pictures.	• Pay attention to the reader's voice.

Checklist

☑ Did I write all my questions in the right order?

☑ Did I end each question with a question mark?

☑ Did I use a capital letter at the beginning of each sentence?

Reflect

- What did you learn about the person you interviewed?
- What did you like best about writing an interview?

Numbers are all around. You use numbers every day.

SALE 75% OFF SALE

100 DOLLARS

ten thousand 10,000

POPULATION
People 98½
Horses 101

$1 .50

one million 1,000,000

NUMBERS COUNT

Look at the pictures.

What do they show?

Work with a partner to find

more numbers around you.

In This Unit

▶ **Language Development**

▶ **Language and Literacy**

▶ **Language and Content**
   Social Science

▶ **Writing Project**

Vocabulary
- Cardinal Numbers
- Ordinal Numbers
- Key Vocabulary

Language Functions
- Ask Questions
- Give Information
- Express Needs

Grammar
- Questions with *Do* and *Does*
- Negative Sentences
- Contractions with *not*

Reading
- Blends and Digraphs
- High Frequency Words
- Comprehension: Identify Problems and Solutions; Identify Details
- Text Features: Tables

Writing
- Fact Sheet

Numbers Everywhere!

▶ **Language: Ask Questions**

Listen and chant. CD

Numbers!

Does it cost ten dollars
To go to the show?
Without numbers
We wouldn't know.

Without numbers
We'd be in a fix.
Does the show start at five?
Or is it at six?

Do we need two tickets?
Or do we need three?
Without numbers,
Where would we be?

> **Questions with Do and Does**
> Use *do* with *I*, *you*, *we*, and *they*.
> **Do you** need two tickets?
> Use *does* with *he*, *she*, and *it*.
> **Does it** cost ten dollars?

EXPRESS YOURSELF ▶ ASK QUESTIONS

1.–4. Work with a partner. Ask 4 questions. Choose words from each column.

Do you	have	five cookies?
Do they	see	two pencils?
Does he	need	seven backpacks?
Does she	want	three markers?

EXAMPLES **1.** Do you need two pencils?
2. Does she see five cookies?

5.–8. Work with a partner. Take turns asking each other questions with *Do* or *Does*.

EXAMPLE **5.** Do you have a highlighter?
No, I do not.

From One to One Million

▶ **Vocabulary: Cardinal Numbers**
▶ **Language: Give Information**

Number Words

0	zero	11	eleven	21	twenty-one	40	forty	100	one hundred
1	one	12	twelve	22	twenty-two	50	fifty	101	one hundred one
2	two	13	thirteen	23	twenty-three	60	sixty	500	five hundred
3	three	14	fourteen	24	twenty-four	70	seventy	550	five hundred fifty
4	four	15	fifteen	25	twenty-five	80	eighty	1,000	one thousand
5	five	16	sixteen	26	twenty-six	90	ninety	1,151	one thousand, one hundred fifty-one
6	six	17	seventeen	27	twenty-seven			5,000	five thousand
7	seven	18	eighteen	28	twenty-eight			10,000	ten thousand
8	eight	19	nineteen	29	twenty-nine			100,000	one hundred thousand
9	nine	20	twenty	30	thirty			500,000	five hundred thousand
10	ten							1,000,000	one million

Beijing, China: seventeen million, four hundred thousand

population 17,400,000

Put commas after the millions place and the thousands place.

ORAL LANGUAGE PRACTICE ▶ GIVE INFORMATION

Work with a partner. Read each fact about China in 2007.
Say a sentence with each fact. Begin your sentence with *China has*.

1. **75,438** kilometers of railways
2. **467** airports
3. **795,300,000** workers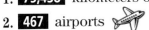
4. **461,100,000** cellular phones
5. **3,240** television stations
6. **448,000,000** televisions

EXAMPLE **1.** China has seventy-five thousand, four hundred thirty-eight kilometers of railways.

WRITTEN PRACTICE

7.–10. **Work with a partner to find numbers in your classroom.**
Write 4 sentences each with the numbers you find.
Write words for the numbers.

EXAMPLE **7.** Our classroom has thirty-three desks.

Language Development

Flight 400 Is Not Late!

▶ **Negative Sentences**

Negative sentences can use *not*, *do not*, or *does not*.

Add *not* after *am*, *is*, or *are*.

He is happy.
She is not happy.

Add *do not* or *does not* before other verbs.

She gets on the flight.
He does not get on the flight.

BUILD NEGATIVE SENTENCES

Read each sentence. Add *not* to make it a negative sentence. Say the new sentence.

EXAMPLE **1.** We are on Flight 400.
We are not on Flight 400.

1. We are on Flight 400.
2. It is 10:00.
3. We are late.
4. People are in a hurry.

Read each sentence. Add *do not* or *does not* to make it a negative sentence. Say the new sentence.

EXAMPLE **5.** The plane leaves at 10:30
The plane does not leave at 10:30.

When you use *does not*, take the *s* off the verb.

5. The plane leaves at 10:30.
6. We walk very fast.
7. We get to Gate 55.
8. A woman talks to us.
9. We miss the plane.
10. The plane leaves without us.

WRITTEN PRACTICE

<u>11.–20.</u> **Write the sentences you made in Items 1–10 above.**

EXAMPLE **11.** We are on Flight 400. We are not on Flight 400.

First, Second, Third…

▶ **Vocabulary: Ordinal Numbers**
▶ **Language: Express Needs**

Ordinal numbers are used to describe the order in which things happen.

ORAL LANGUAGE PRACTICE ▶ EXPRESS NEEDS

1.–6. Who's talking?  CD
Listen. Which person in line is talking?
Point to the correct person.
Tell what the person needs.

EXAMPLE **1.** This is the fifth person.
She needs a magazine.

WRITTEN PRACTICE

7.–14. Write about 8 people in the line.
Tell what each person needs.

EXAMPLE **7.** The first person needs water.

Listen and Read Along

FOCUS ON GENRE

Historical Fiction   Historical fiction is a story that is not true. Although it is not a true story, it is based on events that really happened in history. This story is about a drought in ancient China.

FOCUS ON VOCABULARY

Number Words   You have been learning words like the ones below. Use these words as you talk about *A Year Without Rain*. Collect more words to put in the web.

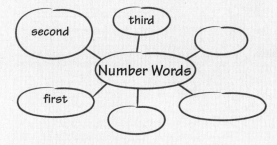

THEME BOOK

Read this historical fiction about a drought.

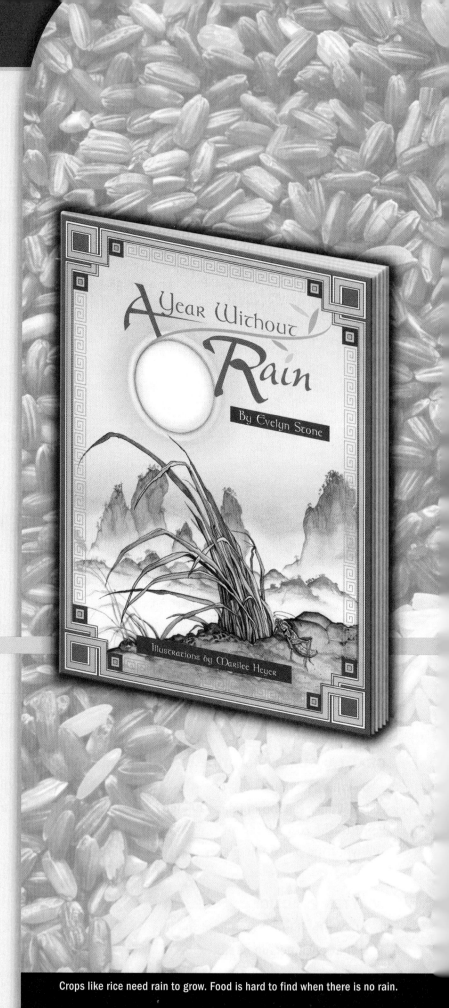

Crops like rice need rain to grow. Food is hard to find when there is no rain.

Think About
A Year Without Rain

IDENTIFY PROBLEM AND SOLUTION

Make a problem-and-solution chart for *A Year Without Rain.* Follow these steps.

1 Think about the story. What is the main problem? Draw a box and write the problem.

> **Problem:** There is no rain. People are hungry.

2 What happens next? Add boxes. Write one event in each box.

> **Problem:** There is no rain. People are hungry.
>
> | 1. The children each give 1 bowl of rice. | 2. | 3. |
> |---|---|---|
> | 4. | 5. | 6. |
>
> Solution:

3 How is the problem solved? Write the solution in the box at the bottom of your chart.

4 Use your completed problem-and-solution chart to take turns telling the story with a partner.

High Frequency Words

▲ People look at their flight numbers in an airport.

REVIEW HIGH FREQUENCY WORDS

Read the words aloud. Which word goes in the sentence?

are	say
year	read
find	from

1. The people _____ in an airport.
2. They _____ the screens.
3. They _____ their flight numbers.

LEARN NEW WORDS

Study these words. Say them as whole words when you read.

leave	Stan and his friend **leave** in June for a vacation.
two	They go for **two** months: June and July.
out	They fly in and **out** of many airports.
three	China, Japan, and Laos are **three** Asian countries.
all	Stan likes them **all.**

PRACTICE

<u>4.–8.</u> **Make a map for each new word. Write the word in the center. Complete the other boxes. Then use the word in a sentence of your own.**

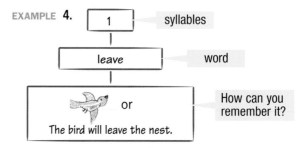

EXAMPLE **4.**

1 — syllables

leave — word

The bird will leave the nest. — How can you remember it?

<u>9.–11.</u> **Write each new word on a card. Sort the cards into these groups:**

9. These 2 words have 5 letters.
10. These 3 words have 3 letters.
11. These 2 words are number words.

Read the words in each group aloud. Make up new groups with a partner.

EXAMPLE **9.**

leave   three

leave
three

More High Frequency Words

REVIEW HIGH FREQUENCY WORDS

Read the words aloud. Which word goes in the sentence?

new	go
too	so
there	many

1. I got _____ shoes yesterday.

2. My sister got new shoes, _____.

3. The store has so _____ colors to choose from!

> **How to Learn a New Word**
> - Look at the word.
> - Listen to the word.
> - Listen to the word in a sentence. What does it mean?
> - Say the word.
> - Spell the word.
> - Say the word again.

LEARN NEW WORDS

Study these words. Say them as whole words when you read.

says	Stan **says**, "Our first stop is China."
second	"Our **second** stop is Japan."
without	Stan never travels **without** his camera.
enough	He takes **enough** film to photograph everything.
more	He brings back **more** pictures of Japan than of China.

PRACTICE

4.–8. Make a map for each new word. Write the word in the center. Complete the other boxes. Then use the word in a sentence of your own.

EXAMPLE 4.

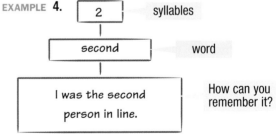

9.–11. Write each new word on a card. Sort the cards into these groups:

9. These 2 words have 6 letters.
10. This word has 7 letters.
11. This word tells number order.

Read the words in each group aloud. Make up new groups with a partner.

EXAMPLE 9.

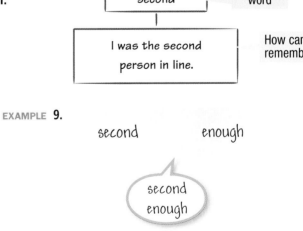

Reading and Spelling

▶ **Blends and Digraphs**

Listen and learn. CD

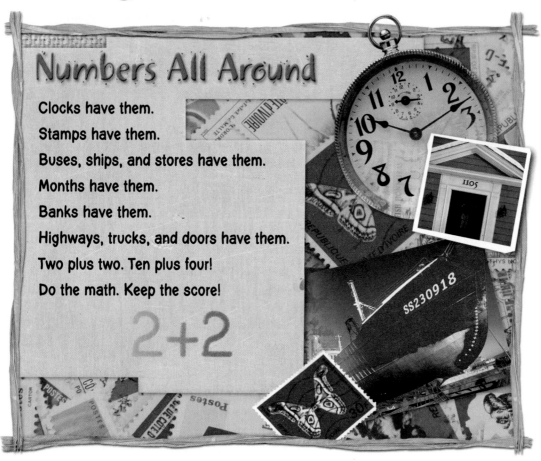

Numbers All Around

Clocks have them.
Stamps have them.
Buses, ships, and stores have them.
Months have them.
Banks have them.
Highways, trucks, and doors have them.
Two plus two. Ten plus four!
Do the math. Keep the score!

2+2

CONNECT SOUNDS AND LETTERS

How many sounds does each word have?

1.

clock

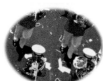

band

nest

truck

2.

fish

bath

check

ring

READING STRATEGY

Follow these steps to read a word.

1 Sometimes 2 consonants stand for 1 sound. When you see **sh**, **ch**, **th**, **wh**, or **ng**, say 1 sound. Then blend all the sounds together to say the word.

<u>sh</u>op   **ba<u>th</u>**

sh + **o** + **p** = **shop**   **b** + **a** + **th** = **bath**

Each word has 3 sounds.

2 When other consonants are together, each usually makes its own sound. Blend all the sounds together to say the word.

<u>dr</u>op   **we<u>nt</u>**

d + **r** + **o** + **p** = **drop**   **w** + **e** + **n** + **t** = **went**

Each word has 4 sounds.

READING PRACTICE

Blend the sounds to read these words.

1. brush   2. bring   3. cash   4. class   5. costs   6. just

Use what you learned to read the sentences.

7. Beth needs a brush for art class this spring.
8. She has three dollars in cash.
9. That is enough for a small brush. It costs just $2.39.
10. A big, long brush costs $5.00.
11. Which brush does Beth bring home?

SPELLING PRACTICE

<u>12.–15.</u> **Now write the sentences that your teacher reads.**

WORD WORK

<u>16.</u> **Write each of these words on a card.**   EXAMPLE   **16.**   *chess*   *catch*

| catch | chess | chin | inch | much |
| match | check | lunch | chat | chop |

Say each word. Group the words that begin with the same sound.
Now group the words that end with the same sound.
Look at these words. What do you notice?

Read on Your Own

FOCUS ON GENRE

Realistic Fiction   Realistic fiction is a story that is not true but is based on events that could happen in real life. This story is about a man who thinks he is late for his flight.

FOCUS ON WORDS

Blends and Digraphs   When you read and come to a word you don't know, blend the sounds together to read it.

Remember that *sh*, *th*, *wh*, and *ng* make one sound. You have learned about words with these spellings:

cl	sh	th	ng
wh	lt	fr	sn

fi<u>sh</u>

High Frequency Words   Say these words as whole words when you read.

leave	two
out	three
all	says
second	without
enough	more

Stan is in a big rush. His plane leaves at 2:00 p.m. The clock says 1:57 p.m. Stan has three minutes to catch his plane. That is not very long! He jumps out of the cab and slams the door. Bang! He drops his bag. All of his things fall out of the bag. Then he drops one more thing—his ticket! A man helps Stan. The first thing he picks up is the bag. The second thing he picks up is the ticket. The man asks Stan, "When does your plane leave?"

Stan says, "I think it just left without me."

The man looks at Stan's ticket. He grins and tells Stan, "You have enough time. Your plane leaves tomorrow at two."

Think About "Rush!"

CHECK YOUR UNDERSTANDING

Make a web. Then complete it. Tell the story to a partner.

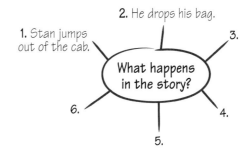

I Don't Want to Pay $10.00!

▶ **Contractions with** *not*

When you make a contraction, you join two words together.

is + not = isn't	do + not = don't
are + not = aren't	does + not = doesn't

no space   Write an apostrophe in place of the *o*.

Use these contractions in negative sentences.

The food at the airport **isn't** very good.
The cookies **aren't** big.
The cake **doesn't** have nuts.
I **don't** want anything to eat.

READ SENTENCES

**Read the first sentence in each item. Then read the second sentence
with the contraction. Listen to how the contraction sounds.**

1. Stan <u>does not</u> want this food. Stan <u>doesn't</u> want this food.
2. The grapes <u>are not</u> green. The grapes <u>aren't</u> green.
3. The sandwich <u>is not</u> fresh. The sandwich <u>isn't</u> fresh.
4. The cookies <u>do not</u> have raisins. The cookies <u>don't</u> have raisins.

**Read each sentence. Change the <u>underlined</u> words to a contraction.
Then say the new sentence.**

EXAMPLE **5.** The salad <u>does not</u> have carrots.
          The salad <u>doesn't</u> have carrots.

5. The salad <u>does not</u> have carrots.
6. The grapes <u>do not</u> taste sweet.
7. The cake <u>is not</u> chocolate.
8. The grapes <u>are not</u> cold.
9. The food <u>is not</u> cheap!
10. Stan <u>is not</u> hungry anymore.

WRITE SENTENCES

<u>11.–14.</u> **Work with a partner. Write 4 new sentences to tell about
the picture above. Use** *isn't, aren't, don't,* **and** *doesn't.*

EXAMPLE **11.** The salad isn't fresh.

Success in Social Science

▶ **Learn About Geography**

Tables

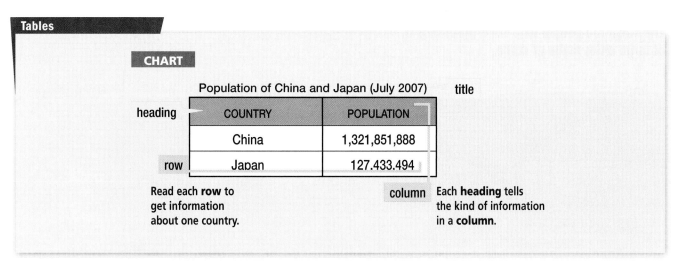

CHART

Population of China and Japan (July 2007) — title

heading

COUNTRY	POPULATION
China	1,321,851,888
Japan	127,433,494

row

Read each **row** to get information about one country.

column

Each **heading** tells the kind of information in a **column**.

Listen to the article and study the chart. Then do the Review.

Compare Populations

• Why do some places have a large population?

South America is a large **continent**. It has many different kinds of land.

Mountains

Rain Forest

The Coast

Most people live near the coast. Not many people live in the middle of the continent because it has many forests and mountains. Roads and towns are difficult to build in places like that, and it is not easy to ship things.

Compare Colombia and Bolivia, for example. These **countries** are of similar size, but their populations are very different. One reason is the location of each country. Bolivia is an inland country with mountains and rain forests. It has only about 2,000 miles of paved roads, so travel is difficult. Colombia has about 10,000 miles of paved roads. The roads make it easy for people to get there. Colombia also has coasts on both the Caribbean Sea and Pacific Ocean. It is easy to ship things by land or sea. People like to live where it is easy to get the things they need.

REVIEW

1. **Check Your Understanding** Why do most people in South America live near the coast?
2. **Vocabulary** In what continent are Colombia and Bolivia located?
3. **Use Charts** How many more people live in Colombia than in Bolivia?

Area and Population of Bolivia and Colombia (2007)

COUNTRY	AREA (in square miles)	POPULATION
Bolivia	424,164	9,119,152
Colombia	440,831	44,379,598

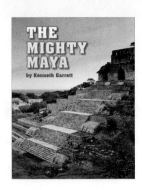

Build Background for "The Mighty Maya"

NUMBERS

The Maya are people who lived thousands of years ago. They built hundreds of large cities made of stone.

▲ The Maya lived in buildings called pyramids.

▲ This map shows where the Maya once lived.

Learn Key Vocabulary

Rate and Study the Words Rate how well you know each word. Then:

1. Pronounce the word. Say it aloud several times. Spell it.
2. Study the example.
3. Tell more about the word.
4. Practice it. Make the word your own.

Rating Scale

1 = I have never seen this word before.

2 = I am not sure of the word's meaning.

3 = I know this word and can teach the word's meaning to someone else.

Key Words

city (si-tē) *noun*

A **city** is a place where many people live and work. Copán is one old Maya **city** that still exists today.

hundreds (hun-dridz) *noun*

When there are **hundreds** of something, it means there are more than 100. This rainforest has **hundreds** of trees.

population (pop-yū-lā-shun) *noun*

POPULATION OF COPÁN AND TIKAL	
City	**Population**
Copán	20,000
Tikal	50,000

The **population** is the number of people who live in one place. Tikal has a higher **population** than Copán.

thousands (thou-zundz) *noun*

Thousands means a number that is higher than 1,000. This pyramid was built **thousands** of years ago.

two (tū) *adjective*

Two is a number that equals one plus one. These **two** Maya men are living today.

Practice the Words With a partner, make a Vocabulary Study Card for each Key Word.

Write the word.

front

city

Tell what it means and use it in a sentence.

back

a place where many people live

Miami

Use the cards to quiz your partner. Take turns answering.

Listen and Read Along

FOCUS ON GENRE

Personal Narrative   A personal narrative is a story about a person's experiences. It is nonfiction. This personal narrative is about a photographer's visit to the place where the ancient Maya once lived.

FOCUS ON COMPREHENSION

Details   Details are used to give more information about a topic. Photographs, pictures, and tables can give details about the text you read. The author of "The Mighty Maya" used pictures and tables to give details about his visit.

POPULATION OF COPÁN AND TIKAL	
City	Population
Copán	20,000
Tikal	50,000

The Ancient Maya once lived in these stone buildings.

THE MIGHTY MAYA

by Kenneth Garrett

VISITING THE MAYA

I **am a photographer.** I want to show people **cities** the Maya lived in many years ago. I went to **San Bartolo** to take pictures.

▼ This is where the Maya once lived.

Mexico and Central America

Palenque ▲   Tikal ▲   San Bartolo ▲

Copán ▲

▼ This pyramid was built by the Maya.

NORTH AMERICA

AREA ENLARGED

SOUTH AMERICA

Key Vocabulary
cities *n.*, places where many people live and work

In Other Words
am a photographer take pictures
San Bartolo a famous city in Central America

▼ The Maya created paintings called murals.

The Maya have lived in these rainforests for **thousands** of years. **In ancient times,** the Maya built large cities with **pyramids** of stone. They also made beautiful paintings on the walls.

Key Vocabulary
thousands *n.*, the numbers between 1,000 and 999,999

In Other Words
In ancient times A long, long time ago
pyramids buildings made with sides shaped like a triangle

Before You Move On
1. **Author's Purpose** Why did the author go to San Bartolo?
2. **Details** What do you know about the Maya?

Two Cities of Stone

The Maya built **hundreds** of cities from stone. I saw **two famous** cities. Parts of both cities still **exist** today.

Copán

Copán was a small city. It grew quickly. When I saw it, I could imagine living there.

▼ The Maya used stone to make art like this.

▲ Tikal was a large Maya city.

Tikal

Tikal was a much larger city. I think that Tikal is the most beautiful Maya city.

Compare the **population** of Tikal and Copán.

POPULATION OF COPÁN AND TIKAL	
City	Population
Copán	20,000
Tikal	50,000

Key Vocabulary
population *n.*, the total number of people living in one area

Before You Move On

1. **Details** Which **city** was the author's favorite?
2. **Text Features** How many more people lived in Tikal than in Copán?

Empty Cities

The cities I saw are empty. Things changed around the year 800. The cities stopped growing. The people stopped building. People **decided to** leave the cities.

▲ The Maya once lived in stone buildings like this.

In Other Words
decided to made a choice to

▲ In ancient times, the Maya liked to fly giant kites. The Maya still fly kites today.

The Maya Today

There are Maya **living today**. They do some of the same things that the Maya did long ago. They still fly colorful kites. They still use Maya words.

I liked talking with the Maya people. I was glad I **had the chance to** take pictures of the old, beautiful cities.

In Other Words

living today alive now
had the chance was able to

Before You Move On

1. **Make Comparisons** How are the Maya today like the Maya from long ago?
2. **Details** What is one thing the Maya still do today?

Language and Content

Think About "The Mighty Maya"

CHECK YOUR UNDERSTANDING

<u>1.–2.</u> **Work with a partner to complete each item.**

1. **Identify Details** Make a chart like the one below. Then complete the chart with details about each **city** using information from the selection.

Tikal	Copán
	population was 20,000

2. **Sum It Up** Use the information in the chart to describe the **two** ancient Maya **cities**.

REVIEW VOCABULARY

<u>3.–7.</u> **Read the paragraph aloud. Add the vocabulary words.**

> _____ of years ago, the Maya built pyramids. They built _____ of cities from stone. I learned about _____ famous cities. Parts of both _____ still exist today. Copán was a small city, but more people went to live there. At one time, the city's _____ was 20,000 people.

Vocabulary
two
hundreds
thousands
population
cities

WRITE ABOUT POPULATIONS

<u>8.</u> Write about how the **population** of your town or a nearby town has changed over the years.

Fact Sheet

WHAT IS A FACT SHEET?

A fact sheet gives information. It can give facts about a person, place, or thing. It can include questions and answers. It usually gives some number facts.

United States

- What is the population of the United States?
  The population of the United States is
  301,139,947.
- How many people are fourteen years old or younger?
  There are 29,777,438 girls 14 years or younger. There are 31,152,050 boys.
- What is the highest place in the United States?
  The highest place is Mount McKinley in Alaska. It stands 20,322 feet high.
- How many miles of rivers does the United States have?
  The United States has 25,482 miles of rivers and other waterways.

A **number fact** answers each of these questions. Use commas in large numbers.

Names of places begin with capital letters.

Use a question mark at the end of each question.

Writing Project

Write a Fact Sheet

WRITING PROMPT What country do you want to study? What number facts do you want to find out? Make a fact sheet with questions and answers to share with the class.

Plan and Write

1 PLAN YOUR FACT SHEET

Choose a country to research. Make a list of what you want to know. What are the most important things? Put a check mark next to the things to focus on. Ben chose to write about China.

> ✓ size
> history
> food
> ✓ population
> ✓ capital

2 FIND ANSWERS

Turn your list into questions. Look at books or on the Internet to find answers to your questions. Ask your teacher or librarian for help. Write the number facts carefully.

> ✓ size ——→ How big is China?
> ✓ population ——→ How many people live in China?
> ✓ name of capital city ——→ What is the capital of China?

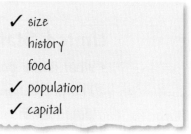

> Beijing is the capital of China.

3 WRITE FACTS

Use your notes to write questions and answers. Add a map to your page.

> **China**
> • How large is China?
>   It is more than 3,700,000 square miles.
> • What is the population of China?
>   The population of China is 1,321,851,888.
> • What is the capital of China?
>   The capital is Beijing.

Check Your Work

Read more of Ben's fact sheet. He needs to make some changes.

- The first question needs a question mark. To add it, he used this mark: $\wedge$.
- The first answer needs capital letters for the name of the river. He put three lines under the letters: $\equiv$.

What other errors does he need to fix?

- What is the longest river in China?
  The yangtze river is the longest.
- What is the population of the capital city
  beijing has 13,800,000 people.

Look back at your fact sheet. Read it aloud. Then ask yourself the questions in this checklist. Mark your changes.

Finish and Share

Use these steps to finish your fact sheet.

1. Write the questions and facts neatly and correctly.
2. Write a title at the top of the page.
3. Add a map.
4. Put all the pages together in a class book about different places.

PRESENT

Share your writing with the class. Use these tips.

Presenting Tips

If You Are the Speaker:	If You Are the Listener:
• Stay on the topic.	• Pay attention to the reader's voice.
• Read loudly and clearly.	
• Show the map.	• Ask questions about the topic.
	• Look at the map.

Checklist

- ✓ Did I use capital letters at the beginning of the names of places?
- ✓ Did I use the correct end marks?
- ✓ Did I only tell facts?

Reflect

- What facts did you learn about your country?
- What other countries would you like to learn about?

There are many things to do in a city.

Welcome to MIAMI

Look at the sign. What does it tell you about this city? Work with a group to make a sign for your city. Describe your sign to the class.

In This Unit

▶ **Language Development**

▶ **Language and Literacy**

▶ **Language and Content**
  Social Studies

▶ **Writing Project**

Vocabulary
- Location Words
- Neighborhoods
- Key Vocabulary

Language Functions
- Ask for and Give Information

Grammar
- Prepositions
- Regular Past Tense Verbs
- Statements with *There is* and *There are*
- Pronoun-Verb Contractions

Reading
- Word Patterns and Multisyllabic Words
- High Frequency Words
- Comprehension: Identify Details
- Text Features: Maps

Writing
- Journal Entry

Language Development

Out and About in the City

▶ **Language: Ask for and Give Information**

Listen and sing. CD

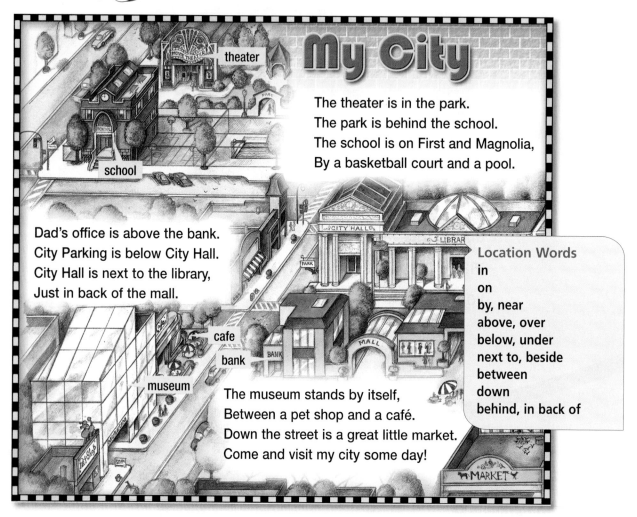

My City

The theater is in the park.
The park is behind the school.
The school is on First and Magnolia,
By a basketball court and a pool.

Dad's office is above the bank.
City Parking is below City Hall.
City Hall is next to the library,
Just in back of the mall.

The museum stands by itself,
Between a pet shop and a café.
Down the street is a great little market.
Come and visit my city some day!

Location Words
in
on
by, near
above, over
below, under
next to, beside
between
down
behind, in back of

EXPRESS YOURSELF ▶ ASK FOR AND GIVE INFORMATION

Work with a partner. Ask each question about your school. Answer in a complete sentence. Use a location word.

EXAMPLE **1.** Where is the library?
It is by the gym.

1. Where is the library?
2. Where is the parking lot?
3. Where is the main office?
4. Where is the cafeteria?
5. Where is the entrance?
6. Where is the gym?

7.–10. Choose 4 places in your school. Tell your partner where each place is. Then listen as your partner tells you where 4 other places in your school are.

EXAMPLE **7.** The gym is by the library.

What Happens Here?

▶ **Vocabulary: Neighborhood**
▶ **Language: Ask for and Give Information**

Hardware Store — sign

Bus Station — bus

Hospital — ambulance

Post Office — flag, mailbox

Library

Fire Station — fire engine

Police Station — patrol car

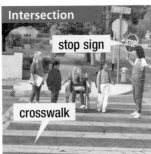
Intersection — stop sign, crosswalk

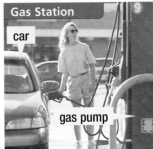
Gas Station — car, gas pump

Store — parking lot

ORAL LANGUAGE PRACTICE ▶ ASK FOR AND GIVE INFORMATION

<u>1.–4.</u> Work with a partner. Ask this question about 4 places in the neighborhood: *What happens at ____?* Answer your partner's questions.

EXAMPLE **1.** What happens at the bus station?
People wait for the bus.

WRITTEN PRACTICE

<u>5.–14.</u> Write a question and answer about each photo above.
Take turns sharing your questions and answers with a partner.

EXAMPLE **5.** What happens at the hardware store?
People buy tools.

Language Development

At the Mall

▶ **Vocabulary: Neighborhood**
▶ **Language: Ask for and Give Information**

ORAL LANGUAGE PRACTICE ▶ ASK FOR AND GIVE INFORMATION

1.–3. Who's talking?  CD

Listen. Where are the people? Point to them in the picture.

Act out each scene with a partner. Ask for and give information.

WRITTEN PRACTICE ✎

4.–8. Write 5 questions about the mall. Then trade papers with a partner and write the answers.

EXAMPLE **4.** Where is the bench?
The bench is next to the information booth.

On My Street

▶ **Regular Past Tense Verbs**

A verb changes to show the past tense.

Fred **cleans** the car.

Fred **cleaned** the car.

BUILD SENTENCES

Look at each picture below. Choose the correct verb to go with each picture. Say the new sentence.

EXAMPLE **1.** She plants the flowers.

She planted the flowers.

1.

She ___(plants/planted)___ the flowers.

2.

She ___(pulls /pulled)___ the weed.

3.

They ___(play /played)___ basketball.

4.

He ___(pumps /pumped)___ the tire.

WRITTEN PRACTICE

5.–8. Write each sentence you made above.

EXAMPLE **5.** She plants the flowers.

She planted the flowers

We Played Football in the Park

▶ **Regular Past Tense Verbs**

You can add -_ed_ to many verbs to tell about an action that happened in the past.

I **wanted** to play football on Saturday.

I **called** my friends.

We **walked** to the park.

WRITE ABOUT THE PAST

Write each sentence. Add the past tense of the word in dark type.

EXAMPLE **1.** We enjoyed a fun day at the park.

1. **enjoy**	We _____ a fun day at the park.
2. **play**	We _____ football on the grass.
3. **miss**	I _____ the ball.
4. **roll**	It _____ by the picnic table.
5. **turn**	Jessie _____ on the radio.
6. **pick**	She _____ a good station.
7. **want**	Emilio _____ to hear his new CD.
8. **ask**	Jessie _____ to hear it, too.
9. **listen**	We _____ to the CD.
10. **jump**	Alvin _____ to the beat.
11. **enjoy**	I _____ it.
12. **laugh**	We all _____.
13. **learn**	Everyone _____ his funny dance.
14. **talk**	We _____ about school.
15. **pass**	The time _____ quickly.

READ ALOUD

<u>16.–30.</u> Work with your teacher. Read aloud each sentence you wrote.

What Is in Our City?

▶ **Statements with *There is* and *There are***

The phrase *There is* talks about one person or thing. The phrase *There are* talks about two or more people or things.

Use *There is* to talk about one person or thing.

> **There is** a bike trail near the park.

Use *There are* to talk about two or more people or things.

> **There are** two girls on the trail.

BUILD SENTENCES

Say each sentence. Add *There is* or *There are*.

EXAMPLE **1.** There are 2 lions.

1. _____ 2 lions.
2. _____ a U.S. flag.
3. _____ some steps.

4. _____ a bus stop.
5. _____ a trash can.
6. _____ people.

WRITE SENTENCES

7.–10. Work with a partner. Write 4 more sentences to tell about the photos above. Add location words.

EXAMPLE **7.** There are 2 lions in front of the museum.

Language Development

Listen and Read Along

FOCUS ON GENRE

Realistic Fiction   Realistic fiction is a story that is like real life, but the story did not really happen. This story is about a boy who helps people.

FOCUS ON VOCABULARY

Neighborhood Words   You have been learning words like the ones below. Use these words as you talk about *More Than a Meal*. Collect more words to put in the web.

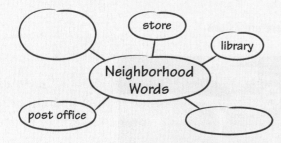

THEME BOOK

Read this realistic fiction about a boy who helps people.

MORE THAN A MEAL

by Suzy Blackaby

These students are making meals for people in their neighborhood.

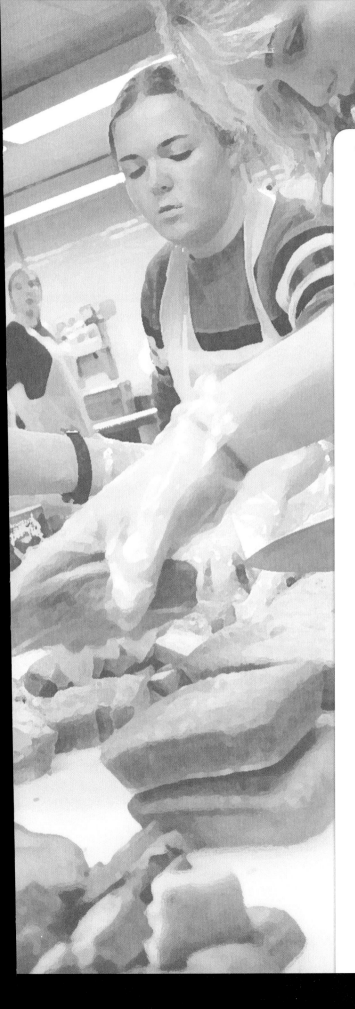

Think About *More Than a Meal*

IDENTIFY DETAILS

**Make a detail chart to tell about *More Than a Meal*.
Follow these steps.**

1 Think about what Carlos did each day in the story. Draw a chart like the one below. Write what Carlos did on Monday.

Day	Events
Monday	delivered meals, took out trash, and fixed a light
Tuesday	
Wednesday	
Thursday	
Friday	

2 What did Carlos do the rest of the week? Complete the chart with more details. Use words from the book.

3 Use your detail chart to tell the story to a partner. Then have your partner tell the story to you.

High Frequency Words

REVIEW HIGH FREQUENCY WORDS

Read the words aloud. Which word goes in the sentence?

Here	Have
where	want
take	things

1. _____ is the bus.

2. This is the bus they all _____ .

3. They _____ this bus every day.

▲ People use the bus in cities around the world.

LEARN NEW WORDS

Study these words. Say them as whole words when you read.

city	Padma lives in the **city** of Chicago.
above	She lives in an apartment high **above** the street.
by	It is on Belmont Street, **by** a Mexican restaurant.
sometimes	**Sometimes** she jogs to Lake Michigan.
her	**Her** dog, Bandit, likes to run, too.

PRACTICE

<u>4.–8.</u> Make a map for each new word. Write the word in the top. Complete the drawing. Then use the word in a sentence of your own.

EXAMPLE **1.**

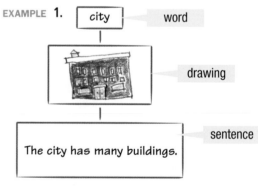

The city has many buildings.

<u>9.–13.</u> Where does each new word fit in the chart? Say the word and spell it.

EXAMPLE **9.**

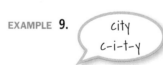

city
c-i-t-y

What to Look For	Word
9. ends with **y**	_ _ _ _
10. starts with **a**	_ _ _ _ _
11. ends with **er**	_ _ _
12. has two smaller words in it	_ _ _ _ _ _ _ _ _
13. means "next to"	_ _

More High Frequency Words

▷ How to Learn a New Word
• Look at the word.
• Listen to the word.
• Listen to the word in a sentence. What does it mean?
• Say the word.
• Spell the word.
• Say the word again.

REVIEW HIGH FREQUENCY WORDS

Read the words aloud. Which word goes in the sentence?

long	large
very	soon
move	different

1. It took a _____ time to finish the project.

2. Other kids finished their projects _____ quickly.

3. My project was very _____ so it took a lot of time.

LEARN NEW WORDS

Study these words. Say them as whole words when you read.

come	Padma's mom says, "**Come** home before dinner."
animals	There is a park for dogs and other **animals**.
people	**People** call it "Bark Park."
down	Bandit runs up and **down** the hill there.
under	Then Padma and Bandit rest **under** a tree.

PRACTICE

4.–8. Make a map for each new word. Write the word in the top. Complete the drawing. Then use the word in a sentence of your own.

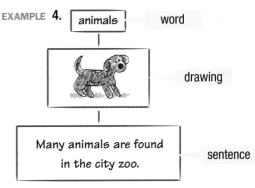

EXAMPLE **4.** animals — word

drawing

Many animals are found in the city zoo. — sentence

9.–13. Where does each new word fit in the chart? Say the word and spell it.

EXAMPLE **9.**

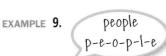

people
p-e-o-p-l-e

What to Look For	Word
9. starts with **p**	_ _ _ _ _ _
10. is the opposite of over	_ _ _ _ _
11. has 3 syllables	_ _ _ _ _ _ _
12. rhymes with some	_ _ _ _
13. means the opposite of up	_ _ _ _

Reading and Spelling

▶ **Word Patterns and Multisyllabic Words**

Listen and learn. CD

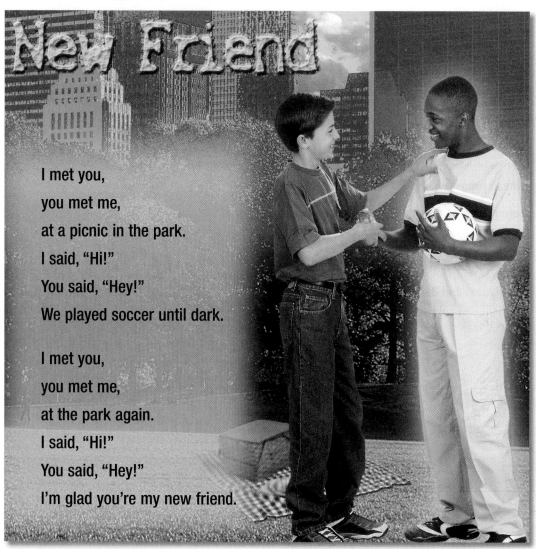

I met you,

you met me,

at a picnic in the park.

I said, "Hi!"

You said, "Hey!"

We played soccer until dark.

I met you,

you met me,

at the park again.

I said, "Hi!"

You said, "Hey!"

I'm glad you're my new friend.

LOOK FOR WORD PATTERNS

Some words have only one vowel at the end. The vowel is usually long.	Some words have one vowel and then one or more consonants. The vowel is usually short.
n<u>o</u> h<u>i</u> m<u>e</u>	<u>o</u>n h<u>i</u>m m<u>e</u>lt

READING STRATEGY

Follow these steps to read a word.

❶ Look for a pattern in the word. Find the vowel.
How many consonants come after the vowel?
Use the pattern to figure out the vowel sound.

g**o**
*The vowel **o** is at the end, so it is long.*

g**o**t
*A consonant comes after the vowel **o**, so the vowel is short.*

❷ Start at the beginning. Blend the sounds together to say the word.

go   **g + o = go**

got **g + o + t = got**

Reading Help

Look for patterns in a long word, too.

First divide the word into parts. Then look for a pattern in each part.

basket   napkin
▲   ▲
bas ket   nap kin

What pattern do you see in each part? Is the vowel long or short?

READING PRACTICE

Use what you learned to read the sentences.

1. Meg is lost. She has to be in the city soon.
2. Meg stops to get gas. She asks for help.
3. A man by the pump gives her a map.
4. He tells her, "Take the tunnel at Elm Canyon."
5. "Then go down the hill to First Street, and go left."
6. "Thank you so much!" Meg answers.

SPELLING PRACTICE

7.–10. **Now write the sentences that your teacher reads.**

WORD WORK

11.–18. **Make a chart. Then read these words:**

| me | sock | be | bed |
| no | men | so | not |

Write each word in the chart. Put it under the word that has the same vowel sound.

go	got	we	web
11.	13.	15.	17.
12.	14.	16.	18.

EXAMPLE **11.**

go
11. no

Read on Your Own

FOCUS ON GENRE

Newspaper Article A newspaper article is written to include facts about a person or an event. This article is about a woman who works with animals.

FOCUS ON WORDS

Words with Short and Long Vowels
When you read and come to a word you don't know, blend the sounds together to read it.

A vowel at the end of a word usually means that the vowel has a long sound. A vowel followed by one or more consonants usually has a short sound. You just learned about words with short and long vowels. You also learned about words with more than one syllable.

he

sock

mattress

High Frequency Words Say these words as whole words when you read.

city	above
by	sometimes
her	come
animals	people
down	under

CITY PEOPLE
Tom Santos

THE

Meet Jo

Jo is brushing Velvet the rabbit.

Jo works at the City Animal Hospital. I asked her to tell me about what she does at her job.

I have a great job. I love to help the animals. Look. This cat got hit by traffic. It is so sad when that happens. I had to make her a special bed. She has to lie down a lot.

Jo put a special collar on this dog.

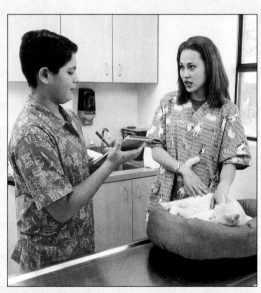

Jo made a bed for this cat.

This is Samson. Samson has a bad rash. He has this thing around his neck so he can't bite the skin under it. Sometimes we play catch. He needs to run a lot. He likes to run down the hill to the park. We rest under the trees. I like to look at the sky above us as Samson sleeps.

This rabbit is Velvet. I like to brush him. He is so soft! Velvet had to get his shots. He needs to rest for a day or two. Then he will go home.

So, that is my job. I help hundreds of animals. It is great to see them get well. I miss them when people come to take them home.

Think About "Meet Jo"

CHECK YOUR UNDERSTANDING

Make a chart. Show what Jo does for each animal. Then tell a partner about Jo's job.

Animal	How Jo Helps
a cat that got hit	Jo makes a special bed.

They're at the Museum!

▶ **Pronoun-Verb Contractions**

Use an apostrophe to put a pronoun and the verb "to be" together to form a **contraction**.

falcon

Contraction	Example
I + am = I'm	**I'm** Mrs. Patch.
you + are = you're	**You're** at the Natural History Museum.
he + is = he's she + is = she's it + is = it's	Look at this bird. **It's** a falcon.
we + are = we're	**We're** happy to have birds like this.
they + are = they're	**They're** wonderful animals.

BUILD SENTENCES

Look at the underlined words in each sentence. Use a contraction in their place. Say the new sentence.

EXAMPLE **1.** Mrs. Patch holds a falcon. It's a big bird.

1. Mrs. Patch holds a falcon. It is a big bird.
2. The children listen to Mrs. Patch. They are very interested.
3. One boy raises his hand. He is afraid of the bird.
4. "You are brave, Mrs. Patch. Does that falcon hurt people?"
5. She is happy to answer his question.
6. "No, falcons are afraid of humans. We are so big."

WRITE SENTENCES

Replace the underlined words with pronouns. Then combine the pronoun and the word *is* or *are*. Write the new sentence.

EXAMPLE **7.** She's helpful.

7. Mrs. Patch is helpful.
8. The boy is not afraid anymore.
9. The visit is over too soon.
10. The students are sad to go.
11. A girl is at the door.
12. Her parents are glad to see her.

Success in Social Science

▶ **Learn About Cities**

Maps

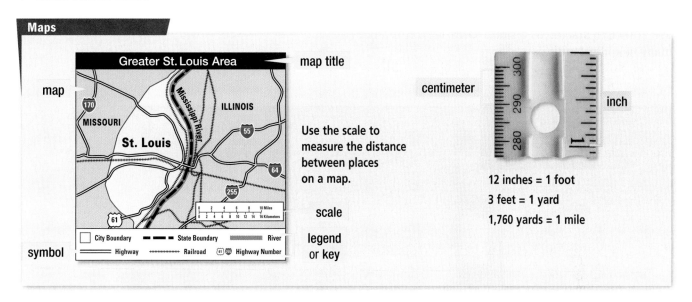

Greater St. Louis Area — map title

map

MISSOURI

ILLINOIS

St. Louis

Mississippi River

170 · 55 · 64 · 255 · 61

Use the scale to measure the distance between places on a map.

10 Miles
16 Kilometers

scale

| City Boundary | State Boundary | River |
| Highway | Railroad | Highway Number |

symbol

legend or key

centimeter · inch

12 inches = 1 foot
3 feet = 1 yard
1,760 yards = 1 mile

Listen to the article and study the chart. Then do the Review.

Saint Louis, Gateway to the West

• How and why has St. Louis changed over the years?

Saint Louis, Missouri, is located near where the Mississippi and Missouri Rivers meet. Fur traders settled in the area in 1764 because boats could easily travel there. Soon the town became the starting point for explorers, fur trappers, and settlers traveling west.

Rivers Connected to the Mississippi

The Great Lakes
Mississippi
Missouri
ST. LOUIS

• City
— River

In the 1850s, the railroads joined St. Louis with other large cities like Chicago. Companies could easily ship goods in and out of the city. From 1840 to 1870, St. Louis' population increased by almost 300,000 people!

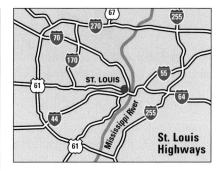

St. Louis Highways

67 · 270 · 255 · 70 · 170 · 61 · ST. LOUIS · 55 · 44 · 64 · 255 · 61

Mississippi River

Highways and bridges across the Mississippi River made it even easier to get to St. Louis. Today St. Louis is one of the leading railway and trucking centers in the United States.

REVIEW

1. **Check Your Understanding** Why did the fur traders choose to settle in the St. Louis area?
2. **Vocabulary** Name some highways that go to St. Louis.
3. **Use Maps** What does the dot symbol on the map of rivers mean?

Build Background for "San Francisco"

NEIGHBORHOODS

San Francisco started as a small town. Now it is a big city with many neighborhoods.

▲ People come to San Francisco to see the Golden Gate Bridge.

▲ San Francisco has many neighborhoods. Chinatown is a San Francisco neighborhood.

Learn Key Vocabulary

Rate and Study the Words Rate how well you know each word. Then:

1. Pronounce the word. Say it aloud several times. Spell it.
2. Study the example.
3. Tell more about the word.
4. Practice it. Make the word your own.

Key Words

buildings (bil-dings) noun

Buildings have a roof, walls, and windows. There are tall **buildings** in San Francisco.

live (liv) verb

People **live** in houses and other kinds of homes. Some people in San Francisco **live** on steep streets.

neighborhood (nā-bor-hood) noun

A **neighborhood** is a place where groups of people live. This map shows San Francisco's many **neighborhoods**.

store (stor) noun

A **store** is a place where you can buy food and supplies. This **store** opened in San Francisco in 1853.

town (toun) noun

A **town** is smaller than a city. San Francisco began as a small **town** with some homes and a church.

Practice the Words Work with a partner. Make a Definition Map for each Key Word.

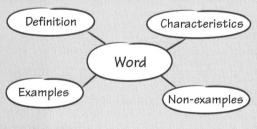

Definition Map

Language and Content

Listen and Read Along

FOCUS ON GENRE

Travel Article   A travel article tells about a place in the world. It tells people why they should visit a certain place. Travel articles are nonfiction. This article is about San Francisco, a city in the state of California.

FOCUS ON COMPREHENSION

Details   Writers add details to help the reader understand a topic. Some writers use details like maps and photos. As you read "San Francisco," look for details that help you understand more about this city.

A view of San Francisco at night.

SAN FRANCISCO

Starting Small

Every city started as a small **town**. In 1776, people from Mexico came to **live** in San Francisco. But they **called the area** Yerba Buena. They built a church and homes.

▲ Mission San Francisco de Asis is the oldest building in San Francisco.

▼ California is near Mexico.

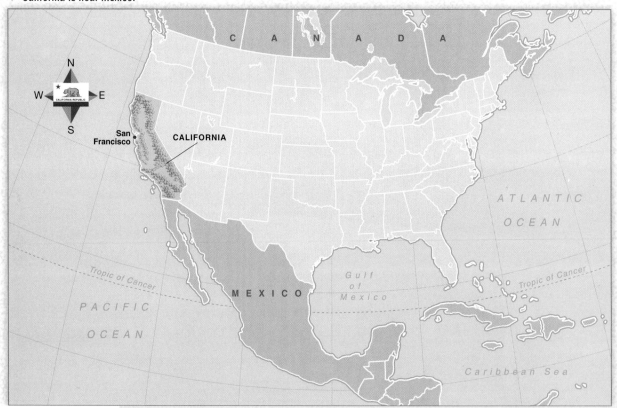

Gold!

In 1848, people **discovered** gold in California. People from all over the world traveled to San Francisco. Many **stores** opened. People opened stores to sell goods to the gold miners.

▲ Levi Strauss opened a store in San Francisco in 1853.

gold

▼ Miners went to San Francisco to look for gold.

Key Vocabulary
 stores *n.*, places where supplies and food are sold

In Other Words
 discovered found

Before You Move On

1. **Details** How did San Francisco change after gold was discovered?
2. **Draw Conclusions** Were the **stores** important? Tell why or why not.

The Earthquake

A terrible earthquake and fire almost **destroyed** San Francisco in 1906. **Buildings** fell and people **lost their homes**. Many people died. But people built San Francisco again.

In Other Words
destroyed ruined
lost their homes had no place to live

▼ San Francisco was almost destroyed after the 1906 earthquake.

Before You Move On

1. **Cause and Effect** What did the earthquake and fire do to San Francisco in 1906?
2. **Details** What did people do after the earthquake?

A Mix of Cultures

Today, San Francisco is a big city with many **neighborhoods** and many different people. The people who live in San Francisco share the art, music, and ideas **from their cultures** with everyone in their neighborhood.

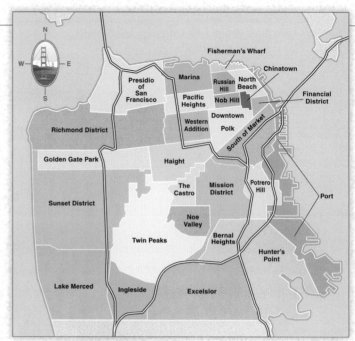

▲ Neighborhoods in San Francisco

▼ Alamo Square is part of the Western Addition neighborhood in San Francisco.

Key Vocabulary
neighborhood *n.*, an area where a group of people live near each other

In Other Words
from their cultures that they learned from their families

▲ Lombard Street in San Francisco is called "the crookedest street in the world." It is in a neighborhood called Russian Hill.

This San Francisco mural was painted by Miranda Bergman and O'Brien Thiele in 1984. The mural is called *I Give You a Song.* ▶

Before You Move On

1. **Details** What do people who live in San Francisco share with other people?

2. **Make Comparisons** How is San Francisco different today than in 1776?

Think About "San Francisco"

CHECK YOUR UNDERSTANDING

<u>1.–2.</u> **Work with a partner to complete each item.**

1. **Identify Details** Make a concept web like the one below.
   Then complete the concept web using information from the
   selection and what you know about San Francisco.

2. **Sum It Up** Use your concept web to tell about San Francisco.
   What are the **buildings** like? What can you buy in the **stores**?

REVIEW VOCABULARY

<u>3.–7.</u> **Read the paragraph aloud. Add the vocabulary words.**

> People who _____ all over the world come to visit San
> Francisco. It started as a small _____. But, soon people built
> many _____ and opened _____. Today, there are many differ-
> ent groups of people who form _____ around the city.

Vocabulary
buildings
live
neighborhoods
stores
town

WRITE ABOUT NEIGHBORHOODS

<u>8.</u> Write about your own **neighborhood**. What would you tell people about
   where you **live**?

Journal Page

WHAT IS A JOURNAL?

A journal is a special book that you keep just for yourself. You tell about your own life when you write in it. You can write about things you do or think about. You can write about how you feel, too.

JOURNAL

Last Monday, I went to soccer practice behind the school.

On Tuesday, I baked cookies at my friend's house.

On Wednesday, I mailed a letter to my aunt at the post office.

On Thursday, I listened to some new CDs in my bedroom at home.

On Friday, I visited Abuelo in the hospital near the mall.

On Saturday, I danced on the new dance floor at the community center.

On Sunday, I cleaned up trash in the park near my house.

Be sure to capitalize **days of the week**.

List the events in the order they happened.

Writing Project

Write a Journal Page

WRITING PROMPT What did you do last week? Write a journal page to tell a friend about something you did each day.

Plan and Write

1 **PLAN YOUR JOURNAL PAGE**

Think about things you did last week. Make a detail chart that shows what you did. Here is Maria's chart.

Day	Events	Place
Monday	walked the dog	in the park
Tuesday	played basketball	on the court at the youth center
Wednesday	skated	next to the school
Thursday	walked	near the library
Friday	cooked soup	in the kitchen
Saturday	washed cars	at the gas station
Sunday	painted a picture	in my bedroom

> **Neighborhood Places**
> store
> gas station
> hospital
> library
> school
> post office

2 **WRITE A JOURNAL PAGE**

Use the detail chart to write a journal page. Start with Monday and end with Sunday.

> Last Monday, I walked the dog in the park.
> On Tuesday, I played basketball on the court
> at the youth center.
> On Wednesday, I skated next to the school.

Check Your Work

Read more of Maria's journal page. She needs to make some changes.

- She needs to capitalize the day of the week in the first sentence. She also needs to capitalize the word **I**. She put three lines under the letter: ≡.
- She needs to add a period to the end of the second sentence. She used a ∧ to add the period.

What other errors does she need to fix?

On thursday, i walked near the library
On Friday, i cooked soup in the kitchen⊙
On saturday, I wash cars at the gas station
On sunday, I painted a picture in my bedroom

Look back at your journal page. Read it aloud. Then ask yourself the questions in the checklist. Mark your changes.

Finish and Share

Use these steps to finish your journal page.

1. Write your journal page neatly and correctly.

2. Add a drawing or photo.

READ ALOUD

Most of the time, you write in a journal just for yourself. You can share this page with your friends. Use these tips.

Presenting Tips

If You Are the Reader:	If You Are the Listener:
• Tell the events in order. • Make eye contact.	• Pay attention to the reader's voice. • Ask questions about things you didn't understand.

Checklist

☑ Did I capitalize the word I?

☑ Did I use a capital letter for the days of the week?

☑ Did I give enough information?

Reflect

- What did you like about writing a journal page?
- How did making the detail chart help you write?

This family is making a
meal together at home.

Empanadas/Tío Beto y Tía Paz, Carmen Lomas Garza, acrylic. Copyright © 1996.

Welcome Home!

Look at the picture. What does each person say? What does each person do? Act out the scene with a partner or a group.

In This Unit

▶ **Language Development**

▶ **Language and Literacy**

▶ **Language and Content**
  Mathematics

▶ **Writing Project**

Vocabulary
- Family
- Rooms in a House
- Household Objects
- Key Vocabulary

Language Functions
- Give Information
- Ask and Answer Questions

Grammar
- Present Tense Verbs (have, has)
- Plural Nouns

Reading
- Long Vowels
- High Frequency Words
- Comprehension: Relate Main Idea and Details
- Text Features: Headings

Writing
- Family Descriptions

Language Development

Meet My Family

▶ **Language: Give Information**

Listen and sing. CD

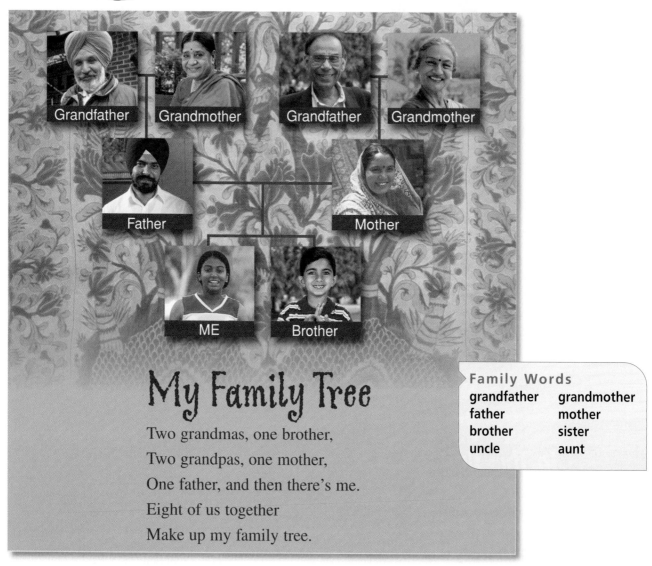

My Family Tree

Two grandmas, one brother,

Two grandpas, one mother,

One father, and then there's me.

Eight of us together

Make up my family tree.

Family Words

grandfather	grandmother
father	mother
brother	sister
uncle	aunt

EXPRESS YOURSELF ▶ GIVE INFORMATION

<u>1.</u> **Change the song to tell about another family.**

<u>2.–3.</u> **Cut pictures of people out of magazines. Use them to make a family tree. Trade papers with a partner. Talk about the family members in your family tree. Then listen as your partner tells you about the people in his or her family tree.**

EXAMPLE **1.** One grandma, two brothers,

One sister, one mother,

One uncle, and then there's me.

Seven of us together

Make up our family tree.

I Have a Great Family

▶ **Present Tense Verbs:** *Have* **and** *Has*

> Use the verb *have* with the pronouns *I, you, we,* and *they*.
> Use the verb *has* with pronouns *he, she,* or *it*.

Hi, I'm Robert. I **have** a sister. I **don't have** any brothers. We **have** a big house. It **has** four bedrooms. My dad **has** an office in our house.

ORAL LANGUAGE PRACTICE

Read each sentence. Add *have* or *has*. Then say the sentence.

EXAMPLE **1.** She has a brother.

1.

She _____ a brother.

2.

They _____ two children.

3.

He _____ an aunt.

4.

"I _____ a wonderful grandmother!"

5.

The house _____ two bedrooms.

6.

The sisters _____ a new brother.

WRITTEN PRACTICE

7.–10. Write 4 sentences about people in your family. Use *have* or *has*. Take turns sharing sentences with a partner.

EXAMPLE **7.** I have a brother.

Let Me Show You My House!

▶ Vocabulary: Rooms in a House
▶ Language: Give Information

roof

Bedroom

closet

guitar

window

Bathroom

toothbrush

mirror

faucet

wall

Living Room

picture

sofa or couch

rug

vacuum cleaner

Kitchen

spoon

pot

ORAL LANGUAGE PRACTICE ▶ GIVE INFORMATION

<u>1.–3.</u> Who's talking? 💿 CD
Listen. Point to the correct person. Then tell where
each person is in the house.

WRITTEN PRACTICE

<u>4.–7.</u> Work in a group of 4. Each person acts out a scene from
above. Tell where each person is and what each person has.
Then write the sentences.

EXAMPLE **4.** Pablo is in the bedroom.
He has a guitar.

What Is in Each Room?

▶ **Vocabulary: Household Objects**
▶ **Language: Ask and Answer Questions**

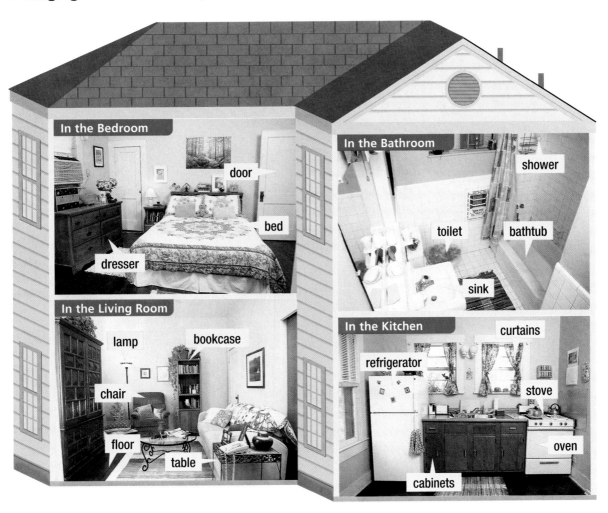

In the Bedroom
door
bed
dresser

In the Bathroom
shower
toilet
bathtub
sink

In the Living Room
lamp
bookcase
chair
floor
table

In the Kitchen
curtains
refrigerator
stove
oven
cabinets

ORAL LANGUAGE PRACTICE ▶ ASK AND ANSWER QUESTIONS

Work with a partner. Take turns asking each question. Answer in a complete sentence.

EXAMPLE **1.** Where is the bed? The bed is in the bedroom.

1. Where is the bed?
2. Where is the refrigerator?
3. Where is the shower?
4. Where is the table?
5. Where are the curtains?
6. Where is the chair?

WRITTEN PRACTICE

7.–10. What kind of house do you want? Draw it.
Then write 4 sentences to tell about your house.
Take turns sharing sentences with a partner.

EXAMPLE **7.** My house has three bedrooms.

Language Development

Listen and Read Along

FOCUS ON GENRE

Photo Essay   A photo essay is a short piece of nonfiction. It uses photographs to give information about the topic. This photo essay is about families.

FOCUS ON VOCABULARY

Family Words   You have been learning words like the ones below. Use these words as you talk about *Families*. Collect more words to put in the web.

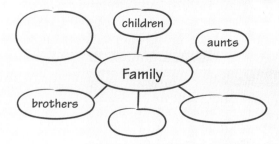

This photo shows a family.

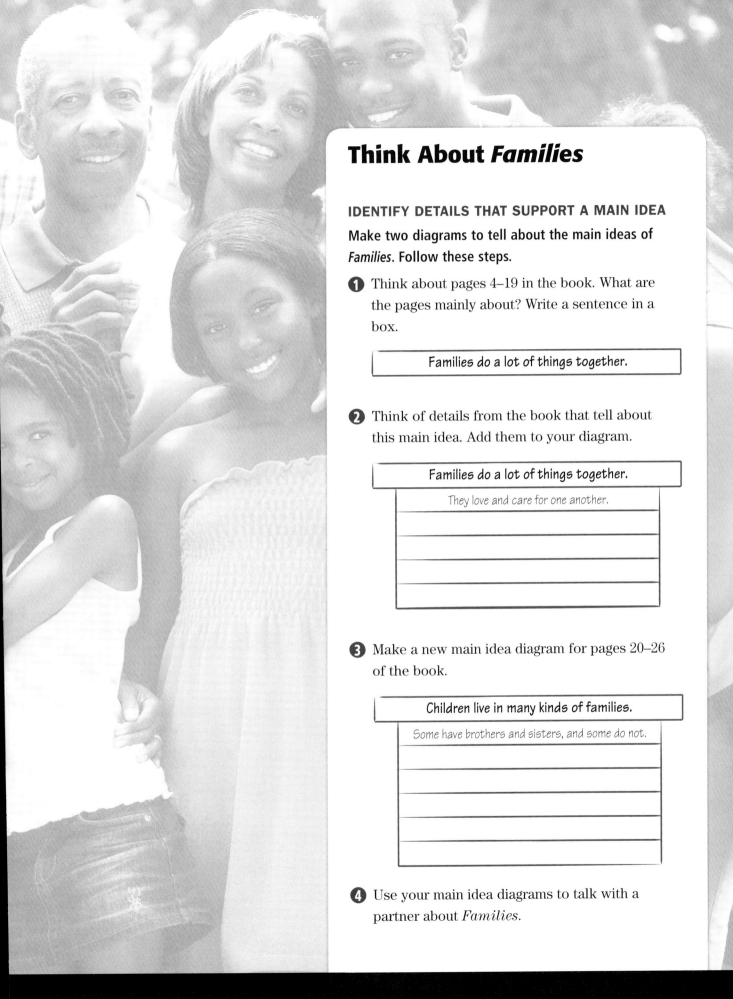

Think About *Families*

IDENTIFY DETAILS THAT SUPPORT A MAIN IDEA

Make two diagrams to tell about the main ideas of *Families*. Follow these steps.

1 Think about pages 4–19 in the book. What are the pages mainly about? Write a sentence in a box.

> Families do a lot of things together.

2 Think of details from the book that tell about this main idea. Add them to your diagram.

> **Families do a lot of things together.**
>
> They love and care for one another.

3 Make a new main idea diagram for pages 20–26 of the book.

> **Children live in many kinds of families.**
>
> Some have brothers and sisters, and some do not.

4 Use your main idea diagrams to talk with a partner about *Families*.

High Frequency Words

REVIEW HIGH FREQUENCY WORDS

Read the words aloud. Which word goes in the sentence?

down	day
small	same
city	see

1. It's a good _____ to ride bikes.
2. The boy rides a _____ bike.
3. They can _____ a bridge.

▲ A boy and his father ride bikes near San Francisco, California.

LEARN NEW WORDS

Study these words. Say them as whole words when you read.

family	There are six people in my **family.**
together	We ride bicycles **together.**
other	We like to do **other** things, too.
really	We **really** like to hike in the woods.
father	My **father** carries a heavy backpack.

PRACTICE

4.–8. Draw a picture to show a family. Write sentences about the picture using all 5 words.

EXAMPLE **4.**

9.–13. Work with a partner. Write each new word on a card. Mix your cards together for the game. Turn them so the words are down. Then:

- Turn over 2 cards.
- Spell the words. Are they the same?
- If so, keep them. If not, turn them over again.
- The player with more cards at the end wins.

EXAMPLE

family

family

f-a-m-i-l-y
f-a-m-i-l-y
These words are
the same.

More High Frequency Words

> **How to Learn a New Word**
> • Look at the word.
> • Listen to the word.
> • Listen to the word in a sentence. What does it mean?
> • Say the word.
> • Spell the word.
> • Say the word again.

REVIEW HIGH FREQUENCY WORDS

Read the words aloud. Which word goes in the sentence?

love	learn	1. I _____ spending time with my family.
carry	face	2. My dad has a big smile on his _____.
went	use	3. We _____ on a long bike ride.

LEARN NEW WORDS

Study these words. Say them as whole words when you read.

mother	My **mother** walks fast. Everyone follows her.
our	She is **our** leader!
watch	We sometimes stop to **watch** the birds.
eyes	Once I saw an eagle with my own **eyes.**
head	It was flying in circles over my **head.**

PRACTICE

4.–8. Draw a picture to show a family on a hike. Write sentences about the picture using all 5 words.

EXAMPLE **4.**

I watch my mother walk ahead of me.

watch
mother

9.–14. Work with a partner. Write each new word on a card. Mix your cards together for the game. Turn them so the words are down. Then:

• Turn over 2 cards.
• Spell the words. Are they the same?
• If so, keep them. If not, turn them over again.
• The player with more cards at the end wins.

EXAMPLE

mother

mother

m-o-t-h-e-r
m-o-t-h-e-r
These words are
the same.

Reading and Spelling

▶ Long Vowels: *a, i, o, u*

Listen and learn. CD

Family Gifts

Mom's smile,
Dad's chin,
And Grandpa's nose.
Mom's eyes,
Dad's hair,
Even Grandma's toes!

Mom's hands,
Dad's ears.
Mine are just the same.
I like these gifts from
My family,
Especially my name!

LOOK FOR WORD PATTERNS

How are the words alike? Is the vowel sound short or long?

c<u>a</u>k<u>e</u>

b<u>i</u>k<u>e</u>

gl<u>o</u>b<u>e</u>

fl<u>u</u>t<u>e</u>s

READING STRATEGY

Follow these steps to read a word.

1 Look for a pattern. The <u>e</u> makes the other vowel say a long vowel sound.

l<u>a</u>k<u>e</u>

2 Start at the beginning. Blend the sounds in your head. Then say the word.

l<u>a</u>k<u>e</u>   **l + a + k + e̶ = lake**

> The **e** at the end of a word has no sound. It tells me that the vowel sound is long.

Reading Help

A few words that end in **e** do <u>not</u> have a long vowel sound.

give   some   have

READING PRACTICE

Use what you learned to read the sentences.

1. My mother likes to make cakes.
2. She says to use pure butter.
3. She melts the butter on the stove.
4. I taste the cake mix. Yum!
5. It's fun to bake a cake at home!

SPELLING PRACTICE

<u>6.–9.</u> **Now write the sentences that your teacher reads.**

WORD WORK

<u>10.–21.</u> **Make a chart. Then read these words:**

map	cake	dot	rope
10.	13.	16.	19.
11.	14.	17.	20.
12.	15.	18.	21.

back	can	made	mad
hop	heat	cane	rob
note	hope	not	bake

Write each word in the chart. Put it under the word that has the same vowel sound.

EXAMPLE **10.**

map
10. back

Read on Your Own

FOCUS ON GENRE

Personal Narrative   A personal narrative is a true story. The author tells about events in his or her life.

FOCUS ON WORDS

Words with Short and Long Vowels   When you read and come to a word you don't know, blend the sounds together to read it.

Remember that an *e* at the end of a word can make the first vowel in the word have a long sound. You just learned about words like this. You also learned about plural words.

cake   **dishes**

High Frequency Words   Say these words as whole words when you read.

family	together
other	really
father	mother
our	watch
eyes	head

When We Came to Wisconsin

La Gigantona in Nicaragua

Pablo and his mother

Hi. My name is Pablo Soto. My mother's name is Sandra. We are from Nicaragua.

In Nicaragua, our family made big puppets to sell. The name of one puppet that we made is *La Gigantona*. We made the head of this puppet with paper and paste. We made the eyes of the puppet really big, with long, thick lashes. We made the arms from long tubes. They swing from side to side. We put a white robe, a cute hat, and other things on the puppet. People like to watch this big puppet in parades.

My mother and I left Nicaragua together and came to Wisconsin. Here, we make piñatas. We make a piñata with paper and paste, just like we made the head of *La Gigantona*. One day, my friend's father came to our store. He asked us to make a big puppet for a parade in Wisconsin. At last, *La Gigantona* is back in our family!

Think About "When We Came to Wisconsin"

CHECK YOUR UNDERSTANDING

Make a diagram. Add details that support the main idea. Then tell your partner how the family made the big puppet.

We made a big puppet.
We made the head with paper and paste.

Boxes and Boxes—We're Moving!

▶ **Plural Nouns**

A noun names a person, place, or thing.

A **singular noun** names one thing.

box

A **plural noun** names more than one thing.

boxes

Study these rules for forming plurals.

To make most nouns plural, just add -s.	boy boys	girl girls	book books	truck trucks
If the noun ends in *x*, *ch*, *sh*, *s*, or *z*, add -es.	box boxes	dish dishes	glass glasses	lunch lunches
Some nouns change in different ways to show the plural.	man men	woman women	child children	foot feet

BUILD SENTENCES

Say each sentence. Use the plural form of the missing words.

EXAMPLE **1.** The women drink from glasses.

1.

glass

woman

The ____ drink from ____.

2.

child

The ____ read on the sofa.

3.

man

sandwich

The ____ eat ____.

4.

boy

book

The ____ pack ____.

5.

box

mover

The ____ carry the ____.

6.

friend

Their ____ wave good-bye.

WRITE QUESTIONS

7.–10. Choose 4 pictures from above. Write a question about each picture. Take turns asking and answering questions with a partner.

EXAMPLE **7.** What do the men eat?

Success in Mathematics

▶ **Learn About Fractions, Decimals, and Percents**

My Family
1. Mama
2. Grandma
3. Sabina, my sister
4. Alex, my brother
5. Tom—me!

FRACTION	DECIMAL	PERCENT
numerator $\dfrac{3}{5}$ denominator	0.6 decimal point	60% percent symbol
Say: three-fifths **Example:** Three-fifths of my family are kids.	**Say:** six-tenths **Example:** Six-tenths of my family are kids.	**Say:** sixty percent **Example:** Sixty percent of my family are kids.

Study the lesson. Then do the Exercises.

Family Math

Think and Discuss

You can use fractions, decimals, or percents to describe the family in the picture.

1 Write a fraction:

Ask yourself how many of the people are kids. This is the numerator. How many people are there in the whole family? This is the denominator.

kids $\dfrac{3}{5}$ whole family

2 Write a decimal:

Divide the numerator by the denominator.

$$5\overline{)3.0}$$ 0.6 — Show the decimal point in the answer.

Add a decimal point and a zero.

3 Write a percent:

Multiply the decimal by 100. Add the percent symbol.

$0.6 \times 100 = 60$

60% — percent symbol

Three-fifths of my family are kids. Six-tenths of my family are kids. Sixty percent of my family are kids.

Exercises

Write a fraction, a decimal, and a percent for each answer.

1

Sabina ate 2 slices of pizza. How much of the pizza is left?

2

How many candles are red?

Build Background for "The Family Reunion"

FAMILY

A family can be more than a mother, father, and children. Cousins, aunts, uncles, and grandparents are all part of the family.

▲ Families like to eat together.

▲ Families live together in their homes.

Learn Key Vocabulary

Rate and Study the Words Rate how well you know each word. Then:

1. Pronounce the word. Say it aloud several times. Spell it.
2. Study the example.
3. Tell more about the word.
4. Practice it. Make the word your own.

Key Words

cousins (ku-zinz) *noun*

Cousins are children of an aunt or uncle. There are many **cousins** in this family.

family (fa-mu-lē) *noun*

A **family** includes people who are related.

grandchildren (grand-chil-drun) *noun*

Grandchildren are the children of a son or daughter. These **grandchildren** hug their grandmother.

parents (pair-ents) *noun*

Our mother and father are our **parents**. These children sing a song with their **parents**.

together (tu-ge-thur) *adverb*

When people are **together**, they are near each other. These people are in a photo **together**.

Practice the Words With a partner, make an Expanded Meaning Map for each Key Word. Ask each other questions like: "What is something that is like a family?"

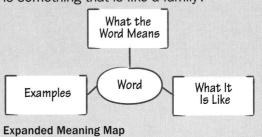

Expanded Meaning Map

Language and Content

Listen and Read Along

FOCUS ON GENRE

Personal Narrative   A writer uses a personal narrative to tell about an event in his or her life. Personal narratives are nonfiction. This one is about a family reunion.

FOCUS ON COMPREHENSION

Main Idea and Details   Writers often give a main idea and then add details to tell about the main idea. As you read "The Family Reunion," look for the details that tell about the main idea.

Main Idea:
Detail:
Detail:
Detail:

THE Family Reunion

by Paz Gonzalez

This painting is called "Barbacoa para Cumpleaños" (Birthday Barbeque) and was painted by artist Carmen Lomas Garza in 1993. It is about a family party.

My Family Reunion

All of my **family** is **together** in San Antonio! Everyone is at my house. My backyard **is filled with cousins**, uncles, aunts, brothers, sisters, and **neighbors**, too. It's a family **reunion**.

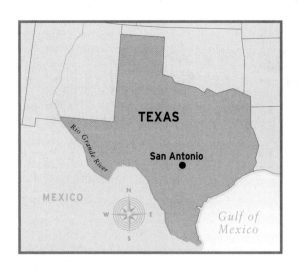

▲ Everyone in my family visits my house once a year.

Key Vocabulary
family *n.*, parents and their children
together *adj.*, gathered in the same place
cousins *n.*, children of an aunt or an uncle

In Other Words
is filled with has
neighbors people who live near us
reunion party

Cooking Together

The kitchen is a busy place. Everyone in my family makes some food. One cousin makes a big bowl of **guacamole**. Another cousin stirs a pot of *frijoles*, or beans, on the stove.

◄ guacamole

▶ frijoles

▲ We all eat together at the reunion.

In Other Words
guacamole food made from avocados, tomatoes, and onions

Before You Move On

1. **Main Idea and Details** What is one thing that happens at the reunion?
2. **Speculate** What other foods might people cook for the reunion?

Games and Dancing

During the day we play lots of games. We make a **piñata** filled with toys and candy. Rosa tries to hit the piñata. She wants all of the candy to fall out!

▲ Rosa tries to hit the piñata.

In Other Words
piñata paper container

In the warm summer evening, we talk and laugh and eat. We sing and dance and tell stories.

▲ I love to dance with my granddaughter.

Before You Move On

1. **Main Idea and Details** What does the family do **together** for fun at the reunion?
2. **Draw Conclusions** Why does Rosa want to hit the piñata?

Stories of the Rio Grande

My **grandchildren** love my family stories. I tell my grandchildren the same story I've told them before. I tell them that my **parents** made their house from **adobe bricks**. I tell them how I would ride **a burro** down to the Rio Grande.

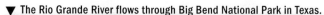

▼ The Rio Grande River flows through Big Bend National Park in Texas.

Key Vocabulary
grandchildren *n.*, children of a son or daughter
parents *n.*, a mother and father

In Other Words
adobe bricks bricks made from earth and straw and dried in the sun
a burro a large animal similar to a donkey

Description

A description of a person gives information about him or her. You can write descriptions about people in your family or anyone else you know.

My Family
by Pia

My stepfather likes airplanes. He has pictures of airplanes in his office. He's able to fly planes, too.

My grandmother likes CDs. She has a special shelf for them in the living room. She's a good singer.

My sister likes basketball. She plays basketball almost every day. She even sleeps with a basketball by her pillow!

My dog likes toys that make noise. He hides them in boxes in the garage. He's a silly dog.

Each description focuses on one person in the family.

The description tells what each person likes and what he or she has. It also tells what the person is like.

Writing Project

Write a Family Description

WRITING PROMPT Write descriptions of family members to put in a family album. Say something special about each person. Share your description with a friend.

Plan and Write

1 PLAN YOUR DESCRIPTION

Think about each person in your family or other people you know. Make a chart like this one. It will help you decide what to say about each person.

Here is Mikhail's chart.

Who?	What the Person Likes	What the Person Has	Where	Something Special About the Person
mother	flowers	flower press	kitchen	good at growing flowers
sister	fish	fishbowl	bedroom	great with pets

Family Words
grandfather
grandmother
father
mother
brother
sister
uncle
aunt

2 WRITE A FAMILY DESCRIPTION

Use the detail chart to write descriptions for your album.

Write 3 complete sentences about each person.

My Family
by Mikhail
My mother likes flowers. She has a flower press. She's going to teach a class about flowers, too.

Check Your Work

Read more of Mikhail's family description. He needs to make some changes.

- The first sentence needs a detail about the games. To add it, he used this mark: ∧.
- He needs to make the last word in the third sentence plural. To add the letter **s**, he used the same mark: ∧.

What other errors does he need to fix?

> a lot of video
> my brother has ∧games. He plays them in the living room. He's an
> expert at playing his game.∧
> My sister likes fish. She has two fishbowl in her bedroom. she likes
> animal and they like her.

Look back at your family description. Read it aloud. Then ask yourself the questions in the checklist. Mark your changes.

Finish and Share

Use these steps to finish your family descriptions and make your album.

1. Write the family descriptions neatly and correctly.
2. Add a drawing or picture for each person you wrote about.
3. Write a title and your name at the top of the first page.
4. Display your family album in your classroom.

READ ALOUD

Share your writing with friends. Use these tips.

Presenting Tips

If You Are the Speaker:	If You Are the Listener:
• Give interesting details.	• Pay attention to the reader's voice.
• Read loudly and clearly.	• Ask questions about things you didn't understand.

Checklist

- ☑ Did I say something special about each person?
- ☑ Did I include enough details?
- ☑ Did I use plural nouns correctly?

Reflect

- How did making the chart help you write your descriptions?
- Did you learn new things about someone you know?

Many different animals can be found in a rain forest.

PACK YOUR BAGS

Look at the picture of the rain forest.

What do you see? Listen to the CD.

What sounds do you hear? 💿 CD

In This Unit

- ▶ **Language Development**

- ▶ **Language and Literacy**

- ▶ **Language and Content**
  Science

- ▶ **Writing Project** ✎

Vocabulary
- Landforms and Transportation
- Weather and Clothing
- Key Vocabulary

Language Functions
- Give and Carry Out Commands
- Describe Places
- Give Information

Grammar
- Commands
- Verbs (can)
- Capitalization: Proper Nouns

Reading
- Long Vowels (ai, ay; ee, ea; oa, ow)
- High Frequency Words
- Comprehension: Classify
- Text Features: Diagrams

Writing
- Travel Guide

Come Along!

▶ **Language: Give and Carry Out Commands**

Listen and chant. CD

Let's Go!

Let's get moving!
Come on, let's go!
Pack your bags,
And dress for snow.

Grab a camera.
Take a hat.
You'll need a parka.
Don't forget that!

Get on the train,
And find your seat.
Let's go traveling.
What a treat!

> **Commands**
> A **command** tells you what to do or what not to do.
> **Pack** your bags.
> **Don't forget**.

EXPRESS YOURSELF ▶ GIVE AND CARRY OUT COMMANDS

Work with a partner. Read the commands from the chant together. Act them out.

1. Pack your bags.
2. Grab a camera.
3. Dress for snow.
4. Take a hat.
5. Get on the train.
6. Find your seat.

7.–10. **Your partner wants to take a trip. Say 4 commands to tell your partner what to do on the trip. Have your partner do the same for you.**

EXAMPLE **7.** Dress for rain.

What Places Can You Explore?

▶ **Vocabulary: Landforms and Transportation**
▶ **Language: Describe Places**

ORAL LANGUAGE PRACTICE ▶ DESCRIBE PLACES

<u>1.–4.</u> Work with a partner. Take turns describing each picture above. Use adjectives.

EXAMPLE **1.** There are tall trees in the green forest. The blue lake is large. The raft is slow.

> **Adjectives**
>
> | blue | tiny | slow | short | hot |
> | green | small | fast | tall | cold |
> | brown | big | | long | wet |
> | white | large | | | dry |

WRITTEN PRACTICE

<u>5.</u> Choose a place to explore. Describe it in a postcard.

EXAMPLE **5.**

Dear Lin,

I am in the mountains. There is a big lake here. A lot of tall trees grow around the lake.

Your friend,
Sanjana

Lin Yang
8362 Hoover Street
New York, NY 10165

Language Development

How Is the Weather There?

▶ **Vocabulary: Weather and Clothing**
▶ **Language: Give Information**

| Sunny and Warm | Hot | Cloudy | Rainy | Windy | Cold |

bathing suit

sandal   sneaker

It is **sunny and warm** at the seashore.

scarf

parka

glove

It is **cold** in the mountains.

coat

skirt

shoe

It is **windy** in the city.

ORAL LANGUAGE PRACTICE ▶ GIVE INFORMATION

1.–3. Who's talking? CD

Listen. Which person is talking? Point to the correct picture.
Tell what the weather is like there.

WRITTEN PRACTICE

Write each sentence. Add words to tell about the weather.

EXAMPLE **4.** I wear a parka when it is cold.

4. I wear a parka when it is _____.
5. I wear sandals when it is _____ and _____.
6. I wear a coat when it is _____.
7. I wear a raincoat when it is _____.
8. I wear gloves when it is _____.

umbrella

raincoat

boot

It is **rainy** in the forest.

We Can Explore All Year Long

▶ Verbs: *Can*

A helping verb is used with a verb. Can is a helping verb that tells what people are able to do.

$$can + hike = can\ hike$$

In this park, we **can hike** up the mountain.

I **can see** some pretty trees.

My friend **can take** a lot of pictures.

Never add -*s* to *can.*

BUILD SENTENCES

Look at each picture below. Make a sentence to go with the picture.
Choose words from each column. Say the sentence.

In the winter, In the spring, In the summer, In the fall,	I can you can he can she can we can they can	sail a boat. hike. ride a bike. ice-skate.

EXAMPLE **1.** In the winter, you can ice-skate.

1.
winter

2.
spring

3.
summer

4.
fall

WRITE SENTENCES

<u>5.–8.</u> Draw a picture for each season. Show what people can do then. Write a sentence to go with the picture. Use words from the box.

swim in a lake	plant a garden
ski in the mountains	eat outside
play soccer	read a book

EXAMPLE **5.** In the spring, we can swim in a lake.

Listen and Read Along

FOCUS ON GENRE

Photo Essay   A photo essay is a short piece of nonfiction. It uses photographs to give information about a topic. This photo essay is about places people can explore.

FOCUS ON VOCABULARY

Weather and Habitat Words   You have been learning words like the ones below. Use these words as you talk about *Explore!* Collect more words to put in the web.

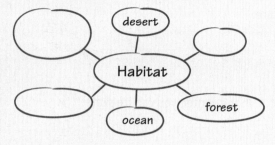

THEME BOOK

Read this photo essay about different places to explore.

A mountain is a place people can explore.

Think About *Explore!*

CLASSIFY INFORMATION

Make a concept map to tell about *Explore!*
Follow these steps.

1 Think about the book. What is it mainly about?

(Places to Explore)

2 What places does the book describe? Add sections to the map. Write the name of a place inside each section.

(Forest)
(Places to Explore)

3 Write words around each place. Tell what you can find there.

leaves   wolves
(Forest)   birds
(Places to Explore)

4 Use your completed map to take turns telling about the book with a partner.

Language and Literacy

High Frequency Words

▲ This family likes to hike together.

REVIEW HIGH FREQUENCY WORDS

Read the words aloud. Which word goes in the sentence?

family	first
says	she
letters	learn

1. The _____ hikes together.
2. Father _____ the names of plants.
3. The children _____ about trees.

LEARN NEW WORDS

Study these words. Say them as whole words when you read.

places	Jean likes to explore unusual **places**.
important	Travel is very **important** to her.
world	She travels all around the **world**.
always	She **always** plans her trips carefully.
or	She travels either by plane **or** by boat.

PRACTICE

4.–8. Draw a picture to show one of the words.
Write a sentence about the picture using the word.

EXAMPLE **4.**

School is a **place** I visit almost every day.

place

9.–11. Work with a partner. Answer each question.
Then use each word in a sentence.

EXAMPLE **9.** important

My family is **important** to me.

9. Which word has 9 letters?
10. Which words have 1 syllable?
11. Which word means "all the time"?

More High Frequency Words

How to Learn a New Word
- Look at the word.
- Listen to the word.
- Listen to the word in a sentence. What does it mean?
- Say the word.
- Spell the word.
- Say the word again.

REVIEW HIGH FREQUENCY WORDS

Read the words aloud. Which word goes in the sentence?

second   enough   **1.** We have _____ time to take a walk.

leave   two   **2.** I see _____ deer in the trees.

out   three   **3.** We got wet walking _____ in the rain!

LEARN NEW WORDS

Study these words. Say them as whole words when you read.

river	Jean sails up the Amazon **River** in a boat.
through	She hikes **through** the Amazon rain forest, too.
once	She goes to Tahiti not **once**, but twice a year.
water	She loves swimming in the clear **water**.
below	She can see hundreds of fish **below** her.

PRACTICE

4.–8. Draw a picture to show one of the words. Write a sentence about the picture using the word.

EXAMPLE **4.**

I like to go swimming in the **river**.   river

9.–11. Work with a partner. Answer each question. Then use each word in a sentence.

9. Which word begins with 3 consonants?

10. Which words have 1 syllable?

11. Which word means "one time"?

EXAMPLE **9.** through

My mom hikes **through** the woods.

Reading and Spelling

▶ Long Vowels: *ai, ay; ee, ea; oa, ow*

Listen and learn. CD

On the Beach

Sailboats sail along the bay
As the sunset ends the day.
Little crabs and starfish play
In the pools along the shore.
Seaweed gathers on the beach.
As the seagulls dive and soar,
Endless waves will sweep the sand
With a whisper or a roar.
The high tide and the low tide
Bring sea gifts to my door.

LOOK FOR WORD PATTERNS

How are the words alike? Are the vowel sounds long or short?

1.
s ai l

t r a y

2.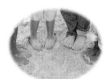
f ee t

sea

3.
b oa t

r o w b oa t

READING STRATEGY

Follow these steps to read a word.

1 Look for a pattern. Do you see two vowels together?

d r e a m

*The two vowels in each word are a team. They make one **long vowel** sound.*

p l a y

2 Start at the beginning of the word. Blend the sounds in your head. Then say the word.

dream   **d + r + ea + m = dream**   **play**   **p + l + ay = play**

Reading Help

Some long words are made up of two small words.

day + dream = daydream

sail + boat = sailboat

sea + shell = seashell

To read these words, find the two small words. Then sound them out and say the two words together.

READING PRACTICE

Use what you learned to read the sentences.

1. Joan and her family spend weekends at the seashore.
2. They keep a rowboat by the beach.
3. Joan likes to swim in the water or row the boat.
4. When it rains, she always stays inside.
5. A good book and hot tea are all she needs.
6. She just sits and reads all day!

SPELLING PRACTICE

<u>7.–10.</u> **Now write the sentences that your teacher reads.**

WORD WORK

<u>11.</u> **Write each word on a card.**

rain	coast	sail	leaf	play	paint
stay	snow	deep	show	grow	road
beach	bee	sweet	read	feet	boat

Then say each word. Sort the words by vowel sound. Make 3 groups.

<u>12.</u> **Now make 6 new groups. Put the words with the same vowel sound *and* spelling together. What do you notice?**

EXAMPLE **12.**

rain

stay

*You can spell **long a** more than one way.*

Read on Your Own

FOCUS ON GENRE

Science Article A science article is nonfiction. Articles include facts about a topic. This article is about wetlands.

FOCUS ON WORDS

Long Vowels When you read and come to a word you don't know, blend the sounds together to read it.

Remember that two vowels together often make one long vowel sound. You learned about long vowel words with these spellings:

ai	ay	ee
ea	oa	ow

feet

rowboat

High Frequency Words Say these words as whole words when you read.

places	important
world	always
or	river
through	once
water	below

EXPLORE A WETLAND

Many animals live near wetlands.

Welcome to Black Creek Wetland. What a great way to spend a Sunday afternoon! My name is Jean Clay. I am your guide. Step into the rowboat. Stay in your seat while we move through the water.

Canada has many wetlands. Black Creek Wetland is one of them. A wetland is a low, wet place. Rainwater and many streams or rivers keep it wet. Black Creek is on the shore of Lake Ontario. Plants such as reeds and cattails grow below the water here. This is an important place for animals, too. Ducks and geese lay their eggs here once each year in May.

Sometimes, people around the world drain the water from wetlands. Then they use the land to grow wheat or other crops. Not here. We always plan to keep this wetland for the ducks, geese, and other animals.

Think About "Explore a Wetland"

CHECK YOUR UNDERSTANDING

Make a web. Tell a partner what you learned about Black Creek Wetland. Then have your partner tell you what he or she learned.

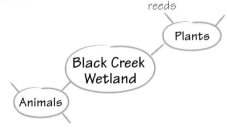

Special Places, Special People

▶ **Capitalization: Proper Nouns**

A **proper noun** names a particular person, place, or thing.

A proper noun begins with a capital letter.

name of a person	<u>J</u>orge is a scientist.
name of a special place, a city, or a country	He will go to **<u>E</u>l <u>Y</u>unque** near **<u>S</u>an <u>J</u>uan**, **<u>P</u>uerto <u>R</u>ico**, to study the birds.
name of a month or a day	He will leave **<u>M</u>onday**, **<u>J</u>uly** 15.

STUDY CAPITALIZATION

Look at the article on pages 198 and 199. Answer these questions.

EXAMPLE **1.** Jean Clay is the name of a person. Joyce Hsu is another person's name.

1. Which 2 words are the name of a person? Tell another person's name.
2. Which word names a country? Name another country.
3. Which word names a month? Name another month.
4. Which word names a day of the week? Name another day of the week.
5. Which words name a special place? Name another special place.

WRITE SENTENCES

Write each sentence correctly. Add the capital letters.

EXAMPLE **6.** Jorge will take a trip to Puerto Rico.

6. Jorge will take a trip to puerto rico.
7. On Monday, july 15, he flies into San Juan.
8. On tuesday, July 16, Jorge takes a bus to the rain forest.
9. The rain forest is called el yunque.
10. It is 40 kilometers from san juan.
11. He will stay there until thursday, july 18.
12. On Sunday, July 21, Jorge flies back to the united states.
13. He goes to his home in miami, Florida.

Jorge studies the birds in the rain forest.

Success in Science

▶ **Learn About Cycles**

A **cycle** is a series of events that happen again and again.

A **diagram** is a drawing. It can show how a cycle works.

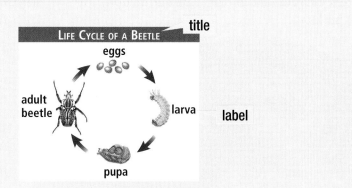

LIFE CYCLE OF A BEETLE — title

eggs

adult beetle — larva — label

pupa

Study the diagram and listen to the article. Then do the Review.

Earth's Amazing Water Cycle

• How does the water cycle work?

The Earth's water can take many forms. It can be a **liquid**, like rainwater, or a **solid**, like ice.

rain

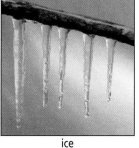

ice

It can even take the form of **vapor**. You cannot see vapor. When water boils, it turns to water vapor.

The Earth's water is recycled. Heat from the sun turns water on the Earth into water vapor. This process is called **evaporation**. The water vapor is carried up by the air. Air that is full of water vapor can cool off. When this happens, clouds form and the water vapor turns into water again. The water falls from the clouds as rain or snow, for example, and becomes part of the water on Earth. Some of this water—in rivers and lakes, for example—evaporates, and the cycle begins again.

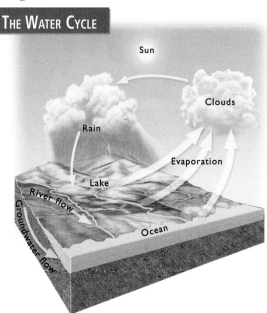

THE WATER CYCLE

Sun

Clouds

Rain

Evaporation

Lake

River flow

Groundwater flow

Ocean

1. **Check Your Understanding** Tell in your own words how the water cycle works. Use the diagram.
2. **Vocabulary** Give an example of another cycle.
3. **Use Diagrams** Draw a diagram to show how another cycle works.

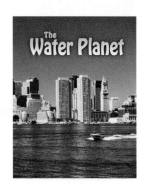

Build Background for "The Water Planet"

LANDFORMS

There are many different kinds of landforms on Earth. The ocean covers most of Earth's surface.

◄ This is what Earth looks like from space.

▲ Ocean water covers most of Earth.

Learn Key Vocabulary

Rate and Study the Words Rate how well you know each word. Then:

   1. Pronounce the word. Say it aloud several times. Spell it.

   2. Study the example.

   3. Tell more about the word.

   4. Practice it. Make the word your own.

Key Words

cold (cōld) *adjective*

Something that is **cold** does not have much heat. The water in the Arctic Ocean is so **cold** that it freezes.

ocean (ō-shun) *noun*

The **ocean** is a big area of salty water. The **ocean** is filled with living things.

surface (ser-fes) *noun*

The **surface** is the outer layer of something. Here you see the oceans and landforms that cover the earth's **surface**.

warm (wôrm) *adjective*

When something is **warm**, it has heat. When the sun shines, the weather gets **warm**.

world (wirld) *noun*

The **world** is where all people live. Our **world** is the planet Earth.

Practice the Words With a partner, make a Vocabulary Study Card for each Key Word.

Write the word.

front

ocean

back

lots of salty water
I love to swim in the _ocean_.

Tell what it means and use it in a sentence.

Use the cards to quiz your partner. Take turns answering.

Language and Content

Listen and Read Along

FOCUS ON GENRE

Expository Nonfiction   Expository nonfiction explains or gives information about a topic. This expository nonfiction tells about Earth's oceans.

FOCUS ON COMPREHENSION

Classify   When you classify ideas, you put them into groups. Grouping ideas can help you remember what you read. As you read "The Water Planet," think about how ideas fit together in groups.

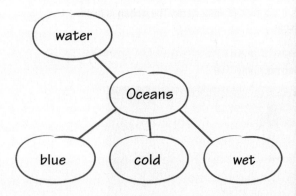

Much of Earth is covered with water.

The Water Planet

Selection Recording

The Water Planet

From space, the **world** looks like a ball of colors: green, brown, white, and blue. The blue parts are **oceans**. The ocean is a big area of water that covers most of Earth's **surface**. People have named different parts of the ocean. Find the names on the map on the next page.

▼ Most of Earth's surface is covered by water.

Key Vocabulary
world *n.*, Earth
oceans *n.*, the salt water that covers more than 70% of Earth
surface *n.*, the outer layer

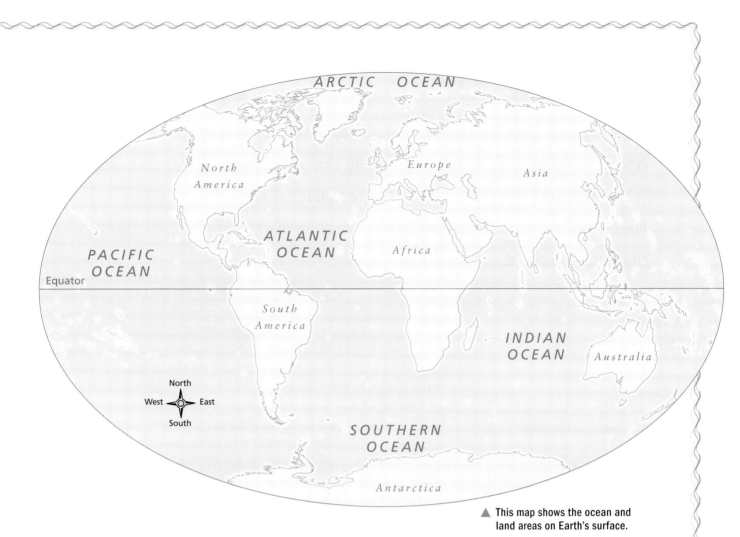

▲ This map shows the ocean and land areas on Earth's surface.

Ocean Sizes

OCEAN	SIZE (in square kilometers)
Pacific Ocean	155,557,000
Atlantic Ocean	76,762,000
Indian Ocean	68,556,000
Southern Ocean	20,327,000
Arctic Ocean	14,056,000

Before You Move On

1. **Main Idea and Details** What covers most of Earth's **surface**? How do you know?
2. **Interpret Tables** Why did the author list the Pacific **Ocean** at the top of the table and the Arctic **Ocean** at the bottom of the table?

Feel the Water

Parts of the Southern Ocean and Arctic Ocean are very **cold**. The water can freeze and form big chunks of ice.

The **warmest** ocean water is near the middle of Earth. Places on land that are near the ocean may be warmer than places **inland**.

▼ Chunks of ice float in the Arctic Ocean.

▼ Earth's warmest water is found near the middle of the planet.

Key Vocabulary

cold *adj.*, having little or no heat

warm *adj.*, having some heat; not hot or cold

In Other Words

inland away from the ocean

Ocean Motion

The water in the ocean is always **in motion**. Winds blowing on the surface of the ocean make the water move. We call this movement **waves**.

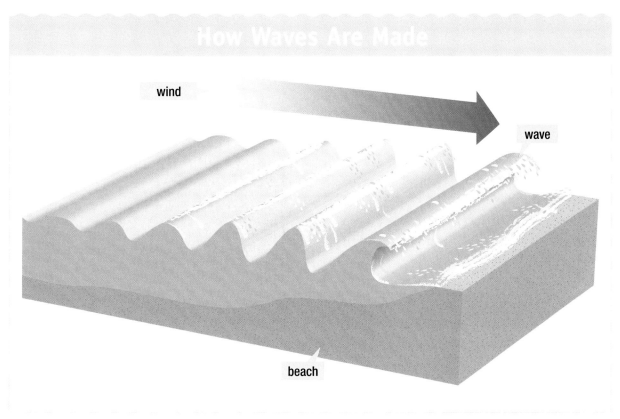

How Waves Are Made

wind

wave

beach

▲ Wind creates waves.

In Other Words
in motion moving
waves rolling areas in the water

Before You Move On

1. **Generalization** Which area of Earth has the **warmest** water?
2. **Cause and Effect** What does wind do to water in the **ocean**?

Exploring the Ocean

Scientists travel around the world to study oceans. They dive deep below the surface.

▲ People go deep into the water to study ocean life.

The Ocean Zones

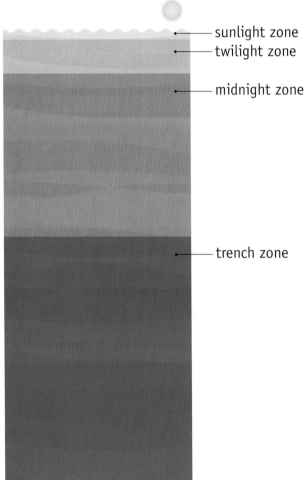

— sunlight zone
— twilight zone

— midnight zone

— trench zone

◀ The ocean has four levels, or zones.

Mostly Ocean

The ocean is a big place. There is a lot to explore in the ocean. Ocean water covers 71% of Earth's surface. That is more than half of the planet! This is why Earth is called "The Water Planet."

▼ Near the ocean

▼ In the ocean

Before You Move On

1. **Interpret Diagrams** Why do you think the third zone of the **ocean** is called the midnight zone?
2. **Main Idea** Why is Earth called "The Water Planet"?

Language and Content

Think About "The Water Planet"

CHECK YOUR UNDERSTANDING

<u>1.–2.</u> **Work with a partner to complete each item.**

1. **Classify** What ideas in the selection go together? Show a group of ideas in a web.

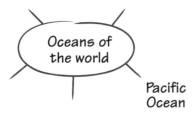

Oceans of the world

Pacific Ocean

2. **Sum It Up** Use the web to retell what you learned about the **ocean**.

REVIEW VOCABULARY

<u>3.–7.</u> **Read the paragraph aloud. Add the vocabulary words.**

> From space, the _____ looks like a ball of colors. The white parts are clouds. The blue is the water in the _____. The ocean covers 71% of Earth's _____. The water in the Arctic Ocean is very _____. The land near the ocean can be _____.

Vocabulary

cold

ocean

surface

warm

world

WRITE ABOUT THE OCEAN

<u>8.</u> **Write about what it would be like to live in the ocean. Would you be cold? Would you miss the rest of the world?**

Writing Project

Travel Guide

WHAT IS A TRAVEL GUIDE?

A travel guide is a piece of paper that tells about a place to visit. It can tell about any place in the world. It tells why that place would be fun to explore.

See Mexico Today!

Explore Mexico! You can take a train to see some **amazing** places. You can hike in the Copper Canyon. You can crawl in **deep**, **dark** caves in Cozumel. You can see the **white**, **sandy** beaches in Cancun. You can taste the **delicious** food in Oaxaca. Visit Mexico soon! You will have the time of your life!

Capitalize proper nouns like **names of places**.

Use **adjectives** to help readers picture the place.

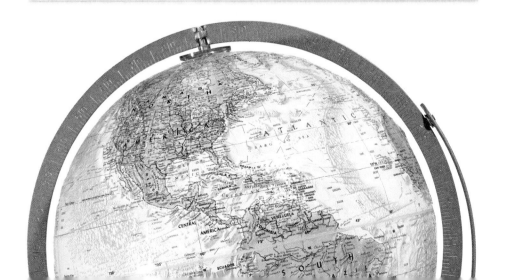

Writing Project

Write a Travel Guide

WRITING PROMPT What place do you want to visit? Write a travel guide that tells about the place. Give information that will make others want to visit there, too.

Plan and Write

1 PLAN YOUR TRAVEL GUIDE

Choose one place you would like to go. Look in books, magazines, or on the Internet for ideas. Use a concept map to take notes. Here is Lee's concept map.

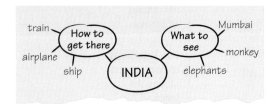

2 WRITE SENTENCES

Turn your notes into sentences. Use adjectives.

Use sentences like these:

Take _____ .

Explore _____ .

You can _____ .

Adjectives		
blue	big	long
green	large	hot
brown	slow	cold
white	fast	wet
tiny	short	dry
small	tall	

> ### See India Now!
> Take an airplane. Explore exciting India!
> You can see beautiful Mumbai. Mumbai is a huge city.

3 WRITE THE TRAVEL GUIDE

Write your sentences on cards. Attach them to a large piece of paper. Add pictures to go with your sentences.

See India Now!
Take an airplane.

You can see Mumbai.
Mumbai is a huge city.

Check Your Work

Read more of Lee's travel guide. He needs to make some changes.

- He needs to add a detail to give more information. To add text, he used this mark: ∧.
- The name of a place in the first sentence needs to start with a capital letter. He put three lines under the letter: ≡.
- Lee needs to make a word plural. He used this mark: ∧.

What other errors does he need to fix?

> You can see ∧tall elephants near calcutta≡. You can hear
> monkey∧s in the jungles.
> You can visit the beaches. You can have great thing to
> eat all around india.

Look back at your travel guide. Read it aloud. Then ask yourself the questions in the checklist. Mark your changes.

Finish and Share

Use these steps to finish your travel guide.

1. Write your sentences on cards neatly and correctly.
2. Be sure you have a title.
3. Attach your cards to a large piece of paper.
4. Add drawings or pictures.
5. Add your page to a class travel book.

PRESENT

Take turns reading the travel guides aloud. Use these tips.

Presenting Tips

If You Are the Speaker:	If You Are the Listener:
• Stay on the topic.	• Pay attention to the reader's voice.
• Read loudly and clearly.	• Ask questions about the topic.

Checklist

- ☑ Did I include enough details?
- ☑ Did I use a capital letter for the names of places?
- ☑ Did I use the singular and plural nouns correctly?

Reflect

- How did the concept web help you decide what to write?
- What did you like best about writing your travel guide?

Friends work together to get the job done.

Friend to **Friend**

Look at the pictures.

Act out the scenes with a partner.

Talk about how each character feels.

In This Unit

▶ **Language Development**

▶ **Language and Literacy**

▶ **Language and Content**
   Mathematics

▶ **Writing Project**

Vocabulary
- Feelings
- Key Vocabulary

Language Functions
- Describe Actions
- Express Feelings

Grammar
- Regular Past Tense Verbs
- Irregular Past Tense Verbs (was, were)
- Negative Sentences and Contractions with Not
- Possessive Nouns

Reading
- Verb Ending: -ed
- High Frequency Words
- Comprehension: Cause and Effect
- Text Features: Bar Graphs

Writing
- Memory Story

Together We Dreamed

▶ **Language: Describe Actions**

Listen and sing. CD

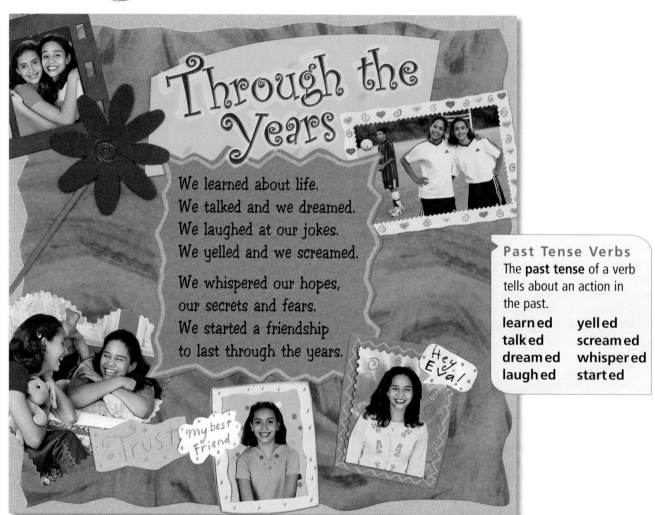

We learned about life.
We talked and we dreamed.
We laughed at our jokes.
We yelled and we screamed.

We whispered our hopes,
our secrets and fears.
We started a friendship
to last through the years.

Past Tense Verbs
The **past tense** of a verb tells about an action in the past.

learn ed	yell ed
talk ed	scream ed
dream ed	whisper ed
laugh ed	start ed

EXPRESS YOURSELF ▶ DESCRIBE ACTIONS

Complete each sentence. Tell what your friends did. You can use a verb from the box above. Take turns sharing sentences with a partner.

EXAMPLE **1.** I finished the race. My friends yelled.

1. I finished the race. My friends _____.
2. I danced a funny dance. My friends _____.

3. I learned a sport. My friends _____ it, too.
4. I shared my dreams. My friends _____, too.

<u>5.–8.</u> **Tell a friend about 4 things you did.**

EXAMPLE **5.** I talked about my idea. My friends listened.

How Do the Friends Feel?

▶ **Vocabulary: Feelings**
▶ **Language: Express Feelings**

Len has lots of friends. Len and his friends use adjectives to describe how they feel.

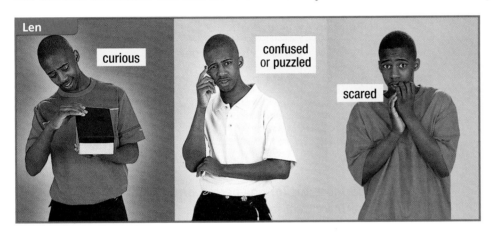

ORAL LANGUAGE PRACTICE ▶ EXPRESS FEELINGS

1.–4. Who's talking? 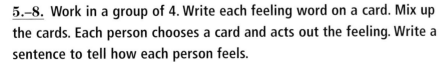 CD

Listen. Who is talking? Point to the correct person.
Act out the scene. Tell how you feel. Use your face and body
to show your feelings, too.

WRITTEN PRACTICE

5.–8. Work in a group of 4. Write each feeling word on a card. Mix up
the cards. Each person chooses a card and acts out the feeling. Write a
sentence to tell how each person feels.

EXAMPLE **5.** Nora is bored.

Were the Friends Happy?

▶ **Irregular Past Tense Verbs: *Was* and *Were***

Was and *Were* are irregular past tense verbs.

Pronoun	Verb	Example
I	was	I **was** happy.
you	were	You **were** excited.
he, she, it	was	He **was** proud.
we	were	We **were** the winning team!
they	were	They **were** good losers, though.

Use *There was* for one person or thing.
Use *There were* for two or more.

> **There was** one girl on their team.
> **There were** two girls on our team.

BUILD SENTENCES

Read each sentence. Change the <u>underlined</u> verb
to the past tense. Say the new sentence.

EXAMPLE **1.** We were at my house.

Present	Past
is	was
are	were

1. We <u>are</u> at my house.
2. We <u>are</u> on the sofa.
3. The sofa <u>is</u> too small for all of us.
4. Len <u>is</u> on the floor.
5. Veronica <u>is</u> on the floor, too.
6. There <u>are</u> no pillows to sit on.
7. Len and Veronica <u>are</u> mad.
8. Finally, there <u>is</u> food to eat!
9. We <u>are</u> all happy again.

WRITE SENTENCES

<u>10.–14.</u> Work with a partner to write 5 sentences
about the past. Tell about a day with your friends.
Use *was* and *were*.

EXAMPLES **10.** Yesterday I was at the library.

11. A lot of my friends were there, too.

The Friends Didn't Scare Len!

▶ **Negative Sentences and Contractions With *Not***

Contractions can be used to build sentences with negative past tense verbs.

Add the word *not* after *was* and *were*.

Len **was not** scared.

Eddie and Miguel **were not** happy.

With other verbs, add *did not* <u>before</u> the verb.

did not
The trick worked.
                    ^

> When you add **did not** to a sentence, take the **-ed** off the main verb.

BUILD SENTENCES

Read the sentences in number 1. Then answer the questions in number 2. Say your answer in a complete sentence. Use *did not, was not,* or *were not.*

EXAMPLE **2.** They did not trick Sofia.

1. The friends tricked Veronica.
   They were proud!
   The snake jumped out.
   Veronica was afraid.
   She screamed.

2. Did the friends trick Sofia?
   Were they proud?
   Did the snake jump out?
   Was Sofia afraid?
   Did she scream?

WRITE SENTENCES

3.–7. Write each sentence you made above. Then write it again. Use contractions to replace *did not, was not,* and *were not.*

EXAMPLE **3.** They did not trick Sofia.
         They didn't trick Sofia.

> **Contractions**
> Contractions combine two words using an apostrophe.
>
> **did + not = didn't**
> **was + not = wasn't**
> **were + not = weren't**

Language Development

Listen and Read Along

FOCUS ON GENRE

Journal A journal tells about the author's thoughts, feelings and experiences. This is a fictional journal.

FOCUS ON VOCABULARY

Feeling Words You have been learning words like the ones below. Use these words as you talk about *Friends Are Like That.* Collect more words to put in the web.

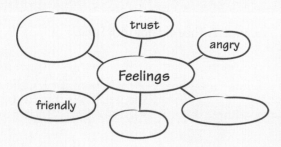

THEME BOOK

Read this journal about friendship.

Some people add pictures and drawings to their journals to express how they feel.

Think About
Friends Are Like That

CAUSE AND EFFECT

Make a cause-and-effect chart for *Friends Are Like That.*
Follow these steps.

1 Copy the following cause-and-effect chart. Think about the story. Write the effect next to each cause.

Cause	Effect
Eva and Veronica are best friends.	They talk about everything.
Veronica saw Eva walking with Eddie.	
Eva asked Veronica to tell her what was wrong.	
Veronica found out that Eva had helped Eddie choose her gift.	

2 Use your completed chart to take turns retelling the story with a partner.

Language and Literacy

High Frequency Words

REVIEW HIGH FREQUENCY WORDS

Read the words aloud. Which word goes in the sentence?

which	watch
around	always
Sometimes	Something

1. The boys will _____ a movie.
2. They _____ buy popcorn at the movies.
3. _____ they get cold drinks, too.

▲ These boys buy popcorn at the movies.

LEARN NEW WORDS

Study these words. Say them as whole words when you read.

saw	Last week I **saw** a movie.
was	I **was** sitting in the first row.
were	A lot of kids from school **were** there.
their	Some kids came with **their** mothers and fathers.
said	"Look, there's Sofia," I **said** to my dad.

PRACTICE

4.–8. Make a map for each new word. Write the word in the center. Complete the other boxes and use the word in a sentence of your own.

EXAMPLE **4.**

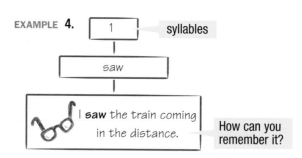

```
[ 1 ] ── syllables
    │
[ saw ]
    │
[ I saw the train coming
  in the distance. ] ── How can you
                         remember it?
```

9.–13. Write each sentence. Add the missing word.

EXAMPLE **9.** My friends were not at school last week.

9. My friends _ _ _ _ not at school last week.
10. My best friend _ _ _ sick for two days.
11. I helped Sofia and Rosa get _ _ _ _ _ homework.
12. I _ _ _ _, "I'm glad you are feeling better."
13. Sofia said, "I _ _ _ the card you sent me."

More High Frequency Words

→ **How to Learn a New Word**
- Look at the word.
- Listen to the word.
- Listen to the word in a sentence. What does it mean?
- Say the word.
- Spell the word.
- Say the word again.

REVIEW HIGH FREQUENCY WORDS

Read the words aloud. Which word goes in the sentence?

animals	down	1. Sam saw many _____ at the city zoo.
city	above	2. He saw a bird flying _____ his head.
by	people	3. Many other _____ saw it, too.

LEARN NEW WORDS

Study these words. Say them as whole words when you read.

began	They shut off the lights, and the movie **began**.
about	The movie was **about** some kids in the 1950s.
dance	I watched them **dance** to old music.
thought	My dad **thought** the music was great.
again	We want to see that movie **again** next week.

PRACTICE

4.–8. **Make a map for each new word. Write the word in the center. Complete the other boxes and use the word in a sentence of your own.**

EXAMPLE **4.**

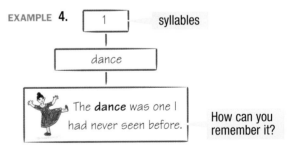

9.–13. **Write each sentence. Add the missing word.**   EXAMPLE **9.** I began telling Sofia about math class.

9. I __ __ __ __ __ telling Sofia about math class.

10. Then I __ __ __ __ __ __ __ about what I was doing.

11. Sofia was __ __ __ __ __ to talk to the teacher.

12. So I just said, "I will talk to you __ __ __ __ __ later."

13. I knew I would see Sofia at the school __ __ __ __ __ that night.

Reading and Spelling

▶ **Verb Ending: -ed**

Listen and learn. CD

Best Friends

My best friend had a bracelet.
I wanted a bracelet, too.
I wished,
I hoped,
I waited,
But my wish did not come true.

My friend gave me a bracelet.
I didn't know she knew!
I smiled,
She laughed,
We hugged.
That's just
    what best friends do.

STUDY VERB ENDINGS

For some verbs, you can just add **-ed**.

    wish + ed = wished

    need + ed = needed

This verb ends in silent **e**.

    smile

When you add **-ed**, drop the e.

    smil~~e~~ + ed = smiled

This verb ends in one vowel and one consonant.

    hug

When you add **-ed**, double the consonant.

    hug̲ged

Follow these steps to read a word with -ed.

1 Look for the ending you know. Cover it.

lifted

lift

2 Look for vowel and consonant patterns to sound out the base word.

lift   **l + i + f + t = lift**

> I see two consonants after the vowel i, so the i is short.

3 Look at the entire word again. Blend the base word and the ending to read the word.

lift + ed = lifted

> Blend **lift** and **ed** to say the word **lifted**.

Reading Help

There are three different sounds for **-ed.**

1. The sound for d

waved	hugged
smiled	rained

2. The sound for t

picked	liked
wished	hoped

3. The sounds for ed

waited	ended
needed	melted

Say each word. Which group has words with two syllables?

READING PRACTICE

Use what you learned to read the sentences.

1. Eddie hated to be sick. He was so bored!

2. He needed something to do.

3. He picked a book to read and flipped through it.

4. Just then, Eddie saw Len at his window.

5. Eddie waved. "I'm so glad you stopped by!" he said.

SPELLING PRACTICE

6.–9. Now write the sentences that your teacher reads.

WORD WORK

10.–15. Read these words. Then write each word on a card. Match the 6 pairs that go together. What do you notice?

> I double the **b** when I add **-ed**.

waited	need	wait
rub	hope	liked
hoped	like	needed
rip	rubbed	ripped

EXAMPLE **10.**

rub   rubbed

Read on Your Own

FOCUS ON GENRE

Realistic Fiction   Realistic fiction is a story that is not true, but could really happen. The characters act like real people. This story is about two girls who are practicing for a show at school.

FOCUS ON WORDS

Verb Ending: *-ed*   When you read and come to a word you don't know, blend the sounds together to read it. You just learned about verbs that end in *-ed*.

hugg<u>ed</u>

High Frequency Words   Say these words as whole words when you read.

saw	was
were	their
said	began
about	dance
thought	again

Eva's LESSON

Eva was mad. She tapped her foot. She looked at the clock above the stove.

"Veronica has ten more seconds to get here," she said. Eva waited and waited.

Veronica was always late.

They had planned to talk about their dance for the school show. Eva thought Veronica was not very good. She thought Veronica needed a lot of help.

While she waited, Eva played the CD for their dance. She clapped her hands and kicked to the beat. She began to sing. She kicked again. This time, she kicked too high. She slipped and landed on the rug! Just then, Veronica peeked in the kitchen window. She saw Eva and rushed to help her. Eva smiled and rubbed her leg. "I thought you were the one who needed help. Now I know I was the one," she joked.

Think About "Eva's Lesson"

CHECK YOUR UNDERSTANDING

Make a chart. Write what happened as a result of each cause. Use the finished chart to tell the story to a partner. Then listen as your partner tells the story.

Cause		Effect
Veronica and Eva wanted to dance in the school show.	→	They needed to practice.
Veronica was late.	→	
Eva kicked too high.	→	
Veronica helped Eva.	→	

Eddie's Friends Do Well

▶ **Possessive Nouns**

| **A singular noun that shows ownership ends in 's.**

Eva and Veronica picked costumes for their show. Eva**'s** costume was purple and green. Veronica**'s** costume was red and blue. Sofia**'s** mom gave them matching caps to wear.

BUILD SENTENCES

Say each sentence. Add 's to the word in dark print.

EXAMPLE **1.** Eva's mom and dad came to the show.

1. Eva _____ mom and dad came to the show.

2. Veronica _____ mom came, too.

3. friend She borrowed her _____ camera to record the show.

4. show Eva and Veronica were the _____ final act.

5. crowd The _____ cheers made them feel good.

6. Eddie Veronica was very proud when she saw _____ big smile.

WRITE SENTENCES

7.–9. Work with a partner. Look at the picture. Write 3 sentences about the picture. Use possessive nouns.

EXAMPLE **7.** Miguel's shirt is orange.

Success in Mathematics

▶ **Learn About Bar Graphs**

Bar Graphs

A **bar graph** compares numbers. It is a good way to see information quickly.

This bar graph shows how many students stay in touch with their friends by visiting, using the telephone, using e-mail, and text messaging.

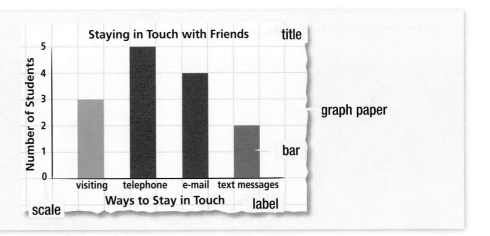

Read the instructions. Then do the activity.

Make a Survey and Graph the Results

You will need: a data chart, graph paper

ACTIVITY STEPS

1 Make a Survey

Interview several students. Ask: "Which languages do you know how to speak?" Record the names and languages in chart.

Languages Spoken					
English	Spanish	Chinese	Vietnamese	Russian	Korean
James	Ernesto	Archie	Duc	Anya	Annette
Annette	Felicia	Jun		Nick	Brian
Ernesto	Martin				Sungmee
Anya	Vanesa				
Archie	Alexandra				

2 Create a Tally

Count the number of students in each category.

3 Make a Bar Graph

• Label the bottom line of your graph: Languages Spoken.

• Label the scale: Number of Students.

• Draw the bars to make the graph.

• Write a title.

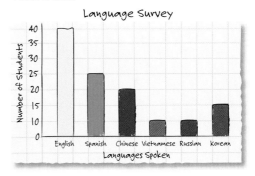

THINK IT OVER

1. Look at your chart. What do the numbers tell you?

2. Is the total number of students across the languages the same as the number of students you interviewed? If not, why?

3. Why is a bar graph a good way to see the results of your survey?

Build Background for "Hand in Hand"

FEELINGS

In Israel, Jews and Palestinians live in different areas. At the Hand in Hand schools, these two groups of people learn to be friends.

▲ Jewish and Palestinian students learn to get along.

▲ This map shows where Israel is located.

Learn Key Vocabulary

Rate and Study the Words Rate how well you know each word. Then:

1. Pronounce the word. Say it aloud several times. Spell it.
2. Study the example.
3. Tell more about the word.
4. Practice it. Make the word your own.

Key Words

angry (āng-rē) *adjective*

When people are **angry**, they feel mad about something. **Angry** people sometimes shout.

different (di-fur-rent) *adjective*

When things are **different**, they are not the same. The players in the blue shirts play for a **different** team than the players in the white shirts.

friendship (frend-ship) *noun*

A **friendship** is when people care about each other. These Palestinian and Jewish children have a close **friendship**.

group (groop) *noun*

A **group** is a collection of the same kind of people. People from different **groups** must learn to live together.

hoped (hōpt) *verb*

The word **hoped** is the past tense of **hope**. The creators of Hand in Hand **hope** to show Jews and Palestinians that they are not that different after all.

Practice the Words Work with a partner. Make a Word Map for each Key Word.

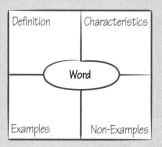

Word Map

Listen and Read Along

FOCUS ON GENRE

Magazine Article   A magazine article can be written to give information. It is nonfiction. It usually includes more pictures, maps, and graphs than a newspaper article. This article is about some schools in Israel.

FOCUS ON COMPREHENSION

Cause and Effect   An effect is something that happens. The cause is the reason why it happened. As you read "Hand in Hand," think about the effects of the schools on the people in Israel.

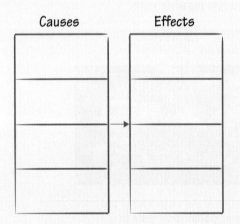

Causes	Effects

This photo shows the city of Jerusalem in Israel.

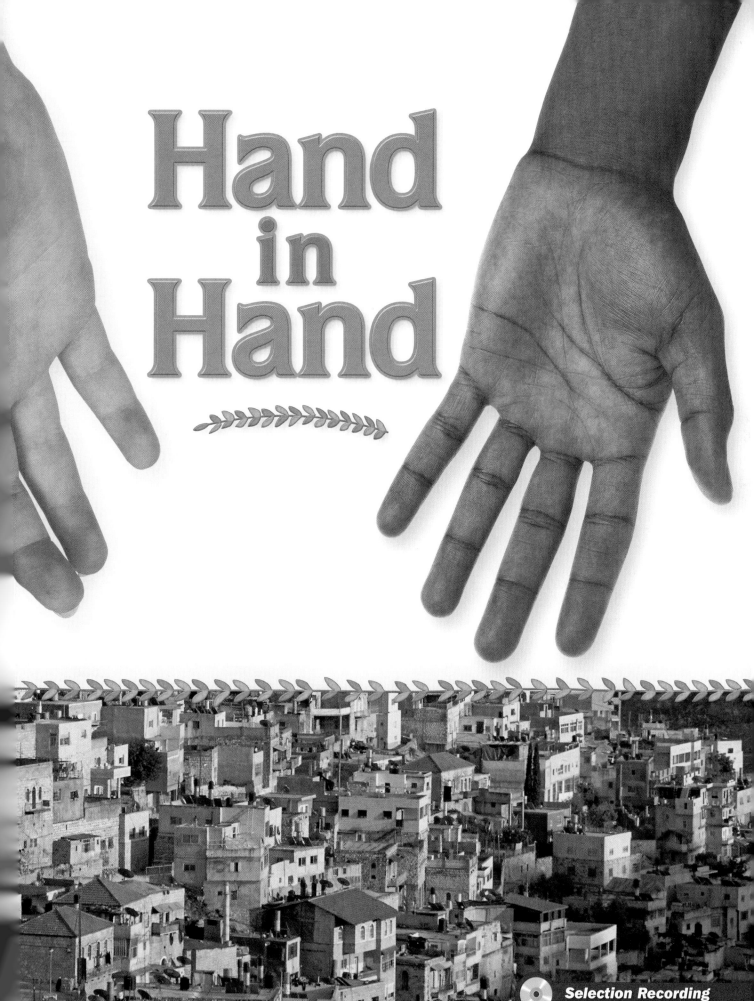

Hand
in
Hand

Selection Recording

Learning Together

Each morning in Israel, 300 kids do something **unusual**. They go to school. What is **the big deal**? Their schools mix two **groups** that are often **angry** with each other.

▲ These Palestinian and Jewish girls are good friends.

Key Vocabulary
group *n.*, people or things that are alike
angry *adj.*, mad

In Other Words
unusual different
the big deal so unusual about this

In Israel, Palestinians and Jews often do not get along. They live in **different** areas. They speak different languages and have different religions. Most don't go to the same schools.

Bringing these groups together is hard. But two friends try.

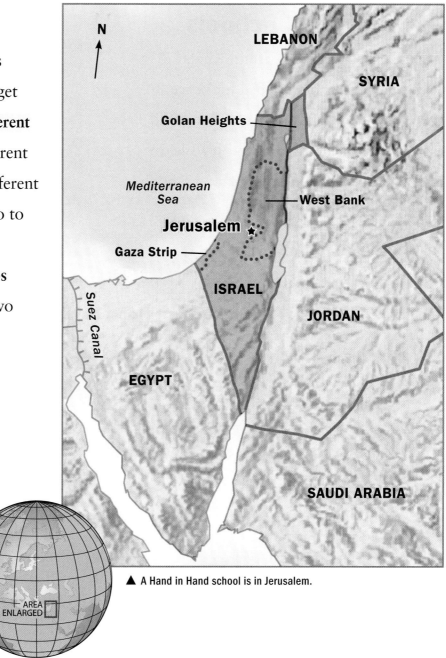

▲ A Hand in Hand school is in Jerusalem.

Before You Move On

1. **Main Idea and Details** What two **groups** of students go to the Hand in Hand schools?
2. **Cause and Effect** Why don't the two **groups** of students in Israel usually go to school together?

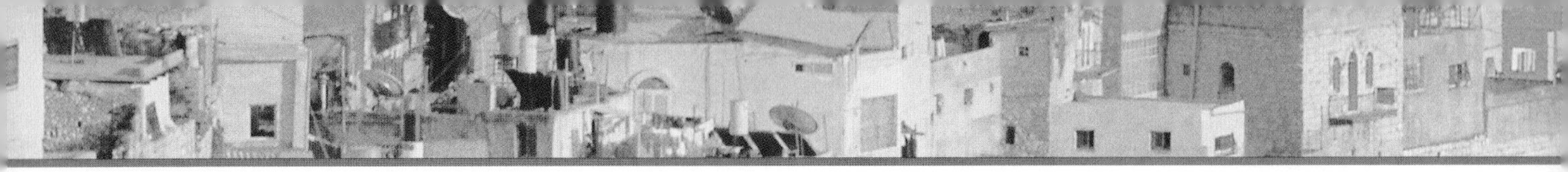

Hand in Hand Schools

Lee Gordon is Jewish. Amin Khalaf is Palestinian. They both **hoped** for peace. In 1996 they **formed** Hand in Hand to build schools where Palestinians and Jews learn together. One of the Hand in Hand schools is in Jerusalem, **Israel's capital**.

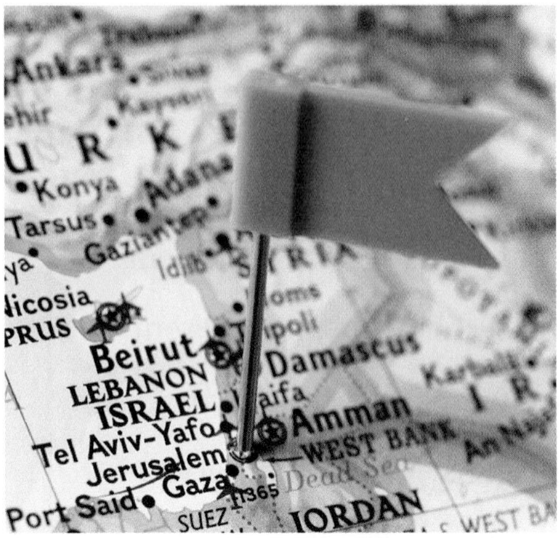

Konya
Tarsus
Beirut
LEBANON
ISRAEL
Damascus
Amman
Tel Aviv-Yafo
Jerusalem
WEST BANK
Gaza
Port Said
SUEZ
JORDAN

▲ Jerusalem is the capital city of Israel. There are Hand in Hand schools in different areas of Israel.

Number of Students at Hand in Hand Schools

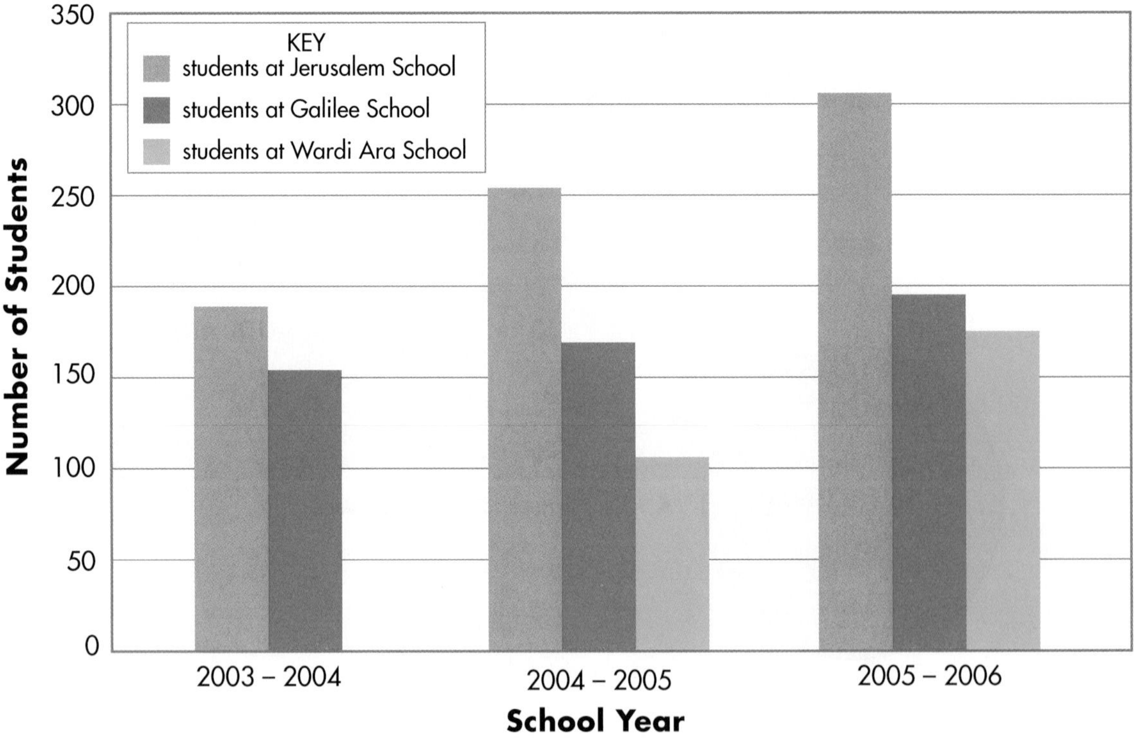

KEY
students at Jerusalem School
students at Galilee School
students at Wardi Ara School
Number of Students
350
300
250
200
150
100
50
0
2003 – 2004
2004 – 2005
2005 – 2006
School Year

Key Vocabulary
hoped *v.*, wanted; wished

In Other Words
formed started
Israel's capital the city where Israel's government is

The students get to school at about 7:30 a.m. Adults are sometimes fighting near the school. The school has **guards** to keep students safe.

The Jewish students speak Hebrew at home. The Palestinian students speak Arabic at home. When class starts, kids hear both languages.

▲ Kids at Hand in Hand school made this poster. It shows the word *spring* in Hebrew and Arabic.

▲ A Palestinian teacher talks with students.

In Other Words

guards people who protect the school

Before You Move On

1. **Text Features** Which Hand in Hand school gained the most students between 2003 and 2006?
2. **Inference** Why are kids at Hand in Hand schools taught in two languages?

At Home, At School

At home, the kids talk about what they are doing at school.

Palestinian kids ask their Jewish friends to come over to visit.

Jewish kids invite their Palestinian friends over to visit.

This is new for the parents. Some families **feel nervous** at first.

Then they get to know each other and start to have fun together!

One **friendship** at a time, they are learning how to get along.

▲ Palestinian and Jewish kids spend time with their families at home.
They spend time with each other at school.

Key Vocabulary
friendship *n.*, a feeling of closeness and kindness between people

In Other Words
feel nervous are not sure that this is right

◀ Kids from different groups build friendships at Hand in Hand schools.

Before You Move On

1. **Cause and Effect** What happens after kids talk to their families about school?

2. **Personal Experience** Have you ever made a new friend who has a very **different** family life than you? Explain.

Language and Content

Think About "Hand in Hand"

CHECK YOUR UNDERSTANDING

<u>1.–2.</u> **Work with a partner to complete each item.**

1. **Identify Cause and Effect** Make a chart like the one below. Then complete the chart by adding causes and effects that you read in the article.

Causes	Effects
Lee Gordon and Amin Khalaf created the first Hand in Hand school.	Palestinian and Jewish children began to learn together.

2. **Sum It Up** Use your chart to tell about the **groups** that go to Hand in Hand schools. Tell about the **different** things that happen and why.

REVIEW VOCABULARY

<u>3.–7.</u> **Read the paragraph aloud. Add the vocabulary words.**

> Jews and Palestinians are _____. Sometimes _____ of people who are different get _____ with each other. At Hand in Hand, Jews and Palestinians form _____. These students _____ that there can be peace.

Vocabulary

angry

different

friendships

groups

hope

WRITE ABOUT FRIENDSHIP

<u>8.</u> **Write about friendship. Describe the ways the friendship has helped you.**

Memory Story

WHAT IS A MEMORY STORY?

A memory story is a story you write about your own life. You can tell other people about one day in your life or your whole life. You can tell about your family and friends.

MEMORY STORY

A Great Day with Mario

Mario and I played basketball at the school gym last Saturday. I was excited when I scored some points. We walked to the music store to check out some new CDs. I was happy to listen to a new CD that Mario told me about. We got some sandwiches at the grocery store. I was really hungry! Then we used the computer at Mario's house. I was sorry when it was time to go home.

Capitalize **proper nouns**.

Use **past tense verbs**.

Write a Memory Story

WRITING PROMPT Write a memory story about a day with a friend. Tell what you did and how you felt. Plan to share it with your class.

Plan and Write

1 PLAN YOUR MEMORY STORY

Think about a special day you spent with a friend. What did you do? Where were you? How did you feel? Make a chart like this one. Add notes to your chart. This is Rosa's chart.

What We Did	Where	My Feelings
shopped	at the mall	excited
talked and laughed	at the mall	happy
had ice cream	at a restaurant	happy
watched a movie	in the theater	surprised

Feelings
curious
confused
scared
proud
happy
angry
sad

2 WRITE SENTENCES

Use your chart to write your memory story. Write about each thing you did. Write about where you were. Write about each feeling you had.

Maura and I shopped at the mall last weekend. I got new clothes. So did Maura. We talked and laughed for hours! We had ice cream. Then we watched a movie. I was surprised at the end of the movie.

Check Your Work

Read more of Rosa's memory story. She needs to make some changes.

- She needs to capitalize names of people. She put three lines under the letter: ≡.
- She needs to capitalize the word **I**. She put three lines under that letter, too: ≡.
- She needs to take out a detail that doesn't go with the topic. To take out this text, she used this mark: ℘.

What other errors does she need to fix?

We went back to her house after the movie. maura tried on her new clothes. Then i tried on my new clothes. ~~My sister got new shoes last week.~~ Later i had dinner with maura's family. We had a great day together

Look back at your memory story. Read it aloud. Then ask yourself the questions in the checklist. Mark your changes.

Finish and Share

Use these steps to finish your memory story.

1. Write the memory story neatly and correctly.
2. Be sure you have a title.
3. Add drawings or pictures.
4. Add your memory story to a class friendship book.

ACT IT OUT

Share your writing with friends. Use these tips.

Presenting Tips

If You Are the Speaker:	If You Are the Listener:
• Tell the events in order.	• Pay attention to the reader's voice.
• Change your voice to show how you felt.	• Ask questions about things you didn't understand.

Checklist

- ✓ Did I capitalize the word I?
- ✓ Did I capitalize the first letter in people's names?
- ✓ Did I take out sentences that are not about my memory?

Reflect

- How did the chart help you write your memory story?
- What did you like best about writing about your life?

Many people dance for exercise.
Many people dance for fun.

Dance!

1. Jump high,   2. jump low,   3. turn,   4. hop, hop.

5. Step forward,   6. step back,   7. turn,   8. kick, kick.

9. Reach up,   10. reach down,   11. wiggle,   12. spin.

Now you try the dance. Come on! Jump in!

Let's Celebrate!

Learn the dance. Try it!
Then use some of the moves to
make up a new dance. CD

In This Unit

▶ **Language Development**

▶ **Language and Literacy**

▶ **Language and Content**
Social Studies

▶ **Writing Project**

Vocabulary
- Actions
- Country Words
- Key Vocabulary

Language Functions
- Ask and Answer Questions
- Describe People

Grammar
- Adverbs
- Present Progressive Verbs
- Phrases with *like to* and *want to*

Reading
- Verb Ending: *-ing*
- High Frequency Words
- Comprehension: Classify
- Text Features: Maps

Writing
- Blog

How Do You Dance

▶ **Language: Ask and Answer Questions**

Listen and chant. CD

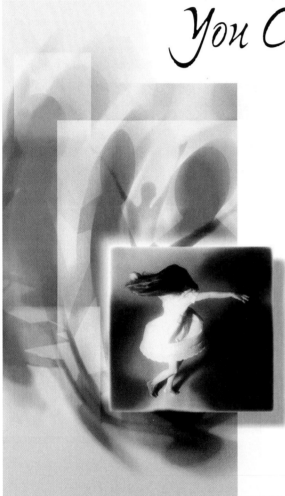

You Can Dance!

Can you dance?
No, I can't dance.
You can't dance?
No! I just can't dance.
Can you jump high?
I can jump high.
Can you jump low?
I can jump low.
Can you step forward?
I can step forward.
Can you step back?
I can step back.
Can you turn quickly?
I can turn quickly.
Then you can dance.
Now you can dance!

> **Adverbs**
> Adverbs tell how, when, or where an action happens.
>
> turn **quickly**
> dance **wildly**
> dance **now**
> step **back**

EXPRESS YOURSELF ▶ ASK AND ANSWER QUESTIONS

Work with a partner. Take turns asking these questions. Answer in a complete sentence. Then act it out.

EXAMPLE **1.** Can you jump high?
Yes, I can jump high.

1. Can you jump high?
2. Can you jump low?
3. Can you step forward?
4. How do you jump?
5. Where do you step?
6. How do you turn?

<u>**7.–10.**</u> **How do you dance? Say 4 sentences to answer the question. Use adverbs to tell how you dance.**

EXAMPLE **7.** I dance fast.

What Are They Doing?

▶ **Present Progressive Verbs**

Present progressive verbs tell what is happening now.

The woman **is jumping**.

The dancer **is standing**.

They **are dancing**.

BUILD SENTENCES

Look at the pictures below. Say sentences to go with each picture.
Choose words from each column.

The boy		jumping.
The girl	is	playing the drums.
The people	are	turning around.
He		kicking.
She		dancing.
They		marching.

EXAMPLE **1.** The girl is turning around.

1.

2.

3.

4.

WRITE SENTENCES

5.–8. Write 2 sentences for each picture. Tell how
the people are moving. Use an adverb in each sentence.
Take turns reading sentences to a partner.

EXAMPLE **5.** The girl is turning around quickly.

She is dancing happily.

> **Adverbs**
>
> high   up
> carefully quickly
> happily   slowly
> loudly   wildly

People Celebrate Around the World

▶ **Vocabulary: Country Words**
▶ **Language: Describe People**

Look at the pictures. Read about the people.

This dragon dance is from **China.** People do the dragon dance to celebrate the **Chinese** New Year.

These dancers are from **Mexico**. They are doing a **Mexican** dance.

These dancers are **English**. They are doing an old dance from **England**.

ORAL LANGUAGE PRACTICE ▶ DESCRIBE PEOPLE

<u>1.–3.</u> **Who's talking?** 💿 CD

Listen. Who is talking? Point to the correct picture.

Then describe the dancers.

Tell what they look like. Tell what they are doing.

WRITTEN PRACTICE ✏️

<u>4.–8.</u> **Interview 3 people from different countries.**
Write 2 sentences to describe each person.

EXAMPLE **4.** Juan is from Cuba.

He is Cuban.

Country	A Person from the Country
India	Indian
Mongolia	Mongolian
Japan	Japanese
Vietnam	Vietnamese
Cuba	Cuban
Guatemala	Guatemalan
Nicaragua	Nicaraguan
Ireland	Irish

Everyone Likes to Dance

▶ **Phrases with *Like To* and *Want To***

Use a verb to complete a phrase with *like to* or *want to*.

| like to | + | verb |

They **like to dance**.

She **likes to perform**.

| want to | + | verb |

They **want to celebrate**.

She **wants to keep** a tradition.

Add an *-s* when you use *he*, *she*, or *it*.

BUILD SENTENCES

Read each sentence. Add the correct form of *like to* or *want to*. Say the new sentence.

EXAMPLE **1.** The dancers like to march.

1.

The dancers _____ march.

2.

He _____ perform.

3.

The men _____ jump.

4.

The dancers _____ move.

5.

She _____ turn.

6.

She _____ celebrate.

WRITE SENTENCES

7.–12. Write 2 sentences for each picture above. Use *like to* or *want to* and a country word.

EXAMPLE **7.** The dancers from China want to celebrate.
The Chinese dancers like to march.

Listen and Read Along

FOCUS ON GENRE

Photo Essay A photo essay gives information about a topic. The photos in this book help to show what the words mean.

FOCUS ON VOCABULARY

Action Words You have been learning words like the ones below. Use these words as you talk about *Let's Dance!* Collect more words to put in the web.

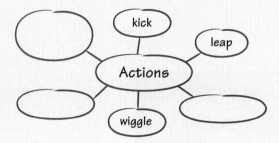

THEME BOOK

Read this photo essay about dance.

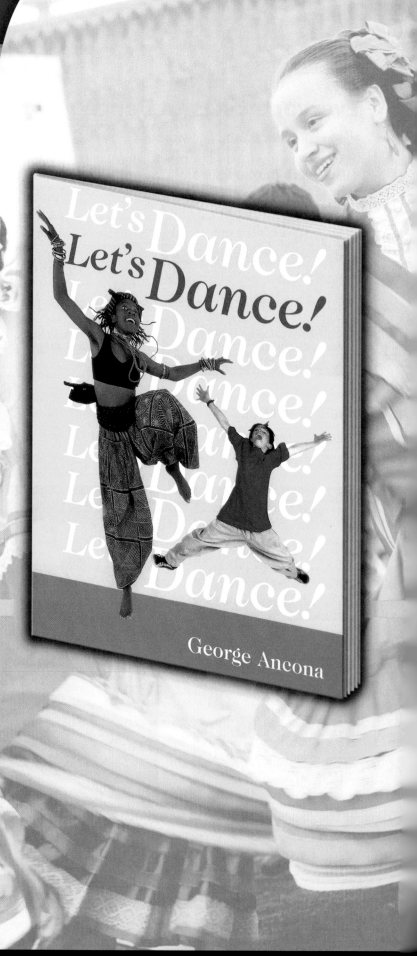

Colorful costumes add to the excitement of the dance.

Think About *Let's Dance!*

CLASSIFY INFORMATION

**Make a concept map to tell about *Let's Dance!*
Follow these steps.**

❶ Think about the book. What is it mostly about?

(Dancing)

❷ Who dances? Add a section to the map. Write
Who? inside. Write the people who dance.

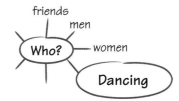

friends
men
(Who?)── women
(Dancing)

❸ What else does the book tell you? Add more
sections with ***Why?***, ***How?***, and ***Where?***

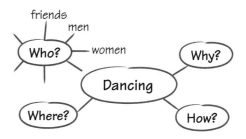

friends
men
(Who?)── women
(Why?)
(Dancing)
(Where?)
(How?)

❹ Add a few words from the book for each section.
Then use your map to discuss the book with a
partner.

friends
men
to celebrate
(Who?)── women
(Why?)
(Dancing)
(Where?)
(How?)
Korea
happily

Language and Literacy

High Frequency Words

▲ A Thanksgiving Day parade

REVIEW HIGH FREQUENCY WORDS

Read the words aloud. Which word goes in the sentence?

enough	through
really	world
above	on

1. The parade goes _____ the streets.
2. The floats are _____ big.
3. This parade is _____ Thanksgiving Day.

LEARN NEW WORDS

Study these words. Say them as whole words when you read.

celebrate	We like to **celebrate**. Today is my sister's birthday.
most	**Most** of her friends are here, but not all of them.
young	Her friends are **young** kids from school.
children	There are about 10 **children** in our yard.
started	The party **started** at 3:00.

PRACTICE

<u>4.–8.</u> **Make a map for each new word. Write the word in the center. Complete the other boxes and use the word in a sentence of your own.**

EXAMPLE **4.**

```
            3          syllables
        celebrate
   We will celebrate my dad's      How can you
   birthday on Saturday.           remember it?
```

<u>9.–13.</u> **Write each sentence. Add the missing word.**

EXAMPLE **9.** In my family, we dance when we celebrate.

 9. In my family, we dance when we _ _ _ _ _ _ _ _ _.
10. I learned the waltz when I was very _ _ _ _ _.
11. I _ _ _ _ _ _ _ to learn it when I was 5.
12. My father wants all his _ _ _ _ _ _ _ _ to know how to dance.
13. _ _ _ _ of us are very good dancers!

More High Frequency Words

> ## How to Learn a New Word
>
> - Look at the word.
> - Listen to the word.
> - Listen to the word in a sentence. What does it mean?
> - Say the word.
> - Spell the word.
> - Say the word again.

REVIEW HIGH FREQUENCY WORDS

Read the words aloud. Which word goes in the sentence?

Our	Other	1. _____ parents like to spend time with us.
family	city	2. The whole _____ likes to do things together.
father	river	3. My _____ and mother are special people.

LEARN NEW WORDS

Study these words. Say them as whole words when you read.

beginning	It is now 4:00, and it is **beginning** to rain.
change	My mother says, "We need to **change** our plans!"
another	"Let's move the party to **another** place!"
only	The house is the **only** place to go.
following	The kids are quickly **following** me inside. This is fun!

PRACTICE

<u>4.–8.</u> **Make a map for each new word. Write the word in the center. Complete the other boxes and use the word in a sentence of your own.**

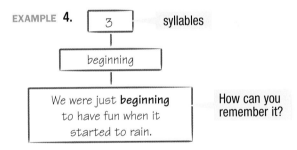

EXAMPLE **4.**

3 — syllables

beginning

We were just **beginning** to have fun when it started to rain.

How can you remember it?

<u>9.–13.</u> **Write each sentence. Add the missing word.**

EXAMPLE **9.** The basic dance steps never change.

9. The basic dance steps never __ __ __ __ __ __.
10. The waltz is not the __ __ __ __ dance I know.
11. My father is teaching me __ __ __ __ __ __ __ dance called the cha-cha.
12. My house is __ __ __ __ __ __ __ __ __ to look like a dance club!
13. I am __ __ __ __ __ __ __ __ __ __ in my father's dancing footsteps!

Reading and Spelling

▶ **Verb Ending:** *-ing*

Listen and learn. CD

Invitation

Tap your foot. Tap your foot.
  You are really tapping.
Jump around. Jump around.
  You are really jumping.
Leap high. Leap high.
  You are really leaping.
Smile for me. Smile for me.
  You are really smiling!

STUDY VERB ENDINGS

For some verbs, you can just add **-ing**.

leap + **ing** = **leaping**

jump + **ing** = **jumping**

This verb ends in silent **e**.

smile

When you add **-ing**, drop the **e**.

smil~~e~~ + **ing** = **smiling**

This verb ends in one vowel and one consonant.

tap

When you add **-ing**, double the consonant.

tapping

READING STRATEGY

Follow these steps to read a word with *-ing*.

1 Look for the ending you know. Cover it.

leaping

leap

2 Look for vowel and consonant patterns to sound out the root word.

leap

l + eå + p = leap

> Remember that **ea** makes one vowel sound. Blend three sounds to say **leap**.

3 Uncover the ending. Blend the syllables to read the entire word.

leap + ing = leaping

> Blend **leap** and **ing** to say the word **leaping**.

Reading Help

Some words end in silent **e**. They have a long vowel sound.

shake

Look at this word and cover the **-ing**.

shaking

You do not see the **e** in the root word, but the vowel is still long.

READING PRACTICE

Use what you learned to read the sentences.

1. The first grade class is getting ready for a show.
2. I am helping with the costumes and taking care of the children.
3. Most of the children are running around. Some are screaming!
4. The music is playing. The show is beginning.
5. Two kids are waving at me. They dance very well!

SPELLING PRACTICE

6.–9. Now write the sentences that your teacher reads.

WORD WORK

10.–15. Read these words. Then write each word on a card. Match the 6 pairs that go together. What do you notice?

jumping	reach	jump
hop	smile	waving
smiling	wave	reaching
make	hopping	making

EXAMPLE **10.**

wave   waving

> I drop the **e** when I add **-ing**.

Read on Your Own

FOCUS ON GENRE

Informational Text   Informational text gives you information about a topic. It is nonfiction. This piece is about people who dance to celebrate important events.

FOCUS ON WORDS

Verb Ending: *-ing*   When you read and come to a word you don't know, blend the sounds together to read it. You just learned about verbs ending in *-ing*.

skate   ska<u>ting</u>

High Frequency Words   Say these words as whole words when you read.

celebrate	most
young	children
started	beginning
change	another
only	following

DANCE TO CELEBRATE!

People celebrate Chinese New Year.

People dance to celebrate a holiday. These people are beginning the Chinese New Year with a dance. They are greeting the Chinese dragon, which brings good luck. Nine men inside the costume are lifting the dragon with long poles. Only one man is beating a drum. He is following the dragon.

Chinese New Year

People dance to celebrate an important day in the family. This bride is having fun at her wedding. Three young men are lifting her in her seat while her husband watches. The family is dancing around them. They are smiling and clapping.

Jewish Wedding

Another time that people dance is during a change in the seasons. May Day is the time to welcome spring. It comes at the beginning of the season. This celebration started a long time ago. These children are weaving ribbons over and under, making a braid around the maypole.

All around the world, people dance to celebrate the most special times in their lives!

May Day

Think About "Dance To Celebrate!"

CHECK YOUR UNDERSTANDING

Write each sentence. Label it *T* for *True* or *F* for *False*.
If it is false, write the sentence again to make it true.

EXAMPLE **1.** There are six men inside the dragon costume. **F**
There are nine men inside the dragon costume.

Chinese New Year

1. There are six men inside the dragon costume.
2. People dance to celebrate a holiday.
3. The Chinese dragon brings bad luck.

Jewish Wedding

4. A wedding is an important day.
5. The bride is standing.
6. The bride is sad.
7. The family is dancing.

English Maypole Dance

8. The children are skipping around the maypole.
9. The children are celebrating summer.
10. The children are weaving ribbons.

EXPAND YOUR VOCABULARY

<u>11.–13.</u> **Tell about each picture on pages 258–259. Use some of these words and phrases.**

wedding	bride	around the maypole	May	dancing
spring	dragon	having fun	costume	in the family

EXAMPLE **11.** People are lifting the dragon.
They are inside the costume.

WRITE ABOUT CELEBRATIONS

<u>14.</u> **Choose a celebration from page 259. Write sentences to describe it.**

EXAMPLE **14.** Children are dancing around a maypole.
They are celebrating spring.

Language and Content

Success in Social Studies

▶ **Learn About Maps**

Maps

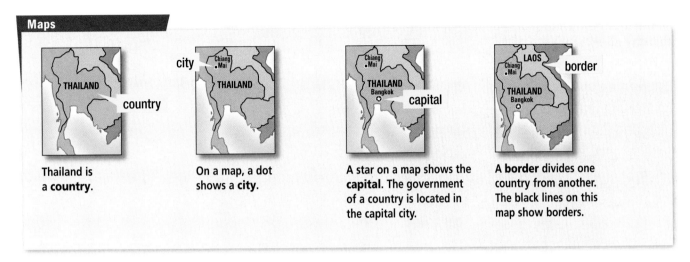

Thailand is a **country**.

On a map, a dot shows a **city**.

A star on a map shows the **capital**. The government of a country is located in the capital city.

A **border** divides one country from another. The black lines on this map show borders.

Listen to the article and study the map below. Then do the Review.

New Year Celebrations in Southeast Asia

• How do people in Southeast Asia celebrate the new year?

People in Southeast Asia celebrate the new year at different times and in different ways. Some countries celebrate in winter after the shortest day of the year. In Vietnam, people celebrate for an entire week in January or early February. During this time, the Vietnamese people of Ho Chi Minh City decorate their homes with small fruit trees full of orange-colored fruit.

Other countries celebrate the new year at the beginning of spring. In Thailand, people celebrate the new year from April 13 to April 15. All over Thailand, especially in the city of Chiang Mai, people splash water on each other to wash away bad luck.

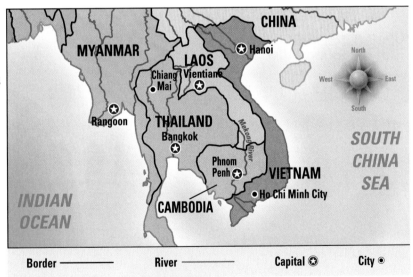

Border ——— River ——— Capital ✪ City ◉

REVIEW

1. **Check Your Understanding** How do people in Thailand and Vietnam celebrate the new year?
2. **Vocabulary** Name a country that has a border with Thailand.
3. **Use Maps** List the capitals shown on the map.

Build Background for "Kite Festival"

ACTION WORDS

At the Kite Festival in Japan, people fly kites of every color. They celebrate this day every year.

JAPAN
Hamamatsu

◀ The city of Hamamatsu is located in Japan.

▲ Kites fly high once a year in Hamamatsu, Japan.

Learn Key Vocabulary

Rate and Study the Words Rate how well you know each word. Then:

1. Pronounce the word. Say it aloud several times. Spell it.
2. Study the example.
3. Tell more about the word.
4. Practice it. Make the word your own.

Key Words

celebrate (se-luh-brāt) *verb*

When people **celebrate**, they get together for a special event. People in Japan started to **celebrate** the Kite Festival in the 1500s.

colorful (cul-er-ful) *adjective*

When something is **colorful**, it has a lot of colors. People at the festival fly **colorful** kites like this.

enjoy (en-joi) *verb*

When you **enjoy** something, you are having a good time. The teams **enjoy** working together to fly the kites.

gracefully (grās-ful-lē) *adverb*

When something moves **gracefully**, it moves smoothly. The kites fly **gracefully** through the air.

started (stär-ted) *verb*

If something has **started**, it has begun. The teams have not **started** to fly their kites yet.

Practice the Words With a partner, make an Expanded Meaning Map for each Key Word. Take turns quizzing each other.

Word and Definition

Things that are like the word

Things that are not like the word

Use the word in a sentence.

Expanded Meaning Map

Language and Content

Listen and Read Along

Magazine Article   A magazine article tells about a current event or a subject that many people want to read about. It is nonfiction. This magazine article is about a kite festival that happens in Japan.

FOCUS ON COMPREHENSION

Classify   When you classify information, you put it into groups. This will help you remember what you read in an article. As you read "Kite Festival," think about the information that belongs in the same group.

Kite Shape	Kite Color

Kite
FESTIVAL

Kites Fill the Air

Each year on May 3rd the sky in Hamamatsu, Japan, is filled with kites.

The Hamamatsu Kite **Festival started in the 1500s** to **celebrate** the birth of a new **prince**. People in Japan **keep this yearly tradition.**

JAPAN
Hamamatsu

Key Vocabulary
started *v.*, began
celebrate *v.*, to have a good time for a special reason

In Other Words
festival special event; party
in the 1500s about 500 years ago
prince son of the king
keep this yearly tradition
   celebrate the kite festival every year

▲ This painting of the Kite Festival was made hundreds of years ago by Utagawa Kunisada.

Before You Move On

1. **Main Idea and Details** Why did people originally **start** the kite festival?
2. **Inference** How do you think the sky looks during the kite festival?

Big Kites, Big Teams

The kites at the festival can be very big. Some are more than 10 feet wide. People work **in teams** to fly the kites. Some teams have up to 100 people!

In Other Words
in teams together in groups

▲ People work in teams to fly these large kites.

Before You Move On

1. **Inference** Why might it take 100 people to fly one kite?
2. **Compare and Contrast** How are the kites in the festival different from a kite you might fly on your own?

Kite Fights

Kites need to be strong to stay in the air. The kites are made from strong paper that is **stretched** over wood. Then kite makers add **colorful patterns** to the kites.

People at the festival watch the kites fly **gracefully** in the sky. Teams pull very long ropes to move the kites. Each team tries to make the other kites fall from the sky.

Some kites fall when their ropes break. Others get knocked down by other kites. Who will win?

▼ Teams get ready to fly their kites.

▼ This team waits for its turn to fly their kite.

Key Vocabulary

colorful *adj.*, to have many colors

gracefully *adv.*, to move smoothly

In Other Words

stretched pulled out
patterns pictures and designs

The Last Kite

The team with the last kite in the air wins. Everyone cheers. But it doesn't matter who wins. **Enjoying** the kites is the most important part of the day.

◀ People watch the kites to see which kite will win.

Key Vocabulary

enjoy *v.*, to take pleasure in; to feel joy

Before You Move On

1. **Summarize** How does a kite maker build a kite for the festival?
2. **Inference** Why do you think teams try to knock the kites of other teams out of the sky?

Think About "Kite Festival"

CHECK YOUR UNDERSTANDING

1.–2. Work with a partner to complete each item.

1. Classify Look at the different types of kites shown in "Kite Festival." Make a chart like the one below. Then complete the chart by classifying the kites by shape and color.

Kite Shape	Kite Color
The kite shown on page 265 is a square.	The kite shown on page 265 is red and white.

2. Use your chart to tell about the **colorful** kites at the festival. Did you **enjoy** the selection?

REVIEW VOCABULARY

3.–7. Read the paragraph aloud. Add the vocabulary words.

> The Hamamatsu Kite Festival _____ in the 1500s to _____ the birth of a new Japanese prince. The people at the festival _____ the _____ kites. The kites fly _____ in the sky.

Vocabulary
celebrate
colorful
enjoy
gracefully
started

WRITE ABOUT CELEBRATIONS

8. Write about a tradition that you know about. Tell when it started and what people do to celebrate it.

Blog

WHAT IS A BLOG?

A blog is like a journal but it is online. It is for everyone to read. You can write about yourself, your family, and your friends. You can write about things you like.

BLOG

The Festival of Lights

Some people from India like to celebrate the Festival of Lights. It takes place in the fall. We put rows of bright oil lamps all over our house. That looks cool! We watch fireworks. We give each other gifts. We eat rice pudding. You would like this celebration, too.

Capitalize the **names of countries**.

Name the **celebration**.

Writing Project

Write a Blog

WRITING PROMPT Interview someone to find out about a celebration. Describe the celebration. Tell what people do. Tell what people wear and what people eat.

How do people celebrate in Mexico?.

We make sugar skulls to honor our ancestors.

Plan and Write

1 PLAN YOUR BLOG

Think of a celebration you want to write about. Make a list of questions to ask someone. Put a check mark by the most important things to focus on. Use names of countries and people.

Gerardo chose to write about a Mexican celebration called "Day of the Dead." Here are his questions.

> 1. How do people celebrate?
> 2. Where do people go?
> 3. What do people eat?

Names of Countries and People

India	→ Indian
Mexico	→ Mexican
Japan	→ Japanese
Ireland	→ Irish
Vietnam	→ Vietnamese
Guatemala	→ Guatemalan

2 INTERVIEW A PERSON

Choose a person to interview. Plan a time you can talk. Ask your questions and write the person's answers.

> 1. How do people celebrate?   They make sugar skulls.
> 2. Where do people go?   to the cemetery

3 WRITE SENTENCES

Use your questions and answers to write your blog.

> My family likes to celebrate the Day of the Dead. It takes place on November 1 and 2. We remember people in our family who have died.

Check Your Work

Read more of Gerardo's blog. He needs to make some changes.

- He needs to capitalize the name of a place in the first sentence. He put three red lines under the letter: ≡.
- He needs to capitalize the name of a month in the second sentence. He put three red lines under that letter, too: ≡.
- He needs to take out a detail that doesn't go with the topic. To take out this text, he used this mark: ℘.

What other changes does he need to make?

Many people from mexico celebrate this day. We go to the cemetery each november. We like to take candles and flowers there, too. We make skulls from sugar. Children like to eat them. I like chocolate cake best. We also eat a special kind of bread. It is called Pan de muertos. day of the dead is one of my favorite mexican celebrations

Look back at your blog. Read it aloud. Then ask yourself the questions in the checklist. Mark your changes.

Finish and Share

Use these steps to finish your blog.

1. Write the blog neatly and correctly.
2. Be sure you have a title.
3. Add a drawing or picture.
4. Put your blog on a bulletin board in your classroom.

READ ALOUD

Share your writing with friends. Use these tips.

Presenting Tips

If You Are the Speaker:	If You Are the Listener:
• Stay on the topic.	• Pay attention to the reader's voice.
• Read loudly and clearly.	• Ask questions about the topic.

Checklist

- ☑ Did I capitalize names of places?
- ☑ Did I capitalize months of the year?
- ☑ Did I leave out information that's not about my topic?

Reflect

- What did you learn about the celebration?
- What did you like best about writing your blog?

Common Core

INSIDE

LANGUAGE · LITERACY · CONTENT

NATIONAL
GEOGRAPHIC
LEARNING

CENGAGE
Learning·

▶ Handbook

Strategies for Learning Language 278

Grammar 280–305

    Sentences 280

    Punctuation Marks 283

    Capital Letters 286

    Nouns 289

    Pronouns 294

    Adjectives 296

    Verbs 301

Handwriting 306–313

    Manuscript Hints 306

    Cursive Hints. 307

    Manuscript Alphabet, Numbers, and Punctuation Marks 308

    Writing Manuscript Letters 309

    Writing Manuscript Words and Sentences 310

    Cursive Alphabet 311

    Writing Cursive Letters 312

    Writing Cursive Words and Sentences 313

The Writing Process 314–319

    Prewrite 314

    Draft and Revise 316

    Edit and Proofread 318

    Publish 319

Using Information Resources 320–333

    How to Find Information 320

    Dictionary 322

    Thesaurus 324

    Parts of a Book 326

    Atlas: Maps 328

    Globe 329

    Internet 330

Strategies for Learning Language

These strategies can help you learn to use and understand the English language.

❶ Listen actively and try out language.

WHAT TO DO	EXAMPLES
Repeat what you hear.	You hear: Way to go, Joe! Fantastic catch! You say: Way to go, Joe! Fantastic catch!
Recite songs and poems.	My Family Tree Two grandmas, one brother, Two grandpas, one mother, One father, and then there's me. Eight of us together Make up my family tree. Two grandmas, one brother,...
Listen to others and use their language.	You hear: "When did you know that something was missing?" You say: "I knew that something was missing when I got to class."

❷ Ask for help.

WHAT TO DO	EXAMPLES
Ask questions about how to use language.	Did I say that right? Did I use that word in the right way? Which is correct, "bringed" or "brought"?
Use your native language or English to make sure that you understand.	You say: "Wait! Could you say that again more slowly, please?" Other options: "Does 'violet' mean 'purple'?" "Is 'enormous' another way to say 'big'?"

❸ Use gestures and body language, and watch for them.

WHAT TO DO	EXAMPLES
Use gestures and movements to help others understand your ideas.	I will hold up five fingers to show that I need five more minutes.
Watch people as they speak. The way they look or move can help you understand the meaning of their words.	Let's give him a hand. Everyone is clapping. "Give him a hand" must mean to clap for him.

❹ Think about what you are learning.

WHAT TO DO	EXAMPLES
Ask yourself: Are my language skills getting better? How can I improve?	Was it correct to use "they" when I talked about my grandparents? Did I add 's to show ownership?
Keep notes about what you've learned. Use your notes to practice using English.	How to Ask Questions • I can start a question with "who," "what," "where," "when," "how," or "why": What will the weather be like today? • I can also start a question with "do" or "does": Do you have my math book?

Sentences

A sentence is a group of words that expresses a complete thought.

TYPES OF SENTENCES	EXAMPLES
A **statement** tells something. It ends with a period.	The football game was on Friday. The coach made an important announcement.
A **question** asks for information. It ends with a question mark.	What did the coach say?

Kinds of Questions

Questions That Ask for a "Yes" or "No" Answer	Answers
Can you tell me what he said?	Yes.
Does everyone know the news?	No.
Is it about the team?	Yes.
Did the team win the game?	Yes.
Are the players sad?	No.
Were the fans surprised?	Yes.

Questions That Ask for Specific Information	
Who heard the announcement?	The team and the fans heard the announcement.
What did the coach say?	He said the team will play in a special game.
Where will the team play this game?	In Hawaii.
When did the coach find out?	Right before the game.
How did he feel?	He felt so happy!
Why was our team chosen?	Our team was chosen because we won a lot of games.
How many games did the team win this year?	All ten of them.
How much will the tickets to the game cost?	Fifteen dollars.

An **exclamation** shows surprise or strong feeling. It ends with an exclamation mark.	That's fantastic news! I can't believe it!

TYPES OF SENTENCES, continued	EXAMPLES
A **command** tells you what to do or what not to do. It usually begins with a verb. It often ends with a period. If a command shows strong emotion, it ends with an exclamation mark.	Give the team my congratulations. Buy a ticket for me, too. Don't forget!

NEGATIVE SENTENCES	EXAMPLES
A **negative sentence** uses a **negative word** like *not*. • Add *not* <u>after</u> *am, is, are, was,* or *were.* • Add *do not, does not,* or *did not* <u>before</u> all other verbs. • Combine the verb and *not* to make a **contraction**.	The game in Hawaii **was not** boring! The other team **did not play** well. Our team **didn't make** any mistakes.

Contractions with *not*

To make a **contraction**, take out one or more letters and add an **apostrophe (')**.

are + n~~o~~t = aren't	The fans of the other team **aren't** happy.
is + n~~o~~t = isn't	Their coach **isn't** happy either.
can + ~~no~~t = can't	The other team **can't** believe they lost.
was + n~~o~~t = wasn't	The game **wasn't** fun for them.
were + n~~o~~t = weren't	The players **weren't** playing their best.
do + n~~o~~t = don't	They **don't** want to go to practice on Monday.
does + n~~o~~t = doesn't	The quarterback **doesn't** want to hear about his mistakes.
did + n~~o~~t = didn't	The other team **didn't** want to lose.

CAPITALIZATION IN SENTENCES	EXAMPLES
Every sentence begins with a **capital letter.**	**O**ur team was very proud. **W**hat do you think of all this? **I**t's a wonderful story!

COMPLETE SENTENCES	EXAMPLES
A **complete sentence** has a **subject** and a **predicate**. A complete sentence expresses a complete thought.	Many people visit our National Parks. Grand Canyon National Park, Arizona
A **fragment** is not a sentence. It is not a complete thought. You can add information to a fragment to turn it into a sentence.	**Fragment:** A fun vacation **Complete Sentences:** You can have a fun vacation. Will we have a fun vacation at the park? Go to a national park and have a fun vacation.

SUBJECT-VERB AGREEMENT	EXAMPLES

The verb must always agree with the subject of the sentence.

A **singular subject** names one person or thing. Use a **singular verb** with a singular subject.	Another popular **park is** the Grand Canyon. **It has** a powerful river.
A **plural subject** tells about more than one person or thing. Use a **plural verb** with a plural subject.	The **cliffs are** beautiful. **We were amazed** by their colors.

Singular and Plural Verbs

Singular	Plural
The park **is** big.	The parks **are** big.
The park **was** beautiful.	The parks **were** beautiful.
The park **has** campsites.	The parks **have** campsites.
The park **does** not **open** until spring.	The parks **do** not **open** until spring.

Punctuation Marks

Punctuation marks make words and sentences easier to understand.

PERIOD	EXAMPLES
Use a **period**:	
• at the end of a statement or a polite command	Georgia read the paper to her mom**.** Tell me if there are any interesting articles**.**

• after an abbreviation	There's a new restaurant on Stone St**.** near our house.
	
	It opens at 10 a.m**.** today.
	
	But: *Do not use a period in an acronym:*
	
	    National Aeronautics and Space Administration **NASA**
	
	Do not use a period in the abbreviation of a state name written in a mailing address:
	
	    Massachusetts **MA** Illinois **IL** Texas **TX**
	    California **CA** Florida **FL** Virginia **VA**

• after an initial	The owner of J**.**J**.** Malone.
• to separate dollars and cents. The period is the decimal point.	The article says lunch today costs only $1**.**50.
• in an Internet address. The period is called a dot.	The restaurant has a Web site at www**.**jjmalone**.**org.

QUESTION MARK	EXAMPLES
Use a **question mark**:	
• at the end of a question	What kind of food do they serve**?**
• after a question that comes at the end of a statement	The food is good, isn't it**?** ***But:*** *Use a period after an indirect question. In an indirect question, you tell about a question you asked.* I asked how good the food could be for only $1.50.

Punctuation Marks, continued

EXCLAMATION MARK	EXAMPLES
Use an **exclamation mark**: • after an interjection • at the end of a sentence to show that you feel strongly about something	Wow**!** One-fifty is a really good price**!**

COMMA	EXAMPLES
Use a **comma**: • to separate three or more items in a series • when you write a number with four or more digits	Articles about the school, a big sale, and a new movie were also in the newspaper. The school will buy a new bus, 10 computers, and books for the library. There was $500,000 in the school budget.
Use a **comma** in these places in a letter: • between the city and the state • between the date and the year • after the greeting • after the closing	144 North Ave. Milpas, AK July 3, 2002 Dear Mr. Okada, I really like computers and am glad that we have them at school, but ours are out-of-date. As principal, can you ask the school board to buy us new ones for next year? Sincerely, Patrick Green

QUOTATION MARKS	EXAMPLES
Use **quotation marks** to show:	
• a speaker's exact words	"Listen to this!" Georgia said.
• the exact words quoted from a book or other printed material	The announcement in the paper was "The world-famous writer Josie Ramon will be at Milpas Library Friday night."
• the title of a song, poem, or short story	Her poem "Speaking" is famous.
• the title of a magazine article or newspaper article	It appeared in the magazine article "How to Talk to Your Teen."
• the title of a chapter from a book	On Friday night she'll be reading "Getting Along," a chapter from her new book.
• words used in a special way	We will be "all ears" at the reading.
Always put **periods** and **commas** inside quotation marks.	"She is such a great writer," Georgia said. "I'd love to meet her."

COLON	EXAMPLES

Use a **colon**:	356 Oak St.
	Milpas, AK
	Sept. 24, 2002
	
	Features Editor
	Milpas Post
	78 Main St.
	Milpas, AK
	
	Dear Sir or Madam:
	
	Please place this announcement in the calendar section of your paper. Friday at 7:15 p.m., the writer Josie Ramón will be speaking at Milpas Library. When people come, they should bring:
	
	    1. Questions for Ms. Ramón.
	    2. Money to purchase her new book.
	    3. A cushion to sit on!
	
	Thank you.
	
	                Sincerely,
	
	                Hector Quintana

• after the greeting in a business letter	
• to separate hours and minutes	
• to start a list	

Capital Letters

A reader can tell that a word is special in some way if it begins with a capital letter.

PROPER NOUNS	EXAMPLES
	A common noun names any person, place, thing, or idea. **A proper noun names one particular person, place, thing, or idea.**
All the important words in a **proper noun** start with a capital letter.	<table><tr><td></td><td>Common Noun</td><td>Proper Noun</td></tr><tr><td>Person</td><td>captain</td><td>Captain Meriwether Lewis</td></tr><tr><td>Place</td><td>land</td><td>Louisiana Territory</td></tr><tr><td>Thing</td><td>team</td><td>Corps of Discovery</td></tr><tr><td>Idea</td><td>destiny</td><td>Manifest Destiny</td></tr></table>

Proper nouns include:

• names of people and their titles	Laura Roberts Captain Meriwether Lewis **But:** *Do not capitalize a title if it is used without a name:* The captain's co-leader on the expedition was William Clark.
• abbreviations of titles	**Mr.** Ramos **Mrs.** Ramos **Dr.** Schuyler **Ms.** Nguyen **Abbreviations of Titles** **Capt.** for the captain of a boat or in the armed forces **Pres.** for the president of a country, a company, a club, or an organization **Sen.** for a member of the U.S. Senate **Rep.** for a member of the U.S. House of Representatives
• words like **Mom** and **Dad** when they are used as names	"**Mom,** can you tell me more about the expedition?" said Laura. **But:** *Do not capitalize names if they follow a word like my.* I ask my **mom** a lot of questions.
• organizations	United Nations Science Club Wildlife Society Lodi City Council
• names of languages, subject areas, and religions	Spanish Mathematics Buddhism Vietnamese Social Studies Christianity

PROPER NOUNS, continued	EXAMPLES

• names of geographical places

Cities and States
Dallas, Texas
Miami, Florida
St. Louis, Missouri

Countries
Iran
Ecuador
Cambodia

Continents
Asia
South America
Africa

Streets and Roads
King Boulevard
Main Avenue
First Street

Landforms
Rocky Mountains
Sahara Desert
Grand Canyon

Public Spaces
Hemisfair Plaza
Central Park
Muir Camp

Bodies of Water
Yellowstone River
Pacific Ocean
Great Salt Lake
Gulf of Mexico

Buildings, Ships, and Monuments
Empire State Building
Titanic
Statue of Liberty

Planets and Heavenly Bodies
Earth
Jupiter
Milky Way

• abbreviations of geographic places

Words Used in Addresses

Avenue	Ave.	Highway	Hwy.	South	S.
Boulevard	Blvd.	Lane	Ln.	Square	Sq.
Court	Ct.	North	N.	Street	St.
Drive	Dr.	Place	Pl.	West	W.
East	E.	Road	Rd.		

Abbreviations for State Names in Mailing Addresses

Alabama	AL	Hawaii	HI	Massachusetts	MA	New Mexico	NM	South Dakota	SD
Alaska	AK	Idaho	ID	Michigan	MI	New York	NY	Tennessee	TN
Arizona	AZ	Illinois	IL	Minnesota	MN	North Carolina	NC	Texas	TX
Arkansas	AR	Indiana	IN	Mississippi	MS	North Dakota	ND	Utah	UT
California	CA	Iowa	IA	Missouri	MO	Ohio	OH	Vermont	VT
Colorado	CO	Kansas	KS	Montana	MT	Oklahoma	OK	Virginia	VA
Connecticut	CT	Kentucky	KY	Nebraska	NE	Oregon	OR	Washington	WA
Delaware	DE	Louisiana	LA	Nevada	NV	Pennsylvania	PA	West Virginia	WV
Florida	FL	Maine	ME	New Hampshire	NH	Rhode Island	RI	Wisconsin	WI
Georgia	GA	Maryland	MD	New Jersey	NJ	South Carolina	SC	Wyoming	WY

• months, days, special days and holidays

January	July	Sunday	New Year's Day
February	August	Monday	Mother's Day
March	September	Tuesday	Thanksgiving
April	October	Wednesday	Hanukkah
May	November	Thursday	Kwanzaa
June	December	Friday	
		Saturday	

Capital Letters, continued

IN LETTERS	EXAMPLES
Capitalize the first word used in the **greeting** or in the **closing** of a letter. Street, city, and state names in the address, as well as their abbreviations, are also capitalized.	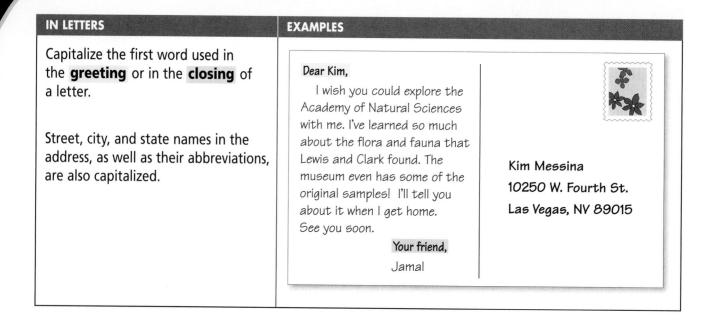

E-Mail

You can use e-mail to send a letter to a friend. E-mail is short for **electronic mail** and is sent by a computer. You can send letters to or receive messages from anyone in the world who has an e-mail address. Here's one kind of computer "mailbox" you might use.

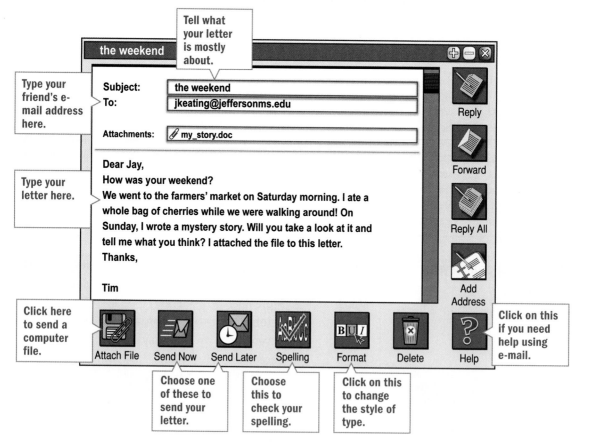

Nouns

A noun names a person, place, or thing.
There are different kinds of nouns.

COMMON AND PROPER NOUNS	EXAMPLES
A **common noun** names any person, place, or thing.	A **teenager** sat by the **ocean** and read a **book**.
A proper noun names one particular person, place, or thing. The important words in a proper noun start with a <u>capital letter</u>.	**Daniel** sat by the <u>A</u>tlantic <u>O</u>cean and read *Save the <u>M</u>anatee*. A manatee

SINGULAR AND PLURAL NOUNS	EXAMPLES

A singular noun names one thing.
A plural noun names more than one thing.

Follow these rules to make a noun plural:					
• Add **-s** to most nouns.	desk desk**s**	book book**s**	teacher teacher**s**	apple apple**s**	line line**s**
• If the noun ends in **x**, **ch**, **sh**, **s**, or **z**, add **-es**.	box box**es**	lunch lunch**es**	dish dish**es**	glass glass**es**	waltz waltz**es**
• Some nouns change in different ways to show the plural.	child **children**	foot **feet**	tooth **teeth**	man **men**	woman **women**

POSSESSIVE NOUNS	EXAMPLES
A **possessive noun** shows ownership. It often ends in **'s.**	Daniel **'s** book was very interesting.

Nouns that Name People

Girls/Women	Boys/Men
great-grandmother	great-grandfather
grandmother	grandfather
mother	father
stepmother	stepfather
sister	brother
stepsister	stepbrother
half-sister	half-brother
daughter	son
granddaughter	grandson
aunt	uncle
cousin	cousin
niece	nephew

My family includes my grandmother, mother, father, sister, cousins, aunts, uncles, and me.

architect

artist
astronaut
athlete
baker
bank teller
barber
bus driver
business person
cab driver
cashier
coach
construction worker

cook
custodian

dancer

dentist
designer
doctor
editor
eye doctor
farmer
firefighter
flight attendant
florist

gardener
guard
historian
lawyer
letter carrier
librarian
mechanic

messenger

model
mover
musician
nurse
office worker

painter
photographer

pilot

plumber
police officer
reporter
sailor
salesperson
scientist
stylist
teacher
veterinarian
writer

Nouns that Name Places

bathroom
bedroom
dining room
garage
garden

kitchen

living room

yard

In Town

airport
bank
basketball court
beauty shop
bookstore

bus stop

cafe
city hall
clothing store

fire station
flower shop
garage
gas station

hardware store

hospital
intersection
jewelry store
library

mall
market
motel
movie theater
museum
music store
nursing home
office building
park
parking garage
parking lot
pet shop
police station
pool

post office
restaurant

school

shoe store
sports stadium
supermarket
theater
toy store
train station

On the Earth

beach
canyon
desert
forest
hill
island
lake

mountains

ocean

plains
pond
rain forest
river
sea
seashore
valley
wetland

SINGULAR AND PLURAL NOUNS	EXAMPLES
Noncount nouns are nouns that you cannot count. A noncount noun does not have a plural form.	My favorite museum has **furniture** and **art**. Sometimes I wonder how much **money** each item is worth.

Types of Noncount Nouns

Activities and Sports

baseball	camping	dancing	fishing
golf	singing	soccer	swimming

Examples

I love to play **soccer**.

Category Nouns

clothing	equipment	furniture	hardware	jewelry
machinery	mail	money	time	weather

My **equipment** is in the car.

Food

bread	cereal	cheese	corn	flour
lettuce	meat	milk	rice	salt
soup	sugar	tea	water	

I'll drink some **water** on my way to the game.

You can count some food items by using a measurement word like **cup**, **slice**, **glass**, or **head** plus the word **of**. To show the plural form, just make the measurement word plural.

I'll drink **two glasses of water** on my way to the game.

Ideas and Feelings

democracy	enthusiasm	freedom	fun	health
honesty	information	knowledge	luck	work

I'll also listen to the radio for **information** about the weather.

Materials

air	fuel	gasoline	gold
metal	paper	water	wood

The radio says the **air** is heavy. What does that mean?

Weather

fog	hail	heat	ice	lightning
rain	smog	snow	sunshine	thunder

Uh-oh! First came the **lightning** and the **thunder**. I want **sunshine** for my next soccer game!

Some words have more than one meaning. Add **-s** for the plural only if the noun means something you can count.	Throw me those **baseballs**. I want to learn to play **baseball**.

ARTICLES	EXAMPLES
An **article** is a word that helps identify a noun. An article often comes before a count noun.	After **the** game, we found **a** coat and **an** umbrella on **the** field.
Use **a** or **an** before **nouns** that are not specific. Use **the** before **nouns** that are specific.	A **boy** walked around the field. The coach's **son** walked around the field.
Use **a** before a word that starts with a consonant sound. Use **an** before a word that starts with a vowel sound.	a **b**all a **g**ate a **p**layer a **o**ne-way street (o is pronounced like w) a **c**ap a **k**ick a **n**et a **u**niform (u is pronounced like y) **a** **e** **i** **o** **u** **silent h** an **a**nt an **e**lbow an **i**nch an **o**live an **u**mbrella an **h**our an **a**pron an **e**el an **i**dea an **o**cean an **a**mount an **e**lection an **o**wl an **a**rtist an **or**ange
Do not use **a** or **an** before a noncount noun.	The soccer ball was made of ~~a~~ leather.
Do not use **the** before the name of: • a city or state • most countries • a language • a day, a month, or most holidays • a sport or activity • most businesses • a person	Our next game will be in **Dallas**. Games in **Texas** are always exciting. We will play a team from **Mexico**. People will be cheering in **Spanish** and **English**. The game will take place on **Monday**. Is that in **February**? Yes, on **President's Day**. That will be a good day to play **soccer**. The fans will have hot dogs to eat from **Sal's Market**. You may even see **Sal** himself.

Pronouns

A pronoun takes the place of a noun or refers to a noun.

PRONOUN AGREEMENT	EXAMPLES
Use the correct **pronoun** for a person or thing. • To tell about yourself, use **I**. • When you speak to another person, use **you**.	 I want to find out about careers.  What career are you interested in?
• To tell about a boy or man, use **he**. • For a girl or woman, use **she**. • For a thing, use **it**.	Scott likes art. **He** wants to be a photographer. Anna likes animals. **She** wants to be a veterinarian. What about music? Is **it** a good career?
• For yourself and other people, use **we**.	 Sam, Jill, and I like music. We might be good musicians.
• When you speak to more than one other person, use **you**.	 Joe and Maylin, what do you want to do?
• To tell about other people or things, use **they**.	Joe and Maylin love children. **They** want to be teachers.

SUBJECT PRONOUNS	EXAMPLES	
Some pronouns tell who or what does the action. They are called **subject pronouns**.	Anna likes animals. **She** works at a pet shop. Ernesto works there, too. **He** is in charge of the fish section. **It** is a big area in the store. Anna takes care of the birds. **They** are in cages.	**Subject Pronouns** **Singular** **Plural** I we you you he, she, it they

OBJECT PRONOUNS	EXAMPLES	
Some pronouns come after an action verb or after a word like *to*, *for*, or *with*. They are called **object pronouns**.	The parrots get hungry at 5 o'clock. Anna feeds **them** every day. The parrots are nice to **her**. One day, Ernesto fed the parrots. They didn't like **him**. The parrots took the food and threw **it** on the floor. Now only Anna can feed **them**.	**Pronouns** **Subject** **Object** **Pronouns** **Pronouns** I ⟶ me you ⟶ you he ⟶ him she ⟶ her it ⟶ it we ⟶ us you ⟶ you they ⟶ them

POSSESSIVE PRONOUNS	EXAMPLES	
A **possessive pronoun** tells who or what owns something. It is sometimes called a **possessive adjective.**	Anna's favorite parrot is a red-and-blue male. **His** name is Repeat. Repeat knows how to say **her** name. Repeat knows Ernesto's name, too. The bird says **their** names over and over again.	**Pronouns** **Subject** **Object** **Pronouns** **Pronouns** I ⟶ my you ⟶ your he ⟶ his she ⟶ her it ⟶ its we ⟶ our you ⟶ your they ⟶ their

Adjectives

An adjective describes, or tells about, a noun. Many adjectives tell what something is like. An adjective can also tell "how many" or "which one".

ADJECTIVES	EXAMPLES
Usually an **adjective** comes <u>before</u> the **noun** it describes.	You can buy **fresh food** at the market. You can buy **colorful fruit**. You can buy **delicious vegetables**.
An **adjective** can come <u>after</u> the **noun** in sentences with verbs like *is, are, was,* or *were*.	The **bananas** are **yellow**. The **tomato** is **round**. The **market** was **busy**. The **shoppers** were **happy**.
Some **adjectives** tell "how many." They always come before the **noun**.	This farmer has **six kinds** of tomatoes. My mom wants **three tomatoes**. She has **five dollars**.
Some **adjectives** tell the order of persons or things in a group. They usually come before the **noun**. They can come after the noun in sentences with verbs like *is, are, was,* and *were*.	Mom looks at the tomatoes in the **first basket**. Then she looks at the tomatoes in the **second basket**. My **mom** is **first** in line to buy them!
Never add *-s* or *-es* to an **adjective,** even if the **noun** it describes is plural.	Look at the **green cucumbers**. Mom wants **two cucumbers**. The **vegetables** tonight will be **delicious**!

Sensory Adjectives

An adjective can tell how something looks, sounds, tastes, feels, or smells.

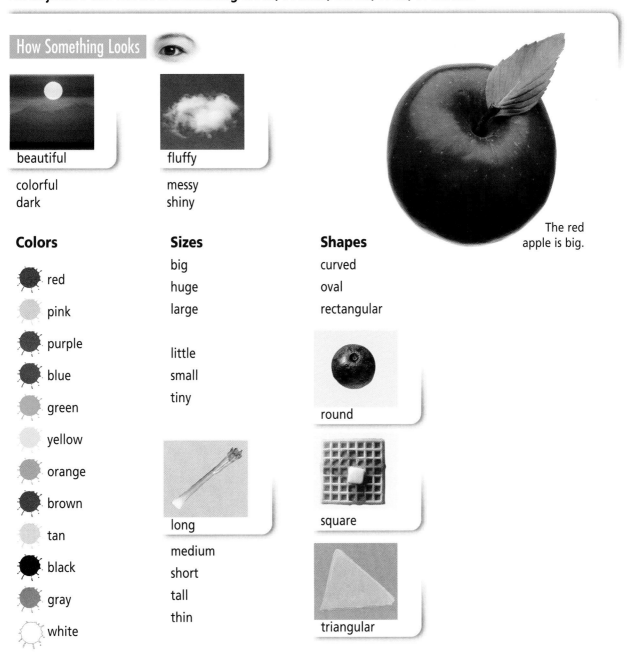

How Something Looks

beautiful

colorful
dark

fluffy

messy
shiny

The red
apple is big.

Colors

red

pink

purple

blue

green

yellow

orange

brown

tan

black

gray

white

Sizes

big
huge
large

little
small
tiny

long

medium
short
tall
thin

Shapes

curved
oval
rectangular

round

square

triangular

Adjectives, continued

How Something Sounds

blaring
crunchy
loud
noisy
quiet
soft
rattling

I like crunchy apples.

How Something Feels

bumpy
dry
hard
hot
rough
sharp
slimy
smooth
soft
sticky
warm

The outside of a pickle feels bumpy.

These cinnamon rolls are very sticky!

How Something Tastes

bitter
delicious
fresh
juicy
salty
sour
spicy
sweet
tasty

These vegetables will taste fresh.

Chili can be very spicy.

How Something Smells

fishy
fragrant
fresh
rotten
sweet

It smells very fragrant here!

Feelings

An adjective can tell how someone feels.

angry

embarrassed

sad

annoyed

excited

scared

bored

happy

shy

confused

nervous

surprised

curious

proud

worried

Numbers

Numbers are a special kind of adjective. They can tell how many.
They can also tell the order of things in a sequence.

Number Words		Order Words	
0 zero	**30** thirty	**1st** first	
1 one	**40** forty	**2nd** second	
2 two	**50** fifty	**3rd** third	
3 three	**60** sixty	**4th** fourth	
4 four	**70** seventy	**5th** fifth	
5 five	**80** eighty	**6th** sixth	
6 six	**90** ninety	**7th** seventh	
7 seven	**100** one hundred	**8th** eighth	
8 eight	**500** five hundred	**9th** ninth	
9 nine	**1,000** one thousand	**10th** tenth	
10 ten	**5,000** five thousand	**11th** eleventh	
11 eleven	**10,000** ten thousand	**12th** twelfth	
12 twelve	**100,000** one hundred thousand	**13th** thirteenth	
13 thirteen	**500,000** five hundred thousand	**14th** fourteenth	
14 fourteen	**1,000,000** one million	**15th** fifteenth	
15 fifteen		**16th** sixteenth	
16 sixteen		**17th** seventeenth	
17 seventeen		**18th** eighteenth	
18 eighteen		**19th** nineteenth	
19 nineteen		**20th** twentieth	
20 twenty			

This woman is the first customer. She buys two
heads of broccoli for $1.98.

Verbs

Every complete sentence has a verb.

THE FORMS OF *BE*	EXAMPLES	
The words **am, is,** and **are** are **verbs.** They are forms of the verb **be.** They tell about something that is happening now, or in the present.	I **am** in New York with my mom. She **is** here for the first time. We **are** excited to see the buildings. They **are** amazing!	**Forms of the Verb *be*** **Present** **Past** I **am** I **was** you **are** you **were** he, she, he, she, it **is** it **was** we **are** we **were** you **are** you **were** they **are** they **were**
The **verbs was** and **were** are also forms of the verb **be.** They tell about something that happened in the past.	I **was** in Central Park yesterday. It **was** beautiful. We **were** with some friends. They **were** very helpful.	

CONTRACTIONS WITH VERBS	EXAMPLES
You can shorten the verbs *am, is,* and *are* to make a **contraction**.	Today **we're** going to Lincoln Center.

> **Contractions with Verbs**
>
> To make a **contraction**, take out one or more letters and add an **apostrophe (')**.
>
> | I + ~~a~~m = I'm | **I'm** glad to be in New York. |
> |---|---|
> | you + ~~a~~re = you're | **You're** going to meet my brother. |
> | he + ~~i~~s = he's | **He's** staying with my aunt. |
> | she + ~~i~~s = she's | **She's** in a performance at Lincoln Center. |
> | it + ~~i~~s = it's | **It's** a ballet. |
> | we + ~~a~~re = we're | **We're** going to watch a ballet practice. |
> | they + ~~a~~re = they're | **They're** coming to our hotel at 3:00. |

ACTION VERBS	EXAMPLES
Most verbs are **action verbs.** They tell what a person or thing does.	The dancers **hop** and **spin.**
When you tell what another person or thing does, use **-s** or **-es** at the end of the **verb.**	The spotlight **shines** on them. One dancer **twirls** around and around. Then she **stretches** a leg and **leaps** gracefully.

Action Verbs

act
add
answer
arrive
ask
bake
bathe
boil
bounce
brush
burn
call

carry

change
check
chop
circle
clap

clean

climb
close
comb
cook
copy
count
cross
cry

dance

deliver
discuss
drop
dry
enter
erase

exercise

fill
finish
fix
fold
hammer
help
introduce
invite
jog
join

jump

kick
laugh

learn
listen
look

mail

mark
mix
mop
move

open

paint
plant
play
point
pour
pull
push
raise
rake
repair
repeat
skate
slice
spell
start
stir
stop
stretch

talk

tie
turn
type
underline
use
vote

walk

wash
watch
water
wipe

work

THE VERBS *CAN, COULD, MAY, MIGHT*	EXAMPLES
You can use the verbs **can, could, may,** or **might** with an **action verb** to express: • the ability to do something • a possibility, or the chance that something may happen	A hurricane **can cause** a lot of damage. Several inches of rain **might fall** in just a few minutes. The wind **may blow** at high speeds. It **might knock** over trees. It **could break** windows.

PRESENT TENSE VERBS	EXAMPLES

The tense of a verb shows when an action happens.

The **present tense** of a verb tells about an action that is happening now, or in the present.	My mom **looks** at her charts. She **checks** her computer screen. She **takes** notes.
The **present tense** of a verb can also tell about an action that happens regularly or all the time.	My mom **works** for the local TV station. She **is** a weather forecaster. She **reports** the weather every night at 5 p.m.
The **present progressive** form of a verb tells about an action as it is happening. It uses **am**, **is**, or **are** and a main verb. The main verb ends in **-ing**.	Right now, she **is getting** ready for the show. "I can't believe it!" she says. "I **am looking** at a terrible storm!" The high winds **are starting** to blow. Trees **are falling** down. Wind damage from Hurricane Floyd, 1999

Verbs, continued

PAST TENSE VERBS	EXAMPLES
The **past tense** of a verb tells about an action that happened earlier, or in the past.	Yesterday, my mom **warned** everyone about the hurricane. The storm **moved** over the ocean toward land. We **did** not **know** exactly when it would hit.
The past tense form of a **regular verb** ends with **-ed**.	The shop owners in our town **covered** their windows with wood. We **closed** our shutters and **stayed** inside.
Irregular verbs have special forms to show the past tense. See page 339 for more examples.	The storm **hit** land. The sky **grew** very dark. It **began** to rain. <table><tr><td colspan="2">**Some Irregular Verbs**</td></tr><tr><td>Present Tense</td><td>Past Tense</td></tr><tr><td>hit</td><td>hit</td></tr><tr><td>grow</td><td>grew</td></tr><tr><td>begin</td><td>began</td></tr></table>

FUTURE TENSE VERBS	EXAMPLES
The **future tense** of a verb tells about an action that will happen later, or in the future. To show future tense, use one of the following: • **will** plus another verb	After the storm, people **will come** out of their houses. They **will inspect** the damage.
• a **contraction** with **will** plus another verb	**They'll uncover** their windows. **They'll clean** up their yards. Some people **won't have** as much work as other people. <table><tr><td colspan="3">**Contractions with *will***</td></tr><tr><td>I + will = I'll</td></tr><tr><td>you + will = you'll</td></tr><tr><td>he + will = he'll</td></tr><tr><td>she + will = she'll</td></tr><tr><td>it + will = it'll</td></tr><tr><td>we + will = we'll</td></tr><tr><td>they + will = they'll</td></tr><tr><td>will + not = won't</td></tr></table>
• the phrase **am going to, is going to,** or **are going to** plus a verb.	I **am going to take** the tree branches out of my yard. The city **is** not **going to clean** every street. We **are** all **going to help** each other.

Irregular Verbs

These verbs have special forms to show the past tense.

Present	Past
become	became
begin	began
bend	bent
blow	blew
break	broke
build	built

Present	Past
buy	bought

catch	caught
come	came
cut	cut
do	did
draw	drew

drink	drank

eat	ate
fall	fell
feel	felt

Present	Past
find	found
fly	flew
get	got

give	gave

grow	grew
go	went
have	had
hear	heard
hide	hid
hit	hit

hold	held
keep	kept
know	known
lead	led
leave	left

make	made

Present	Past
pay	paid
put	put
read	read

run	ran

say	said
see	saw
sing	sang
sit	sat
speak	spoke
stand	stood
swim	swam
take	took
throw	threw
wear	wore

write	wrote

It's important to use your best **penmanship**, or handwriting. That way your audience will be able to read what your write.

HANDWRITING HINTS

You can **print** your words or write in **cursive**. Printing is sometimes called **manuscript**.

MANUSCRIPT

Manuscript is less formal than cursive and is usually easier to read at a glance. That makes manuscript good to use for filling out forms and for writing things like posters, ads, and short notes. When you write in manuscript, hold the pencil and paper this way.

Left-handed

Right-handed

CURSIVE

Cursive is good to use for longer pieces, such as letters or stories, because you can write faster. You don't have to lift your pencil between letters. Also, cursive writing gives your finished pieces a polished look. When you write in cursive, hold the pencil and paper this way.

Left-handed

Right-handed

Manuscript Alphabet

CAPITAL LETTERS

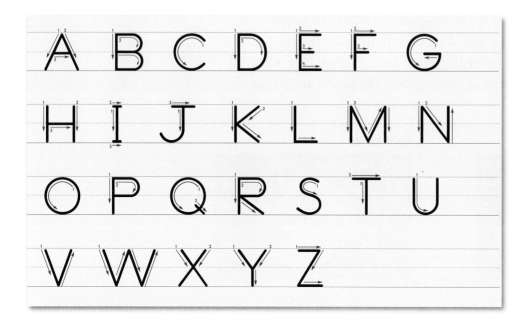

LOWERCASE LETTERS, NUMBERS, AND PUNCTUATION

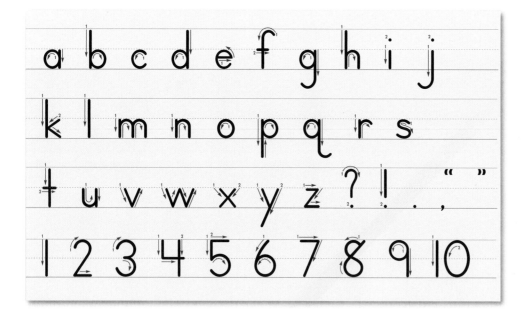

Writing Manuscript Letters

- Make letters sit on the **baseline**, or bottom line.
  Make letters the same size.

NOT OK

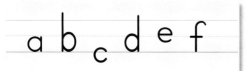

OK

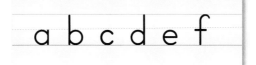

- Letters that go past the **midline**, or middle line, should all be the same height.

NOT OK

OK

- Make your capital letters touch the **headline**, or top line.
  Make half-size letters touch the midline.

NOT OK

OK

- Letters should be **vertical**, or standing up straight.

NOT OK

OK

WRITING WORDS AND SENTENCES

- Put the same amount of space between each word.

  NOT OK

  Votefor Juji for ClassPresident!

  OK

  Vote for Juji for Class President!

- Put the right amount of space between each letter.

  NOT OK

  She wil l work hard for our school.

  OK

  She will work hard for our school.

- Write smoothly. Do not press too hard or too light.
  Make your lines the same thickness.

  NOT OK

  Who will you **vo**te for?

  OK

  Who will you vote for?

Cursive Alphabet

CAPITAL LETTERS

LOWERCASE LETTERS

Handwriting, continued

Writing Cursive Letters

Be careful not to make these common mistakes when you write in **cursive**.

MISTAKE	NOT OK	OK	IN A WORD
The **a** looks like a **u**.	*u*	*a*	*again*
The **d** looks like a **c** and an **l**.	*d*	*d*	*dad*
The **e** is too narrow.	*e*	*e*	*eagle*
The **h** looks like an **l** and an **i**.	*h*	*h*	*high*
The **i** has no dot.	*ı*	*i*	*inside*
The **n** looks like a **w**.	*w*	*n*	*none*
The **o** looks like an **a**.	*a*	*o*	*onion*
The **r** looks like an **i** with no dot.	*ı*	*r*	*roar*
The **t** is not crossed.	*l*	*t*	*title*
The **t** is crossed too high.	*t*	*t*	*that*

Writing Words and Sentences

- Slant your letters all the same way.

NOT OK

My Chinese-language class today was interesting.

OK

My Chinese-language class today was interesting.

- Put the right amount of space between words.

NOT OK

I learned how togreet   adults.

OK

I learned how to greet adults.

- Write smoothly. Do not press too hard or too lightly.

NOT OK

I practiced on my teacher. He was impressed.

OK

I practiced on my teacher. He was impressed.

The Writing Process

Writing is one of the best ways to express yourself. The steps in the Writing Process will help you say what you want to say clearly, correctly, and in your own unique way.

PREWRITE

Prewriting is what you do before you write. During this step, you collect ideas, choose a topic, make a plan, gather details, and organize your ideas.

❶ Collect Ideas Writing ideas are everywhere! Think about recent events or things you've read or seen. You can brainstorm more writing ideas with your classmates, friends, and family. Collect your ideas in a computer file, a notebook or a journal. Then when you're ready to write, check your idea collections.

❷ Choose a Topic Sometimes you have a lot of ideas you want to write about. Other times, your teacher may give you a writing prompt, or a writing assignment. You will still need to decide exactly what you write about. Make a list of possible writing ideas. Then circle the one that is the most important or interesting to you. That idea will be your topic.

> I could write about...
>   a concert my friends and I went to
>   (when my grandparents arrived in the U.S.)
>   why we need more school dances
>   why the eagle is a popular symbol

❸ Plan Your Writing An FATP chart can help you organize your thoughts and focus on the details that you'll need for your writing.

The **form** tells you the type of writing. Study examples of the form to help you decide how to craft your writing.

A specific **topic** will help you collect only those details you need.

FATP Chart

HOW TO UNLOCK A PROMPT

Form: personal narrative

Audience: my teacher and classmates

Topic: when my grandparents arrived in the U.S.

Purpose: to describe a personal experience

If you know your **audience**, you can choose the appropriate style and tone. For example, if you are writing for your friends, you can use friendly, informal language.

The **purpose** is why you are writing. Your purpose can be to describe, to inform or explain, to persuade, or to express personal thoughts or feelings.

❹ Gather Details To write about a personal experience, you can just list the things you remember about an event. For other kinds of writing, you may need to talk about your topic with others or do research to gather information.

There are many ways to show the details you've gathered. You can

- make charts, lists, or webs
- draw and label pictures
- take notes on notecards
- make a story map
- use a gathering grid to write down answers to your questions

Gathering Grid

Topic: Vietnam	Get to Know Vietnam (book)	Internet
What is the population?		
What fuels the economy?		

Show your details in a way that works best for you and for your topic.

❺ Get Organized Review your details and plan an interesting way to write about your topic. Put the details in the best order for your writing.

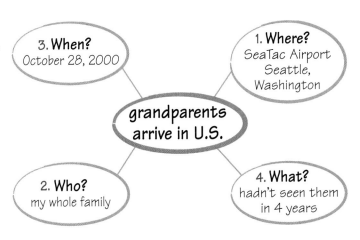

- Sometimes you can organize the details as you write them down.
- Other times, you can use numbers to order events in time sequence or to order the details from the most to least important.
- You could also make an outline to show main ideas and supporting details.

DRAFT

Now you are ready to start writing. At this stage, don't worry about making mistakes—just get your ideas down on paper! Turn your details into sentences and paragraphs. As you are writing, you'll probably think of new ideas. Add those to your draft.

Trang Bui's Draft

> My family stood by the windows and watched the plane land at SeaTac airport in Seattle on October 28, 2007. We were so exsited to see the plane. The people started coming through the door, we lined up so we could see. I had to lift my little sister up so she could see. Suddenly everyone was hugging and crying. My little sister tried to hide. My sister didn't know my grandparents. She was feeling shy.

Write your ideas in a first draft.

REVISE

A first draft can always be improved. When you revise a draft, you make changes to it.

❶ **Read Your Draft** As you read your draft, ask yourself questions about the most important ideas. Make sure your ideas are clear, complete, and presented in the best way.

Revision Checklist

☑ Did I follow the plan on my FATP chart? Is the language appropriate for the writing form and audience? Did I stick to the topic?

☑ Does my writing have a beginning, a middle, and an ending?

☑ Are my details organized in the best way? Should I change the order of any details?

☑ Did I include details to make my ideas clear? Should I add or cut any details?

☑ Did I use the best words to say what I mean? Did I avoid using the same words over and over again?

❷ Mark Your Changes

Mark Your Changes What changes do you want to make to your draft? Use the Revising Marks or special features in your computer's word-processing program to show the changes.

Trang Bui's Revisions

My family stood by the [big, glass] windows and watched the plane land at SeaTac airport in Seattle on October 28, 2007. We were so exsited[!] ~~to see the plane.~~ [When the passengers] ~~The people~~ started coming through the door, we lined up so we could see. I had to lift my little sister up so she could [look over the heads of the people in front] ~~see~~. Suddenly everyone was hugging and crying. My little sister tried to hide. My [because she] ~~sister~~ didn't know my grandparents. [and] ~~She~~ was feeling shy. [It took four long years, but my grandparents finally arrived!]

Revising Marks

∧	Add.
↶○	Move to here.
⋀‾	Replace with this.
—⁀	Take out.

The Writing Process, continued

EDIT AND PROOFREAD

After you revise your draft for content, it's time to check it for mistakes.

1 Check Your Sentences When you edit, check that your sentences are clear, complete, and correct. Ask yourself:

- Does each sentence have a subject and a predicate?

2 Check for Mistakes Proofread to find and correct errors in capitalization, punctuation, grammar, and spelling. Look especially for:

- capital letters, end marks, apostrophes, and quotation marks
- subject-verb agreement
- use of pronouns
- misspelled words.

3 Mark Your Corrections Use the Editing and Proofreading Marks to show your corrections or make the corrections when you find them in your document on the computer.

4 Make a Final Copy Rewrite your work and make the corrections you marked. If you are using a computer, print your corrected copy.

Trang Bui's Proofread Draft

My family stood by the big, glass windows and watched the plane land at SeaTac airport in Seattle on October 28, 2007. We were so exsited When the passengers started coming through the door, we lined up so we could see. I had to lift my little sister up so she could look over the heads of the people in front. Suddenly everyone was hugging and crying. My little sister tried to hide because she didn't know my grandparents and was feeling shy. It took four long years, but my grandparents finally arrived!

Editing and Proofreading Marks

∧	Add.
ℒ	Take out.
∧̄	Replace with this.
◯	Check Spelling.
≡	Capitalize.
/	Make lowercase.
¶	Make new paragraph

318 Handbook

PUBLISH

Now that you have corrected your work, share it with others!

- E-mail it to a friend or family member.
- Make a home video of you reading it.
- Put it on a poster, add pictures, and display it in your classroom.
- Send it to your favorite magazine or publication.

The Best Day of My Life
by Trang Bui

My family stood by the big, glass windows and watched the plane land at SeaTac Airport in Seattle on October 28, 2007. We were so excited! When the passengers started coming through the door, we lined up so we could see. I had to lift up my little sister so she could look over the heads of the people in front. Suddenly everyone was hugging and crying. My little sister tried to hide because she didn't know my grandparents. It took four long years, but my grandparents finally arrived!

EVALUATE YOUR WRITING

Save examples of your writing. Date them and collect them in a portfolio. Look through your portfolio from time to time to see how you are doing as a writer.

❶ Organize Put your writing in order by date. Make sections for works written for the same purpose or audience. Group your writing by form—stories, research reports, or poems.

❷ Survey the Work Each time you add new work, ask yourself:

- How does this writing compare to other work I've done?
- Am I getting better in certain areas?
- Are there things that I didn't do as well this time? Why?

❸ Think About How You Write Think about the words you like to use, the kinds of sentences you write, and what you like to write about. All of those things together are your writing style.

Using Information Resources

HOW TO FIND INFORMATION

You can use different resources to find information about your topic. Resources can be experts, or people who know a lot about a topic. Resources can also be nonfiction books, textbooks, magazines, newspapers, or the Internet. You can find resources all around you.

Expert

Nonfiction Books

Magazines and Newspapers

Encyclopedia

Dictionary

Almanac

Atlas

Internet

Think about your research questions. Some resources may be more helpful than others, depending on what kind of information you need about your topic.

- Do you need to look up facts or scientific data?
- Do you want to know about something that happened recently?
- Are you interested in someone's opinion or experience?
- Do you want to see pictures?

These questions will help you decide which resources to use.

Whatever your topic is, try exploring the library first. There you'll discover a world of resources and information!

Using Information Resources, continued

DICTIONARY

Think of the **dictionary** as a tool you can use to learn everything you need to know about a word. Dictionaries tell you how to spell, say, and use words. From a dictionary you can learn how to divide a word into syllables, what part of speech a word is, and how to write different forms of a word. You can also learn the history of a word. Look for examples of all of these types of information on these dictionary pages.

ward slope of the mountain. *Adjective.*
south·ward (south′wərd) *adverb; adjective.*
southwards Another spelling of the adverb southward: *They drove southwards.* **south·wards** (south′wərdz) *adverb.*
southwest 1. The direction halfway between south and west. 2. The point of the compass showing this direction. 3. A region or place in this direction. 4. the Southwest. The region in the south and west of the United States. *Noun.*
○ 1. Toward or in the southwest: *the southwest corner of the street.* 2. Coming from the southwest: *a southwest wind. Adjective.*
○ Toward the southwest: *The ship sailed southwest. Adverb.*
south·west (south′west′) *noun; adjective; adverb.*
souvenir Something kept because it reminds one of a person, place, or event: *I bought a pennant as a souvenir of the baseball game.* **sou·ve·nir** (sü′və nîr′ or sü′və nîr′) *noun, plural* **souvenirs.**
sovereign A king or queen. *Noun.*
○ 1. Having the greatest power or highest rank or authority: *The king and queen were the sovereign rulers of the country.* 2. Not controlled by others; independent: *Mexico is a sovereign nation. Adjective.*
sov·er·eign (sov′ər ən or sov′rən) *noun, plural* **sovereigns;** *adjective.*
Soviet Union Formerly, a large country in eastern Europe and northern Asia. It was composed of 15 republics and was also called the U.S.S.R. The

largest and most important of the 15 republics was Russia.
sow¹ 1. To scatter seeds over the ground; plant: *The farmer will sow corn in this field.* 2. To spread or scatter: *The clown sowed happiness among the children.*
Other words that sound like this are sew and so. **sow** (sō) *verb,* **sowed, sown** *or* **sowed, sowing.**
sow² An adult female pig. **sow** (sou) *noun, plural* **sows.**
soybean A seed rich in oil and protein and used as food. Soybeans grow in pods on bushy plants. **soy·bean** (soi′bēn′) *noun, plural* **soybeans.**
space 1. The area in which the whole universe exists. It has no limits. The planet earth is in space. 2. The region beyond the earth's atmosphere; outer space: *The rocket was launched into space.* 3. A distance or area between things: *There is not much space between our house and theirs.* 4. An area reserved or available for some purpose: *a parking space.* 5. A period of time: *Both jets landed in the space of ten minutes. Noun.*
○ To put space in between: *The architect spaced the houses far apart. Verb.*
space (spās) *noun, plural* **spaces;** *verb,* **spaced, spacing.**
spacecraft A vehicle used for flight in outer space. This is also called a spaceship. **space·craft** (spās′kraft′) *noun, plural* **spacecraft.**
space shuttle A spacecraft that carries a crew into space and returns to land on earth. The same

space shuttle

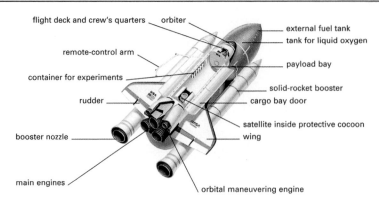

flight deck and crew's quarters ⎯ orbiter
remote-control arm
container for experiments
rudder
booster nozzle
main engines

external fuel tank
tank for liquid oxygen
payload bay
solid-rocket booster
cargo bay door
satellite inside protective cocoon
wing
orbital maneuvering engine

space shuttle can be used again. A space shuttle is also called a shuttle.

space station A spaceship that orbits around the earth like a satellite and on which a crew can live for long periods of time.

spacesuit Special clothing worn by an astronaut in space. A spacesuit covers an astronaut's entire body and has equipment to help the astronaut breathe. **space·suit** (spās'süt') *noun, plural* **spacesuits**.

Astronauts take spacewalks to repair satellites and vehicles.

spacewalk A period of activity during which an astronaut in space is outside a spacecraft. **space·walk** (spās'wôk') *noun, plural* **spacewalks**.

spacious Having a lot of space or room; roomy; large. —**spa·cious** *adjective* —**spaciousness** *noun*.

spade¹ A tool used for digging. It has a long handle and a flat blade that can be pressed into the ground with the foot. *Noun.*
○ To dig with a spade: *We spaded the garden and then raked it. Verb.*
spade (spād) *noun, plural* **spades**; *verb,* **spaded, spading**.

spade² **1.** A playing card marked with one or more figures shaped like this. **2. spades.** The suit

thin strings. It is made of a mixture of flour and water. **spa·ghet·ti** (spə get'ē) *noun.*

Spain A country in southwest Europe. **Spain** (spān) *noun.*

spamming The sending of the same message to large numbers of e-mail addresses or to many newsgroups at the same time. Spamming is often thought of as impolite behavior on the Internet. **spam·ming** (spa'ming) *noun.*

span **1.** The distance or part between two supports: *The span of that bridge is very long.* **2.** The full reach or length of anything: *Some people accomplish a great deal in the span of their lives. Noun.*
○ To extend over or across. *Verb.*
span (span) *noun, plural* **spans**; *verb,* **spanned, spanning**.

This bridge spans a wide river.

spaniel Any of various dogs of small to medium size with long, drooping ears, a silky, wavy coat, and short legs. The larger types are used in hunting. **span·iel** (span'yəl) *noun, plural* **spaniels**.

Spanish **1.** The people of Spain. The word *Spanish* in this sense is used with a plural verb. **2.** The language spoken in Spain. It is also spoken in many countries south of the United States as well as in parts of the U.S. *Noun.*

THESAURUS

A **thesaurus** is similar to a dictionary, but instead of giving word meanings, it lists synonyms and antonyms. A thesaurus can be especially useful when you are looking for just the right word to use. For example, you might want to describe how *good* of an experience NASA's Space Camp® is for kids—but without using that tired, overworked adjective. You could look up *good* in a thesaurus and find an entry that looks like this:

Synonyms are words with almost the same meanings.

fine

good adjective **1** *a good product* FINE, superior, quality; excellent, superb, outstanding, magnificent, exceptional, marvelous, wonderful, first-rate, first-class, sterling; satisfactory, acceptable, not bad, all right; *informal* great, OK, A1, jake, hunky-dory, ace, terrific, fantastic, fabulous, fab, top-notch, blue-chip, blue-ribbon, bang-up, killer, class, awesome, wicked; smashing, brilliant. ANTONYM bad.

Antonyms are words with opposite meanings.

bad

2 *a good person* VIRTUOUS, righteous, upright, nding, moral, ethical, high-minded, principled; e........lary,

from *Oxford American Writer's Thesaurus.* Christine A. Lundberg. By permission of Oxford University Press, Inc.

Which synonym would you decide to use?

A thesaurus can also be helpful when you are trying to decide how to express your thoughts about a big idea or topic. If you can't seem to come up with the right words, look up the subject—for example, *universe*—and see what you find.

universe noun **1** *a collection of stars* COSMOS, creation, nature, heavens, luminaries, constellations, celestial, stellar.

These are only a few of the words listed in one thesaurus for that subject. Just think about how helpful these words might be.

A thesaurus might give more information than simple lists of words.

- This thesaurus looks very similar to a dictionary. It includes a definition for each **entry word**. The definition is followed by a **sample sentence** featuring the word. This thesaurus also includes **guide words** at the top of the page.

baby

beautiful

baby *n.* a very young child or animal: The *baby* is only ten months old.
Synonyms
infant a child too young to walk or talk: You need to carry an *infant*.
newborn a baby that has just been born: The *newborn* and her mother go home from the hospital.

beat *n.* a repeated sound, usually with a regular occurrence: Tap your foot to the *beat*.
Synonyms
pounding I could feel the *pounding* of my own heart.
rhythm The *rhythm* of the rain put me to sleep last night.

- This thesaurus does not include definitions, only sample sentences.

wakeful adjective **1** *he had been wakeful all night* AWAKE, restless, restive, tossing and turning. ANTONYM asleep.

2 *I was suddenly wakeful* ALERT, watchful, vigilant, on the lookout, on one's guard, attentive, heedful, wary. ANTONYM inattentive.

walk verb **1** *they walked along the road* STROLL, saunter, amble, trudge, plod, dawdle, hike, tramp, tromp, slog, stomp, trek, march, stride, sashay, glide, troop, patrol, wander, ramble, tread, prowl, promenade, roam, traipse; stretch one's legs; *informal* mosey, hoof it; *formal* perambulate.

PARTS OF A BOOK

There are many different kinds of books. All books share some features that make it easier for readers to find what they need. Let's look at the parts of a book.

Title Page

The **title page** is usually the first page in a book.

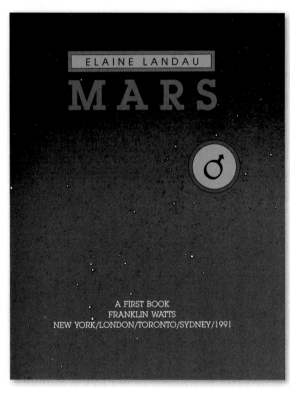

The **title page** gives the **title** of the book and the **author**.

It tells the **publisher** and often names the cities where the publisher has offices.

Copyright Page

The **copyright (©) page** gives the year when the book was published.

Check the **copyright** to see how current the information is.

Landau, Elaine
    Mars / by Elaine Landau
        p.cm. — (First book)
    Includes bibliographical references and index.
    Summary: Uses photographs and other recent findings to
        describe the atmosphere and geographic features of Mars.
    ISBN 0-531-20012-4 (lib. bdg)—ISBN 0-531-15773-3 (pbk)
    I. Mars (Planet)—Juvenile Literature. [1. Mars (Planet)]
1. Title.   II. Series.
QB641.L36 1991
523.4'3—dc20   90-13097 CIP AC

            Copyright © 1991 Elaine Landau
                All rights reserved
        Printed in the United States of America
                    6 5 4 3

Table of Contents

The **table of contents** is in the front of a book. It shows how many chapters, or parts, are in a book. It tells the page numbers where those chapters begin. Look at the chapter names to see which ones might be useful to you.

A table of contents can be much more detailed than the one shown here. For example, it might list sections within chapters, important visuals, or special sections found in the book.

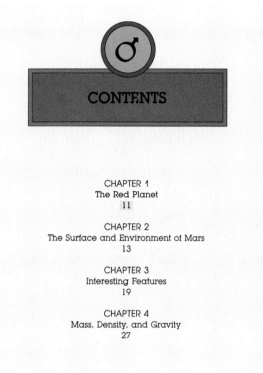

A **chapter title** tells what the chapter is mostly about.

The **page number** tells where the chapter begins.

CONTENTS

CHAPTER 1
The Red Planet
11

CHAPTER 2
The Surface and Environment of Mars
13

CHAPTER 3
Interesting Features
19

CHAPTER 4
Mass, Density, and Gravity
27

Chapter Headings

Once you have found a chapter you are interested in using from the table of contents, you will turn to the chapter. The first page in the chapter will contain a header describing what you will find in the chapter. Often, chapters are numbered.

THE RED PLANET

CHAPTER ONE

The planet Mars appears as a rusty red ball in the nighttime sky. Because of its reddish color, the ancient Romans named the planet after their god of war—Mars. In fact, the fighting god's shield and spear are still used as the planet's symbol.

Mars is one of the nine planets that make up the *solar system*. The solar system consists of the sun and the planets, moons, and other objects that revolve around it. Mars is the fourth planet from the sun. Earth, Mars's neighbor, is the third planet from the sun.

Mars is not a very large planet. Its diameter is

Using Information Resources, continued

You can find different types of maps inside atlases. You can use the different maps for different purposes. Let's see what some of them look like.

PHYSICAL MAPS

A **physical map** shows the geographical features of a place, such as bodies of water and landforms.

Mapmakers often use techniques that make mountains look like they are rising off the page.

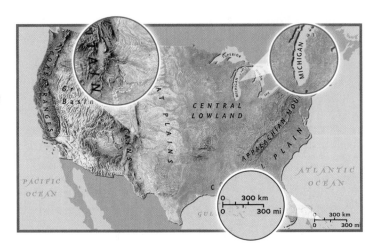

Landforms, like mountains or lakes, are often labeled.

The **scale** shows that this distance on the map is equal to 300 miles on land.

PRODUCT MAPS

A **product map** uses pictures and symbols to show where products come from or where natural resources are found.

The **compass rose** shows the directions north, south, east, and west.

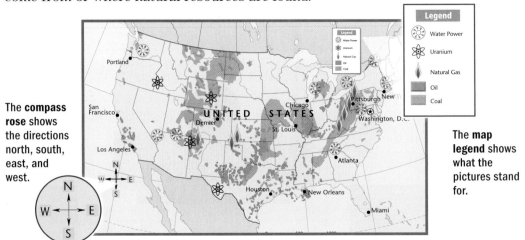

The **map legend** shows what the pictures stand for.

POLITICAL MAPS

A **political map** shows the boundaries between countries, states, and other areas. It also shows capitals and other major cities. **Road maps** are usually set up like political maps.

A **grid system** is used on these maps to make it easy to find a particular place. Look up the place name in the index to find the right map and a code to the exact location on the map. For example, L-6 for this map is the square at which the row L and the column 6 intersect. Can you find Orlando somewhere in the square?

GLOBE

A globe is a small model of the Earth. A globe has a round shape like the Earth does. It gives a better picture of Earth than a flat map does.

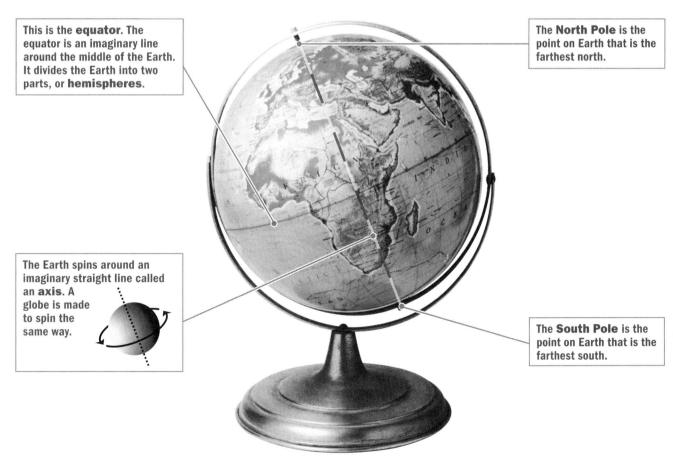

This is the **equator**. The equator is an imaginary line around the middle of the Earth. It divides the Earth into two parts, or **hemispheres**.

The **North Pole** is the point on Earth that is the farthest north.

The Earth spins around an imaginary straight line called an **axis**. A globe is made to spin the same way.

The **South Pole** is the point on Earth that is the farthest south.

Finding Information on the World Wide Web

The Internet is an international network, or connection, of computers that share information with one another. The World Wide Web allows you to find, read, go through, and organize information. The Internet is like a giant library, and the World Wide Web is everything in the library including the books, the librarian, and the computer catalog. The Internet is a fast way to get the most current information about your topic! You'll find resources like encyclopedias and dictionaries, as well as amazing pictures, movies, and sounds.

HOW TO GET STARTED

Check with your teacher for how to access the Internet from your school. Usually you can just double click on the icon, or picture, to get access to the Internet and you're on your way!

DOING THE RESEARCH

Once the search page comes up, you can begin the research process. Just follow these steps.

❶ Type your subject in the search box and then click on the Search button.

If you already know the address of a Web site, you can type it in the address box, instead of a search box, at the top of the screen. A Web site address is also called the URL (Uniform Resource Locator).

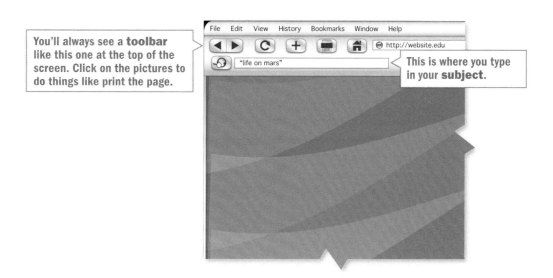

You'll always see a **toolbar** like this one at the top of the screen. Click on the pictures to do things like print the page.

This is where you type in your **subject**.

❷ Read the search results.

All underlined, colored words are links, or connections, to other sites. They help you get from page to page quickly.

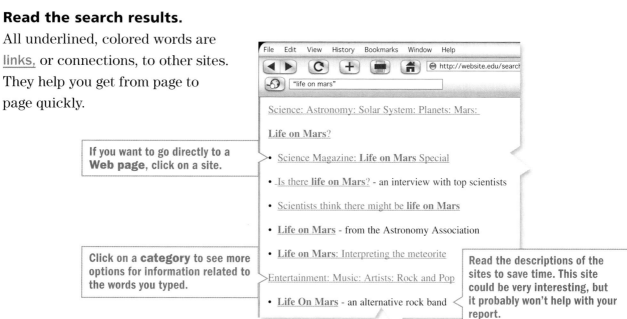

If you want to go directly to a **Web page**, click on a site.

Click on a **category** to see more options for information related to the words you typed.

Read the descriptions of the sites to save time. This site could be very interesting, but it probably won't help with your report.

❸ Select a site, and read the article.

You might want to pick a new site or start a new search. If so, click on the **back arrow** to go back a page to the search results.

If you want to go to another Web page, click on a **link**.

❹ You may choose to print the article if it is helpful for your research. Later on, you can use the article to take notes.

File   Edit   View   History   Bookmarks   Window   Help

http://www.redplanet.com/article_

"life on mars"

Anything you ever wanted to know about the planet Mars is on this site! Is it really red? Does it really have water? Information about the appearance of the planet is only the beginning. Articles are about the planet's history, from its discovery to the most recent evidence scientists have gathered about this interesting planet. Search the list by title or by topic.

MORE ON MARS: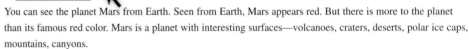

● **The Red Planet**
You can see the planet Mars from Earth. Seen from Earth, Mars appears red. But there is more to the planet than its famous red color. Mars is a planet with interesting surfaces—volcanoes, craters, deserts, polar ice caps, mountains, canyons.

● **Mariner 4**
In 1965, scientists believed Mars was covered with liquid similar to our oceans. In recent years, scientists have been able to gather evidence about the liquid history of Mars.

● **Orbiting Mars**
Mars has more spacecraft circling it than any other planet: Mars Odyssey, Mars Express, and Mars Reconnaissance Orbiter. Mars also has two Exploration Rovers: *Spirit* and *Opportunity*.

● **Phobos and Deimos—Mars has Two Moons**
Some people believe these are not really moons. Some think they are asteroids.

● **Life on Mars?**
What would life be like on Mars? Scientists thought they had the answer.

● **Models of Mars Missions**
Experience a mission to Mars! Click the link to watch video and read scientific analysis of the planet's properties.

CHOOSING DATA FROM THE INTERNET

You may find much more information on the Internet than you need.
Follow these steps to help you choose data for your research.

➊ Choose your key words carefully.

If your words are too general, the search results might show hundreds or even thousands of sites to choose from. Narrow your search by choosing specific key words.

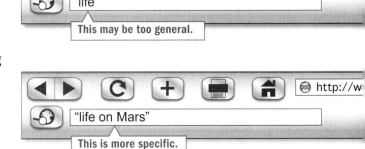

"life"

This may be too general.

"life on Mars"

This is more specific.

➋ Look back at your research questions.

Skim and scan a Web site to see if it answers at least some of your questions. If it does, save it under "Favorites" or "Bookmarks." You can come back to it later to read more carefully.

➌ Check facts and sources.

Use more than one source to **verify your facts**, or make sure they are true. Try to find the same fact in at least two Web sites or in an encyclopedia. Think about the source, too. A well-known scientific Web site probably has more **reliable**, or true, information than a personal Web site.

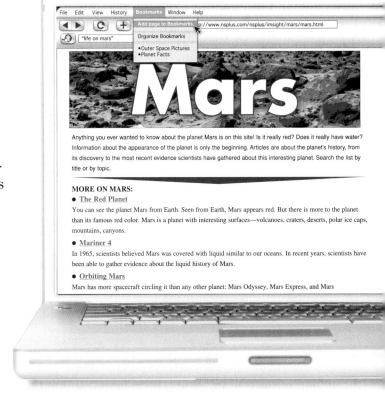

File   Edit   View   History   Bookmarks   Window   Help

Add page to Bookmarks   p://www.nsplus.com/nsplus/imsight/mars/mars.html

"life on mars"   Organize Bookmarks

• Outer Space Pictures
• Planet Facts

Mars

Anything you ever wanted to know about the planet Mars is on this site! Is it really red? Does it really have water? Information about the appearance of the planet is only the beginning. Articles are about the planet's history, from its discovery to the most recent evidence scientists have gathered about this interesting planet. Search the list by title or by topic.

MORE ON MARS:

● **The Red Planet**
You can see the planet Mars from Earth. Seen from Earth, Mars appears red. But there is more to the planet than its famous red color. Mars is a planet with interesting surfaces—volcanoes, craters, deserts, polar ice caps, mountains, canyons.

● **Mariner 4**
In 1965, scientists believed Mars was covered with liquid similar to our oceans. In recent years, scientists have been able to gather evidence about the liquid history of Mars.

● **Orbiting Mars**
Mars has more spacecraft circling it than any other planet: Mars Odyssey, Mars Express, and Mars

A Lap, a Cat Nap, and a Pal

Pam stands at the window and claps.

"Dad! Dad! I can see a van, and I can see a man in a tan cap. The man has a fat cat. Can I go and gab, Dad?" Pam asks.

Dad hangs up a damp rag and says, "Okay, Pam. I can go, too."

Pam ran fast to the van. Pam says, "Hi. I am Pam. I saw your van and your cat."

"I am Frank," says the man in the tan cap. "And my cat is Max. This is our brand new home." Dad and Frank shake hands.

"Can I pat Max?" asks Pam.

"You can pat Max," Frank says. "Max is a fan of pats, and Max is a fan of laps, too."

Pam had a plan.

Pam sat down, and Max sat on her lap. Max had a cat nap on Pam! Max is a fan of laps and naps! Pam, Frank, Dad, and Max are pals. Pam is glad.

Words with short *a*

and	claps	Frank	has	naps	rag
asks	Dad	gab	lap	pal	ran
at	damp	glad	laps	pals	sat
brand	fan	had	man	Pam	stands
can	fast	hands	Max	pat	tan
cap	fat	hangs	nap	plan	van
cat					

Unit 1 High Frequency Words

go	home	new

Jan Has Hot Dogs!

Dad, Mom, Tad, Sal, Tom and Rob sit at a hot dog hut. Jan, a gal in a cap, gets a menu for Dad. Then, Jan gets one for Mom, Tad, Tom, Sal, and Rob. Dad, Mom, Tad, Tom, Sal, and Rob read. Next, Jan runs and gets a fat pad. "Hot dogs?" Jan asks.

"Hot dog!" answers Dad.

"Hot dog!" answers Mom.

"Hot dog!" answers Tad.

"Hot dog!" answers Sal.

"No hot dog," Tom answers.

"No hot dog?" Mom asks Tom.

"No hot dog?" Dad asks Tom.

"No hot dog!" answers Tom. "A can of ham, fat yams, hot cod, toast and jam. Jam on top—not a pat, not a dab—a gob!"

That leaves Rob. Rob sits up. "Hot dog!" says Rob. "A fat, fat hot dog!"

Jan gets hot dogs for Dad, Mom, Sal, and Tad. Jan gets a big, fat hot dog for Rob. And for Tom, Jan gets a can of ham, hot cod, a fat yam, and toast with a gob of jam on top.

Words with short *o*

cod	gob	Mom	on	Tom
dog	hot	not	Rob	top

Unit 1 High Frequency Words

next	one	then

A Dog and a Cat at Last

Tom and Pam are pals. Pam has a fat cat, Max, and Tom has a dog, Bob. "A cat is a blast," says Pam. "But I wish I had a dog *and* a cat! A dog can jog and romp with you. A cat can not jog or romp." Tom is glad he has a dog and not a cat. Tom is not fond of cats at all.

Soon, Bob the dog has puppies. Bob is a gal, not a guy, and now Bob is a mom. Tom brings Pam a small, tan dog in a box. Pam is glad to see Tom.

Max is glad, too. Max hops on Tom's lap. "Scat, Max!" says Tom, but Max is a brat. Max likes the spot on Tom's lap and will not scat. Max flops flat and has a nap.

"You can pat Max," says Pam. "Max will not snap at you." Tom pats Max.

"You can pat the dog, Pam," says Tom, and Pam pats her brand new dog, Spot.

Spot pants fast and wags a lot. "Spot likes me!" claps Pam. "I am very glad."

Tom nods. "I am glad, too," says Tom.

Pam is glad. She has a fat cat and a dog—at last.

Words with short *a*, short *o*

a	brat	flat	hops	nap	romp
am	can	flops	jog	nods	scat
and	cat	fond	lap	not	snap
at	claps	gal	last	on	Spot
blast	dog	glad	lot	Pam	tan
Bob	fast	has	Max	pants	Tom
box	fat	had	mom	pats	wags
brand					

Unit 1 High Frequency Words

new

Dip Tips

Tim has six tips on how to fix hot dip:

1. First grab a pad. Jot down what you will need. Is it a lot? Did you jot ham, a can of yams, jam, cod, hot dogs, or a bag of figs? Dill is tasty with hot dip. Add dill to the pad.
2. Fix the dip. Ham can have a lot of fat on it. Fat is bad. Lop it off. Do not miss a bit. Big figs can have pits. Get rid of the fig pits. Cod can have fins. Rip off the fins. Add a bit of dill.
3. Next mix the dip in a big pot or in a large pan. Do not mix it in a box. Do not mix it in a can. Do not fill it to the top.
4. Fit a lid on the pot. It can be a glass lid or it can be a tin lid.
5. Mix the dip six times: mix, mix, mix, mix, mix, mix. Do not sit. Do not miss a mix! It is a big, hot job.
6. Then sit. Try a bit of dip. Do not eat a lot.

Using Tim's six tips, your dip can not miss! His dip is tops!

Words with short *i*

big	fig	his	mix	rip	Tim's
bit	figs	is	pig	sit	tips
dill	fins	it	pits	six	will
dip	fix	miss	rid	Tim	

Units 1–2 High Frequency Words

First	Then	Next	large

Jim and Big Gus

Jim is in a bad, bad rut. He wants to fix a hot meal for his pal, Big Gus. He wants to mix up something fun to eat at six. But, what will it be? Jim has to think fast.

Can he fix a pan of hot ham? Jim bit his lip. A pan of hot ham is not bad, but it is not great. "Hot ham is a bit of a risk," Jim thinks.

Will Gus like clam dip? No. Clam dip will be a dud!

Jim thinks. Will Gus like crab crisp? No. Crab crisp is not a fun meal.

Will Gus eat a vat of ox stew? No. Ox stew is a bit bland.

Just then, Jim has an idea. Jim grabs a pot and drops a big pat of butter and an egg into it. Jim drops in a cup of flour and a bit of mint. And then, Jim drops in something secret! Finally, Jim puts a lid on the pot and sits.

At six, there is a rap, rap, rap on the door. It is Big Gus.

"It is six, and here I am!" says Big Gus.

"Sit, Gus!" says Jim. "I will grab the pot."

Big Gus had a small bit of the food.

"What is in it?" Big Gus asks.

"Fig!" answers Jim.

"Fig?" asks Big Gus.

"Fig," says Jim. "It is fig pudding."

"Mmm," says Big Gus.

"Is it good and fun?" asks Jim.

"It is!" answers Big Gus.

Words with short *u*				
but	dud	Gus	rut	up
cup	fun	nut	sun	

Units 1–2 High Frequency Words				
eat	small	something	then	there

Dig into a Bun!

Tim put a mat on the table for Bud. Then Tim got Nan a mat and one for himself. Tim put a small plate on each mat. Tim put a large mug on each mat. Then Tim got a big jug of milk.

"Sit!" said Tim. "Go on! Sit! Sit! Sit!" Bud sat and Nan sat, but Tim did not sit. Tim said, "I will sit, but I must get something first. "What is it?" ask Bud and Nan. "Is it a gift for us?"

Tim got a big, flat pan. "It is not a gift, but you will like it. It is six plum buns in a pan! I made six plum buns for us!"

"Do not drop the pan, Tim!" said Nan. "Do not slip or trip, Tim!" said Bud. Tim did not trip or slip, and he did not drop the plum buns. Tim sat and took a big, fat, hot bun. "Have one," said Tim. "Dig in! Eat up!" Bud took a big, fat, hot bun.

Bud has a sip and lifts a bun to his lips. "Mmm," said Bud. "A hot bun is not bad with milk! I will dunk my bun in milk, and I will try to not drip it on the rug!"

"Grab a bun, Nan!" said Bud. "Grab a big, fat, hot bun, and dunk it in milk!

"I will!" said Nan. And that is just what she did! What fun!

Words with short *i*, short *u*

big	drip	his	just	plum	Tim
Bud	dunk	hot	lifts	rug	trip
buns	flat	in	lip	sip	us
but	fun	is	milk	sit	will
did	gift	it	mug	slip	
dig	grab	jug	must	six	

Units 1–2 High Frequency Words

eat	go	one	something
first	large	small	then

Chad Can Chop

Mom asks, "Chad, I know it is dull, but will you help make lunch?"

Chad says, "You bet I will! I can cut a big bunch of carrots. I can chop nuts for a batch of cookies. I can mix a jug of red punch. It is not dull. It will be fun!" Chad is such a good kid.

Mom tells Chad, "Fetch a bunch of carrots, a bag of chips, and the red punch mix." Chad did.

"Can I eat a chip?" Chad asks. Mom nods. Chad munches. Munch, munch, munch!

Chad got a bit of chip on his chin.

"You can mix the punch, Chad," says his mom. "Add a pinch of sugar to the punch. I will fix us a big batch of cookies. We can munch on them at lunch. Sit on the bench. We can chat."

Chad sat. Mom got a cup of chips. Mom got a cup of nuts. Buzz— hot cookies! Chad sets the cookies up on the sill to chill." Mom gets napkins. Chad digs in.

"Yum, yum, yum!" Chad says. The cookies are not rich, but Chad has his fill. Chad hugs his mom.

Words with *ch, tch*

batch	Chad	chin	chop	munches	punch
bench	chat	chip	lunch	pinch	rich
bunch	chill	chips	munch		

Units 1–2 High Frequency Words

eat	make	says

Hens on Eggs

Eggs sell like pop in July—fast. As it is the job of a hen to sit on eggs, we hens get fed well. At six, when the sun is up, we get let out of our pen to fill up on bugs. I love to catch wet, rich gobs of bugs! At ten, when the sun is hot, we get fed corn in a big box. (Yes, it is less tasty than bugs.) At six at night, when the sun sets, we get fed corn in our pen.

Life as a hen is fun, yet it is a bit hard at times. Let me tell you about Meg. Meg is not a pet dog or a cat. Meg is not a pig. Meg is not the vet. Meg is a red fox! A fox and a hen are not pals!

On Sunday, the latch in our pen fell open. A cat yell got me up from bed, and I met Meg in the pen. Well, you can bet I let out a yell. But, Meg and I had a chat. Meg had a den that was such a big, wet mess. The hen pen was not a mess. Hens are not pigs! Meg did not need eggs. Meg did need a bed. I let Meg nap until six, but I did not let her get one egg!

Well, Meg and I became pals, but I can tell you, it is not all bugs, naps, and fun as a hen. A hen has a job—it is to sit on eggs.

Words with short e

bet	get	Meg	pet	tell	wet
den	hen	mess	red	ten	yell
eggs	hens	met	sell	vet	yes
fed	let	pen	sets	well	yet
fell					

Units 1–3 High Frequency Words

from	love	one	open	when

Get Set, Run

Ted pats his dog, Jem. There is a big web with bugs on it and a lot of wet logs, but no sun. Ten minutes pass. The rain has not let up yet, but Ted and his dog set off for home.

Ted's wet hat and wet bag sag. The path is wet, too; it is much like a mud pit. "Do not sit in the mud, Jem!" Ted tells Jem, but Jem sits and gets wet. She is a big wet mess. "Stop it, Jem!" yells Ted. Jem rubs mud on Ted. Ted has gobs of mud on him. It will be a big job to get the mud off his legs.

Suddenly, his hair stands up in the chill air. Jem sits up, too. Ted and Jem can hear a hiss on the hill. I bet it is a fox cub! "Jem," Ted begs, "we must get out of here. Get set, run!"

Jem runs and runs. "Jem!" yells Ted. "Get Mom!" Ted runs as fast as his legs can go, but his bag pops open. His bug net is in the bag. "Yes," thinks Ted. "I can catch it with this." Ted runs behind a big tree and gets the net set. Something runs by, and Ted runs at it with his net.

It is a chipmunk, and Ted did not catch it! "I am such a silly kid!" says Ted. "Well, I am glad Jem can not see my red face."

Words with short e

begs	hems	mess	Ted	well	yet
bet	Jem	net	tells	wet	
get	legs	red	ten	yell	
gets	let	set	web	yes	

Units 1–3 High Frequency Words

face	go	home	open	something	there

Bad Luck

Chuck has bad luck. When he was a baby, Chuck sat on a duck. The duck got very mad and bit him. As a little boy, Chuck fell in a large, wet patch of mud and muck. He had as much mud and muck on him as a rock, so a duck sat in his lap and, when Chuck let out a yell, the duck bit him. As a kid, Chuck pet a pup on the back, and something made the pup run. The pup ran by a duck and scared it. Yes, the duck got mad and bit Chuck.

Jack has bad luck as well. As a baby, Jack pet a cat on the neck, and the cat got mad and bit Jack. As a tot, Jack put his socks in the sun, and the socks got hot. A cat had a nap on those hot socks, and when Jack tried to get his socks back, the cat bit him. As a kid, Jack had a big red sack. A cat got in it, and yes, it bit Jack as Jack tried to pick it up.

Well, get this—now Chuck is a vet, and Jack is a vet, too! A vet has to help sick pups, cats, hens, chicks, ducks, and pigs. If a hen pecks a vet, the vet has to help. If a pig kicks a vet, the vet has to help. You can bet Chuck will get bit by ducks and Jack will get bit by cats. There are no ifs, ands, or buts about it—Chuck and Jack have bad, bad luck!

Words with *ck*

back	duck	luck	neck	rock	sick
Chuck	Jack	muck	pick	sack	socks

Units 1–3 High Frequency Words

large	something	there	when

A Fish Wish

Our ship sits in fog. I am sad, for I can not see any fish in fog, and it is my wish to catch a big fish.

As I wish for sun in the chill, dim hush, Dad yells. "Tish! Get a mop. We can't fish, but we can mop decks. We can dab muck in gaps to fix the hull. "I wish I did not have to dash to get a mop and a tub of muck, which I'll use to fill holes in the hull. But, the sun is not up yet, so I get a mop and a tub of muck.

Dad asks, "Can you fix a mesh net? It has a big gash in it." I pick up the net and rush to find a sewing kit. I wish I did not have to patch a net. Fog has us shut in and we can not fish, so I patch the gash in the mesh.

I am in shock. The sun has gotten rid of the fog! I fetch a pole and net. Will I get my wish and catch a big fish? I shut my eyes and wish for a bit of luck.

We pass wet rocks. Ducks dip, gulls chat, and shells catch the sun. A fin pops up. It is a fish.

"Dad!" I yell. "It is a big fish!" I tug. The fish tugs back, but I win. With a tap, a large cod hits the deck. It fills a net and rips the mesh. But I am not mad. I got my wish to catch a fish.

Words with *sh*

dash	gash	mesh	shells	shock	Tish
fish	hush	rush	ship	shut	wish

Units 1–3 High Frequency Words

find	large	use

Seth at Six

Seth ran up the path. Seth rang the bell. His mom and dad had told him to meet them at this house at six. Seth had to dash to get there at six. It was six on the dot when he rang the bell. Seth rang the bell again—RING, RING—but did not hear a thing. Then he sat on a bench in a patch of hot sun with his back to the door. A fat cat jumped up and sat on his lap. Seth sang a song as he sat in the hot sun with that cat.

Then a thin, fit man with a tan dog ran from a red house. This man sang a song as he ran, but it was a different song than Seth had sung. When the thin man and the tan dog ran by, the fat cat hid from the dog behind a shed.

Seth had turned back to catch the cat when he heard a thud, then a BONG, then a BAM, BONG, BONG! The thin man had whacked a trash can with a big lid as he ran. The lid went BING, BONG, BONG when it hit the ground. Then the man fell on the lid. Seth got up to help the thin man.

When the cat came back, Seth sat in the sun with the cat on his lap. It was now ten past six. Seth wished his mom and dad would show up.

Words with *th*

path	than	them	thin	this	with
Seth	that	then	thing	thud	

Words with *wh*

whacked	when

Words with *ng*

bang	bong	ring	song	thing

Units 1–4 High Frequency Words

different	from	then	there	when

My Next Trip

When I plan my next trip, I will pack a trunk and hope it will be grand. Where will I end up? I do not yet know.

Will I cross the sea in a blimp? Will I hop on a tram? Will I go two or three miles? Will I go 200? And, will I land where colts run in the tall grass? Where I can stroll on the sand and catch a crab in a trap for lunch? Where I can splash in a pond? I do not yet know.

Will I stop for 10 days? Will I stop for 20? Will I find enough different things to snack on? Will I drink milk in a glass? Will I flop onto beds of brass and silk? Will I rest on mats in the dust? Will my trip be bliss or just bland? I do not yet know.

When I get back, will I be sad? Will I brag to my pals? Will I hug my dog and cat and be glad to plop onto a soft bed that I know?

Until I go on my next trip, I will not know if it will stink or if it will be the best. But I will tell you when I get back. In fact, the first thing I will do when I go on my next trip is this: I will grab a stamp and send you a letter.

Words with initial and final blends

best	cross	glad	milk	silk	stop
bland	drink	glass	plan	snack	stroll
blimp	drop	grab	plop	soft	tram
brag	dust	grand	pond	splash	trap
brass	end	grass	rest	stamp	trip
colts	flop	land	sand	stink	trunk

Units 1–4 High Frequency Words

different	enough	final	three	two	when

The Quest for Gold

Gold! One reason that men try to find brand new land is that they hope to find gold. When bold men try to find an old city with a lot of gold, they hope that they will be rich. The quest for gold and land can make even a kind man go wild. The quest for gold and land can give even a kind man a cold, cold heart.

An old book from the past tells of a rich king who has a lust for gold. He would grind his gold until it became dust. He would mix the gold dust with mud and rub the wet stuff on his skin. Then, he would bolt into a big, cold pond. All the people thought that he had lost his mind!

That tale of the gold king became a tale about a golden city with thick gold walls. A long brick path winds through this golden city. In the city, an adult or a child can stroll past golden homes, hop on top of golden posts, and ride in rigs down long golden streets.

You cannot tell men on a quest for gold that golden cities do not exist and never have. In the past, those men did not see that they could go to the end of the map, but they would not find a land of gold. So, the king, his pond, and the golden city can only be found in books and in rich minds.

Words with word patterns and multisyllabic words

be	child	go	he	old	the
became	cold	gold	kind	posts	wild
bold	even	golden	mind	so	winds
bolt	find	grind	minds	stroll	

Units 1–5 High Frequency Words

all	find	home	new	then
city	from	long	one	use
down	go	make	people	when

Jane Doesn't Help!

Jane's father told her that she had to help him clean out the attic tomorrow. Jane had other plans, so she was not happy. As Jane came up the steps, she saw a crib, a bed, games, pots and pans, a hose, skates, and picture frames. Then she saw a lampshade, a desk, a rake, a box of old plates, a cane, fake plants, a fake snake, and a globe. Her father said, "If we work together, we can get rid of this junk in no time!"

Jane looked around. "That's the pole I had to catch my first fish. Those are my first skates. And, this is the bat I had to hit a home run. I made this puppet in second grade! This stuff is not junk! What's in this box, Dad?" asked Jane.

"Family pictures," said Dad. This is Grandma Rose as a baby. And, this is Grandpa Gabe when he was ten."

"Save them!" yelled Jane.

"Look at these, Jane. Grandma brought these plates and cups from Finland when she came here on a ship. Grandma's wedding dress is in this big box."

"Save those things! I will take them!" said Jane as she looked around. "I can put this crate next to my bed and set a vase on it. And, save this globe, this lamp, this game, this rug, this puppet, this shell, this jump rope, this red cape, and this whole case of plastic cups."

"You are not helping a bit, Jane!" laughed Dad. "I'll just do this job alone."

Words with long a

came	crate	game	Jane's	rake	snake
cane	fake	games	made	save	take
cape	frames	Jane	plates	skates	vase
case	Gabe				

Words with long o

alone	home	pole	Rose	whole
globe	hose	rope	those	

Units 1–6 High Frequency Words

family	from	home	other	second	together
father	her	next	out	then	when
first					

Five Things a Fine Home Has

Most fine homes include many fine things. Some are things that people just like to have. Others are things they *must* have. Here are five things a home must include.

A fine home has a stove. A stove is used to make healthful food, on which a family likes to dine. A stove can be used to bake cupcakes, make an egg for lunch, and make a bedtime snack. People can take pride in the cakes they bake.

Next, a fine home has a clock. People use clocks to get the time. Some clocks chime to help them wake up. It is rude to be late for a plane, a game, or a date! A clock's size is not important. Big clocks and little clocks can all do the same fine job! My small clock wakes me at nine!

What home lacks a sink and a tub? A fine home has a spot for people to take a bath. It also has a spot to scrub pots, pans, dishes, glasses, teeth, and hands!

Another thing a fine home includes is light. The light can shine in from a big window. It can also come from a bulb in a bedside lamp or a desk lamp. But in a storm, you might have to use a flashlight!

To finish, what is a home without a bed? A fine home can include many kinds of beds. The beds can be bunk beds, twin beds, wide beds, cribs, and cots. A bed is a fine spot to take a nap, read a book, and listen to a tune!

Words with long *i*, long *u*

bedside	five	like	prune	size	use
bedtime	fine	likes	rude	time	used
chime	include	nine	shine	tune	wide
dine	includes	pride			

Units 1–6 High Frequency Words

all	from	make	next	same	use
come	home	many	people	small	without
family					

Spike Escapes

I have a pet snake. His name is Spike. Spike lives in a big glass tank in my bedroom, and I give him mice to eat. I think snakes make great pets, but my mother doesn't. She has one strict rule. Spike must be in his tank all the time. I follow that rule, but sometimes Spike does not. Last night, he got out of his tank. I knew I had to find him before Mom did. Spike is quite big, so I didn't think that would be a problem. But it was—it was a big problem!

I bent down and felt around in the dark closet. I gave something a poke, but it was just a sock. Under the bed I saw one skate, two dimes, three cubes from a game, and five pens, but no snake.

I looked in the kitchen cabinets behind plates, cups, glasses, and a box of cake mix. Then I searched inside the stove, under the table, and in a spot next to the mops.

In the bathroom, I looked in the tub and under piles of towels. Under the sink, I just saw a thick black and white striped pipe. Then I thought about that. The pipe under the sink isn't striped—it's white. Spike has stripes—that was a snake on the pipe! I learned my lesson. When I put him back in his tank, I set a large rock on the tank's mesh top. Spike will not escape again very soon!

Words with long *a*, long *o*, long *i*, long *u*

cake	game	named	poke	snake	striped
cubes	gave	piles	quite	snakes	stripes
dimes	inside	pipe	rule	Spike	time
escapes	make	plates	skate	stove	white
five					

Units 1–6 High Frequency Words

all	find	make	out	three	under
down	from	mother	something	two	when
eat	large	one	sometimes		

Fun Time at Home

Time at home can be spent at work and play. As a rule, the work comes first, and then it's time for fun.

Jobs at home can be endless. In the winter, most jobs take place inside the home. All the people in a family can take part—both adults and kids. They can mop a floor until it shines. Even kids can scrub a tub and shake the dust out of rugs and drapes.

But even in winter, time at home is not just about work. There is time for fun games inside, such as jacks, chess, and "Go Fish." You can play a tune on a flute, sing a tune, or bake a batch of cupcakes. You can also go outside to slide on your sleds or skate on the ice.

Then in the spring, jobs can include things you do outside. In the bright sunshine, you can rake and dig a plot for plants. You can give your deck a rinse and then a new coat of paint. You can pick up all those sticks and branches that broke off the trees and rake them into a big pile.

But you can also have fun in the sun when it's hot! You can ride bikes, skate on the sidewalk, catch a ball, and fly a kite. You can make a grid on the pavement. Then get a rock or a stone and use it to play hopscotch. You can get a rope and jump rope with a pal.

Which activity do you like best when you have time at home?

Words with long *a*, long *i*

bake	games	kite	rake	shines	sunshine
bike	inside	pavement	ride	skate	take
cupcakes	make	pile	shake	slide	time
drapes					

Units 1–6 High Frequency Words

all	first	make	people	use
come	go	new	then	when
family	home	out	there	

Far Away

"Some day," Ray tells Gail, "I plan to take a trip far, far away."

"Where will you go?" asks Gail.

"Maybe I will sail to Spain," says Ray. "I'd like to go this very day. Spain is way across the sea. It has big mountains and wide plains. I can play in Spain, if it does not rain very much. I will ride the subway and the fast train. I will stay until May. It will be a fine holiday."

"Can you go to Australia?" asks Gail. "That's even farther away than Spain."

"How can I get there?" Ray asks.

"You can take a plane, or you can sail," says Gail, "but you cannot take a train. Australia is a continent in the southern hemisphere. The mainland is a big island. You can play in the sand and hike on trails. You can stay for days and days, and you can mail me notes from there. You may get to play with a kangaroo that has a big tail!"

"That will be fun," says Ray, "but maybe I'll go even farther away."

"You don't say?" asks Gail.

"Yes, I just may aim for a trip to space," Ray says.

"That's great," says Gail, "but how will you get all that way?"

"I will find a way. I may ride a rocket ship."

"Explain how you will pay for your fun trip to space," Gail says.

"I will find a way," says Ray. "And, I just can't wait!"

Words with long _a_ spelled _ai_ and _ay_

aim	holiday	maybe	rain	Spain	trails
away	mail	pay	Ray	stay	train
day	mainland	plains	sail	subway	wait
explain	May	play	say	tail	way
Gail					

Units 1–7 High Frequency Words

all	from	or	says
find	go	say	there

Six Tips Before You Leave

Let's say that you must pack for a trip that will last a week, and your goal is to take only a big backpack. What will you take? These six tips can show you how to squeeze everything that you need in just one backpack. Have faith. You won't fail. It will be a real breeze!

Tip 1 Make a list of the things you need. Greed can make you pack too much! Don't take a load of stuff you don't need. Match things that go together. Ask yourself: Will I use that yellow jacket? Will I really need three sweatshirts in that heat?

Tip 2 Wear the big stuff. Don't pack a coat—wear it. Slip on those jeans, too. Jeans take up a lot of room in a backpack.

Tip 3 Be neat, and don't just throw stuff in. Roll up things like socks, jackets, and pants. Clothes take up much less space when they're rolled, not folded.

Tip 4 Take some laundry soap, and use it to wash your things while you're away. It takes just ten seconds to soak your pants and tops to get them clean. Then you can wear each thing two or three times.

Tip 5 Each pair of shoes takes up a lot of space in a backpack. Pack just one extra set of shoes, not more. Your feet won't mind a bit!

Tip 6 Take your time as you pack. Don't just throw things in the bottom of the backpack. If you rush, you will end up with things that you don't need on the trip.

Now that you know these tips for how to pack, it's time to load up your backpack and go!

Words with long o spelled oa, ow

coat	load	soak	soap	throw	yellow
goal	show				

Words with long e spelled ea, ee

breeze	feet	jeans	neat	real	three
clean	greed	leave	need	squeeze	week
each	heat				

Units 1–7 High Frequency Words

go	more	really	then	two
leave	one	say	three	use
make	or	second	together	when

Camp in the Snow

It's fun to backpack in the summer, but it's great to backpack when it snows! You can see nature like never before. A hush blankets the trails, and the landscape is so white that it gleams.

When you know how to camp, it is a treat to camp in the snow. But, you must know what to bring. Let me teach you how to beat the cold. When the wind blows, it can feel well below zero degrees. Cold can make a dream trip become a nightmare!

Don't leave home without a coat that keeps out the rain and snow. Coats made of down, or goose feathers, keep in heat so hikers can feel as warm as toast! Waterproof boots help, too. Special heels and soles protect the feet to make a hike fun and safe.

A hiker needs to sleep well. A warm sleeping bag is a must so you won't freeze. The best bags are filled with down. It is always painful to sleep on the ground. A thick foam pad beneath the bag will help.

It is important to eat well when you camp. You just can't beat a small gas stove. It can heat water for hot drinks like tea. You can prepare hot meals by pouring hot water into a bag that contains dried food. The sealed bags contain many different treats, like cheese, milk, beans, peas, grains, and meat. Just unseal the bag, and add water. Be sure to throw some G.O.R.P. in your backpack. G.O.R.P is a sweet treat made from good old raisins and peanuts!

So, if you want to camp and hike in the snow on your next holiday, plan away! You will not regret it!

Words with long e spelled ee, ea; long a spelled ai, ay; long o spelled oa, ow

always	coat	freeze	leave	raisins	teach
away	contains	gleams	meals	sealed	throw
beans	degrees	grains	meat	see	toasts
beat	dream	heat	needs	sleep	trails
below	eat	heels	painful	sleeping	treat
beneath	feel	holiday	peanuts	snow	treats
blows	feet	keep	peas	sweet	unseal
cheese	foam	keeps	rain	tea	

Units 1–7 High Frequency Words

always	down	important	next	want
below	eat	leave	or	water
by	from	many	out	when
different	home	make	small	without

Sailing Ships

The ship glides through the water and up to the dock. The sails flap and groan as the boat slows down, as if to protest the landing. Teens tie the vessel with ropes. Mothers and fathers wait ten feet away. Each student is greeted with a smile. The teens seem relaxed as the ship reaches the coast.

Each spring, at least 40 students sail ships on the open sea with SEA, Sea Education Association. In a lab at sea, students study fish, plankton, sea plants, and the sea itself. The teens finish the course at the end of May. By then, they have grown to love the sea.

Sailing can be difficult at times. The students had to clean the sailboat once a day. They had to scrub the decks and shine the brass railings each week. They helped prepare all the food for each meal.

Each day, a team of students had to keep watch for six hours. Being on watch was demanding. A student had to take the wheel and make sure the boat stayed on course. A helmsman had to pay attention each second. One mistake could mean a real problem.

Students had to watch for boats within three miles away. Between sunset and sunrise, students had to take turns looking for boats on the horizon.

By the end of the trip at sea, each student had learned to sail a huge ship, raise the main sails, and name 200 rope knots. These teens can say they are real sailors.

Words with long e spelled ee, ea; long a spelled ai, ay; long o spelled oa, ow

away	each	main	reaches	say	team
between	feet	May	real	sea	teens
boat	greeted	meal	sail	seamen	three
boats	groan	mean	sailboat	seem	wait
clean	grown	pay	sailing	slows	week
coast	keep	railings	sails	stayed	wheel
day	least	raise			

Units 1–7 High Frequency Words

all	learned	mother	open	study	through
by	love	once	say	then	watch
down	make	one	second	three	water
father					

They Hiked at a Lake

Mack and Zack liked to take long hikes at a lake. One of the best paths was at the west end of the lake. There, they hiked past a big grove of pine trees. Mack collected pinecones. He used them to make gifts for his mom and dad.

The next best path at the lake was the east end. There the boys hiked up a big hill. Zack collected rocks. He used them to line the paths at his home. His dad liked the way the stones looked along the paths.

One day, Mack and Zack needed a change. This time, they hiked past the big lake. They looked for pinecones but did not find any. They looked for rocks to collect but did not find pretty stones. They stopped to look at frogs as they jumped in the reeds. They looked at ducks as they dived in the water. They gazed at a stream as it flowed into the lake.

At three, Mack and Zack went home. Zack's dad asked about stones for his paths. Mack's mom asked to see more pinecones. Then the boys told Mack's mom and Zack's dad about the things they saw at the lake. Mack's mom said that friends were better than gifts and stone paths. Zack's dad agreed.

Words with verb ending -ed

asked	dived	gazed	jumped	needed	used
collected	flowed	hiked	liked	stopped	

Units 1–8 High Frequency Words

about	long	next	saw	three	water
find	make	one	then	use	were
home	more	said	there	was	

Glossary

The definitions in this glossary are for words as they are used in the Language and Content selections in this book.

angry (**āng**-grē) *adj. to feel mad*

Angry people sometimes shout.

buildings (**bil**-dings) *n. structures with windows and a roof, such as houses and offices; usually with more than one level*

There are tall **buildings** in San Francisco.

celebrate (**se**-luh-brāt) *v. to remember something in a happy and fun way*

People in Japan started to **celebrate** the Kite Festival in the 1500s.

cities (**sit**-ēz) *n. a place where many people live and work*

Copán is one old Maya **city** that still exists today.

cold (**cōld**) *adj. having little or no heat*

The water in the Arctic Ocean is so **cold** that it freezes.

colorful (**cul**-er-ful) *adj. to have many colors*

People at the festival fly **colorful** kites like this.

Glossary

colors (**kuh**-lers) *n. red, blue, yellow, and any other shade*

Vegetables can be many different **colors**.

cousins (**kuh**-zinz) *n. children of aunts and uncles*

There are many **cousins** in this family.

different (**di**-fur-rent) *adj. not the same; separate*

The players in the blue shirts play for a **different** team than the players in the white shirts.

enjoy (en-**joi**) *v. to take pleasure in; to feel joy*

The teams **enjoy** working together to fly the kites.

family (**fa**-muh-lē) *n. parents and their children*

Sometimes a **family** lives in a house.

first (**furst**) *adj. before anything else*

This person is **first** in line.

foods (**fudz**) *n. anything that you eat or drink*

There are many kinds of **foods** at a farmers' market.

friendship (**frend**-ship) *n. a feeling of closeness and kindness between people*

These children have a close **friendship**.

gracefully (grās-ful-lē) *adv. to move smoothly*

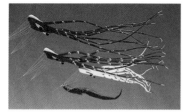

The kites flew **gracefully** through the air.

grandchildren (**grand**-chil-drun) *n. children of sons or daughters*

These **grandchildren** hug their grandmother.

groups (**grüps**) *n. different kinds of people, such as people from different lands*

People from different **groups** must learn to live together.

home (**hōm**) *n. the place where you live*

This is one kind of **home**.

hoped (**hōpt**) *v. wanted; wished*

The creators of Hand in Hand **hope** to show Jews and Palestinians that they are not that different after all.

hundreds (**hun**-dridz) *adj. the numbers between 100 and 1,000*

This rainforest has hundreds of trees.

learn (**lurn**) *v. to gain knowledge or skill*

These people **learn** about rocks.

live (**liv**) *v. to dwell; to have a home*

Some people in San Francisco **live** on steep streets.

Glossary

meet (**mēt**) *v. to see; to come upon*

These students **meet** at school.

neighborhood (**nā**-bôr-hood) *n. the areas where a group of people live near each other*

This map shows San Francisco's many **neighborhoods**.

next (**nekst**) *adv. following right after*

This person is **next** in line.

ocean (**ō**-shun) *n. the salt water that covers more than 70% of the earth*

The **ocean** is filled with living things.

parents (**par**-ents) *n. mothers and fathers*

These children sing with their **parents**.

people (**pē**-pul) *n. human beings*

There are many **people** to talk to in a neighborhood.

population (pop-yū-**lā**-shun) *n. the total number of people living in one area*

POPULATION OF COPÁN AND TIKAL	
City	Population
Copán	20,000
Tikal	50,000

Tikal has a higher **population** than Copán.

rock (**rok**) *n. a stone of any size*

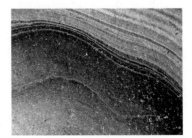

Some **rock** has layers.

scientist (sī-yun-tist) *n. a person who has expert knowledge about a science*

A **scientist** who knows about rocks is a geologist.

shapes (shāps) *n. forms, such as circles or squares*

People make bread in different **shapes**.

sizes (sīz-ez) *n. how big or small objects are*

Fruits can be many different **sizes**.

started (stär-ted) *v. came to be*

If something has started, it has begun. The teams have not **started** to fly their kites yet.

store (stôr) *n. a place where supplies and food are sold*

In 1849, many people came to San Francisco to open **stores** like this one.

study (stuh-dē) *v. to learn about; to think deeply about*

These people **study** by reading books.

surface (ser-fes) *n. the outer layer*

Here you see the oceans and landforms that cover the earth's **surface**.

Glossary **361**

Glossary

thousands (**thow**-zundz) *adj. the numbers between 1,000 and 999,999*

This pyramid was built **thousands** of years ago.

together (tuh-**geh**-thur) *adj. gathered in the same place*

When people are **together**, they are near each other.

town (**town**) *n. a place where people live; smaller than a city*

San Francisco began as a small **town** with some homes and a church.

two (**tō**) *adj. the amount that equals one plus one*

These are **two** Mayan people living today.

use (**yūz**) *v. to do something with*

Geologists **use** tools to take samples of rocks.

visit (**vih**-zit) *v. to go somewhere and stay for a short time*

He **visits** his parents at home.

warm (**warm**) *adj. having some heat; not hot and not cold*

The oceans near the equator are **warm**.

world (**wirld**) *n. the earth*

Our **world** is the planet Earth.

Index of Skills

VOCABULARY

Academic vocabulary 19, 49, 79, 109, 141, 171, 189, 201, 231, 250, 261
Antonyms 12–13, 135
Basic vocabulary
  Abbreviations 286–288
  Actions 39, 66, 246–249, 301–302
  Animals 199
  Cardinal numbers *See* Numbers.
  Careers 66–69, 74, 76–77, 290
  Clothing 190
  Colors 36–38, 297
  Commands 188, 281
  Communication words 9, 10
  Days of the week 200, 287
  Describing words 36–38, 189–190, 250, 296–300
  Family 158–159, 162–166, 171, 290
  Feelings 216–217, 219, 299
  Food 36–41, 46–49
  Habitats 186–187, 189, 198–200, 291
  Homes and household objects 160–161, 170, 291
  Landforms 189, 198–199, 201, 291
  Location words 126–128, 131, 291
  Money 96
  Months of the year 200, 287
  Negative words 48, 98, 221, 281
  Neighborhood 126–131, 291
  Numbers and basic operations 19, 94–95, 97, 99, 104–105, 109, 171, 231, 296, 300
  Order words 13, 16–17, 99, 296, 300
  Ordinal numbers *See* Order words.
  People 158–159, 162–166, 250 *See also* Careers and Family.
  Personal information 2–3, 8
  Plants 189, 198–199
  Question words 68, 78, 96, 278–280
  Rooms in a house *See* Homes and household objects.
  Sensory words 297–298
  Shapes 36–37, 48, 297
  Sizes 36–38, 297
  Social courtesies 4
  Tools 64–65, 69, 76–77
  Transportation 127, 129, 131, 188–189, 191, 196
  Weather 188–191, 201
Classify words 37–38, 40, 42–43, 49, 66, 69, 70, 76–77, 79, 97, 99, 100, 102–103, 126–128, 132, 158, 160–162, 189–190, 192, 198–199, 219, 222, 252–253
Content-area words *See* **Academic vocabulary**.
High frequency words 12–13, 15–17, 42–43, 45–47, 72–73, 75–77, 102–103, 105–107, 134–135, 137–139, 164–165, 167–169, 194–195, 197–199, 224–225, 227–229, 254–255, 257–260
Key Vocabulary 21, 30, 51, 60, 81, 90, 111, 120, 143, 152, 173, 182, 203, 212, 233, 242, 263, 272
Relate words 10, 12–13, 40–43, 70, 102–103, 105, 132–135, 137, 162–163, 167, 192–195, 197, 227, 252–253, 257
Synonyms 126, 134–135, 194–195
Word maps and webs 10, 40, 70–71, 81, 100, 132, 143, 162, 173, 192–193, 204, 222, 233, 252–253, 263

LANGUAGE FUNCTIONS

Ask and answer questions 68–69, 78, 96, 161, 170, 248
Ask for and give information 78, 126–128, 161, 170
Describe 36, 38, 189, 218, 250, 260
Express feelings 219
Express likes and dislikes 36
Express needs, wants, and thoughts 99
Express social courtesies 4
Give and carry out commands 188
Give information 8, 66, 97, 158, 160, 163, 190, 193, 253 *See also* **Ask for and give information**.
Have a discussion 163, 253
Order an item 8
Read aloud and recite 4,12–14, 19, 36, 42–44, 66, 72–74, 96, 102–104, 126, 130, 134–136, 158, 164–166, 188, 194–196, 218, 224–226, 248, 254–256
Retell a story 10–11, 40–41, 70–71, 100–101, 132–133, 222–223
Use the telephone 9

LANGUAGE PATTERNS AND STRUCTURES, MECHANICS, AND SPELLING

Action verbs 39, 66–67, 251, 301–302
Adjectives
  Descriptive 36–38, 189–190, 250, 296–300
  Number words 19, 94, 96–99, 102–105, 109, 171, 296, 300
  Possessive 295
  That appeal to the senses 297–299
Adverbs 248–249
Capitalization
  Beginning of sentences 18, 33, 63, 93, 281
  Pronoun *I* 155, 245
  Proper nouns 123, 154, 200, 215, 245, 275, 286–287, 289
Commands 188, 281
Common nouns 170, 289–292
Contractions 108, 140, 221, 281, 301
Exclamatory sentences 18, 280, 284
Irregular verbs 220, 304, 305
Modals
  can 68, 191, 303
  could 303
  may 303
  might 303
Negative sentences 48, 98, 108, 221, 281
Nouns
  Capitalization of 200, 286–287, 289
  Common 170, 289–292
  Possessive 230, 289
  Proper 200, 286–287, 289
  Singular and plural 170, 292
Phrases with
  like to 251
  want to 251
Plural nouns 170, 292
Plural verbs 6–7, 66, 96, 131, 159, 220, 251, 280, 301, 303, 304
Possessives
  Adjectives 295
  Nouns 230, 289
  Pronouns 295
Prepositions 126–128, 131
Progressive forms of verbs 249, 256–257, 303
Pronouns
  Agreement 4–5, 68, 294
  Object 295
  Possessive 295
  Singular and plural 4–5, 68, 294
  Subject 4–5, 295
Proper nouns 200, 286–287, 289
Punctuation
  Apostrophe 108, 140, 221, 230, 281, 289
  Exclamation mark 18, 280, 284
  Period 18, 283
  Question mark 68, 283
Questions
  with *yes/no* answers 68, 96, 280
  with *Who, What, When, Where* 78, 280
  with *Do* and *Does* 96
  with *How Much* or *How Many* 280
  with *How* 280
  with *Why* 280
Sentences 18, 131, 188, 280–282 *See also* **Questions, Commands**, and **Writing**.
Singular verbs 6–7, 39, 66–67, 96, 159, 220, 251, 301, 303, 304

Spelling 14–15, 44–45, 74–75, 104–105, 136–137, 166–167, 196–197, 226–227, 256–257
Statements 18, 280
  with infinitives 251
  with *There is/are* 131
Subject pronouns 4–5, 295
Subject-verb agreement 6–7, 39, 66–67, 96, 159, 220, 251, 282
Verbs
  Action 39, 66–67, 251, 301–302
  do/does 96
  Forms of *be* (*am, is, are, was, were*) 6–7, 220, 301
  Future tense 304
  has, have 159
  Irregular 220, 304–305
  Modals 68, 191, 303
  Past tense 129–130, 218, 220, 226–227, 301, 304
  Present tense 6–7, 67, 159, 301, 303
  Progressive forms of 249, 256–257, 303
  Singular and plural 6–7, 39, 66–67, 96, 159, 220, 251, 280, 301, 303, 304

Learning to Read

Associate sounds and spelling
  Short vowels
    /a/ *a* 14–15
    /e/ *e* 74–75
    /i/ *i* 44–45
    /o/ *o* 14–15
    /u/ *u* 44–45
  Short vowel phonograms
    –at, –an, –ad, –ag, –ap 14–15
    –et, –en, –ed 74–75
    –ig, –it, –in 44–45
    –og, –op, –ot 14–15
    –ut, –ug, –up 44–45
  Double consonants and *ck* 74–75
  Blends 104–105
  Digraphs
    /ch/ *ch, tch* 44–45, 104–105
    /ng/ *ng* 104–105
    /sh/ *sh* 74–75, 104–105
    /th/ *th* 104–105
    /TH/ *th* 104–105
  Long vowels
    /ā/ *a_e* 166–167
    ai, ay 196–197
    /ē/ *ee, ea* 196–197
    /ī/ *i_e* 166–167
    /ō/ *o_e* 166–167
    oa, ow 196–197
    /ū/ *u_e* 166–167
    /yōō/ *u_e* 166–167

Decodable text 15–17, 45–47, 75–77, 105–107, 137–139, 167–169, 197–199, 227–229, 257–260
Decoding strategies
  Blending 15, 45, 75, 105, 137, 167, 197, 227, 257
  Divide words into syllables 137, 197, 257
  Identify root words and endings 227, 257
  Sound out words 15, 45, 75, 105, 137, 167, 197, 227, 257
  Use letter patterns 105, 197
  Use word patterns 136–137, 167, 197
Divide words into syllables *See* **Decoding strategies**.
High frequency words 12–13, 42–43, 72–73, 102–103, 134–135, 164–165, 194–195, 224–225, 254–255
Inflectional endings
  -ed 129–130, 218, 226–227
  -ing 249, 256–257
  plurals 170
Multisyllabic words
  Compound words 197
  With inflectional endings 129–130, 170, 218, 226–227, 249, 256–257
  With two consonants between two vowels 137
Phonemic awareness 14, 44, 74, 104, 136, 166, 196, 226, 256
Phonics *See* **Associate sounds and spelling** and **Decoding strategies**.
Plurals *See* **Inflectional endings**.
Reading and spelling 14–15, 44–45, 74–75, 104–105, 136–137, 166–167, 196–197, 226–227, 256–257
Reading fluency See The Teacher's Edition for pages 16–17, 46–47, 76–77, 106–107, 138–139, 168–169, 198–199, 228–229, 258–259
Root words 226–227, 256–257
Sounds for *-ed* 227
Syllabication *See* **Multisyllabic words**.
Syllable types
  Open 136–137
  Closed 136–137
  Vowel team 196–197
Word analysis *See* **Associate sounds and spelling**, **Inflectional endings**, **Multisyllabic words**, and **Decoding strategies**.
Word building 15, 45, 75
Word families 14–15, 44–45
  See also **Decoding strategies**, Use letter and word patterns.

Word parts *See* **Root words**.
Word recognition *See* **High frequency words**.
Word sorts 12–13, 42–43, 102–103, 105, 134–135, 167, 194–195, 197, 227, 257
Word work 12–13, 15, 42–43, 45, 72–73, 75, 102–103, 105, 134–135, 137, 164–165, 167, 194–195, 197, 224–225, 227, 254–255, 257

Reading and Learning Strategies, Critical Thinking, and Comprehension

Activate prior knowledge 2–3, 34–35, 64–65, 94–95, 124–125, 156–157, 186–187, 216–217, 246–247
Analyze information 49, 79, 94, 231
Ask questions 68–69, 78, 96, 161, 170, 248
Build background 2–3, 20, 34–35, 50, 64–65, 80, 94–95, 110, 124–125, 141, 142, 156–157, 172, 186–187, 201, 202, 216–217, 232, 246–247, 262
Cause and effect 222–223, 228–229, 234, 242
Classify 49, 52, 60, 79, 94, 192–193, 198–199, 204, 212, 231, 252–253, 264, 272
Comparisons 79, 109, 231
Details 70–71, 76–77, 82, 90, 106–107, 112, 120, 132–133, 138–139, 141, 144, 152, 162–163, 168–169, 258–261
Draw conclusions 49, 79, 124–125, 231
Follow instructions 79, 231
Generate ideas 2–3, 35, 65, 95, 125, 157, 187, 201, 212, 217, 247
Graphic organizers
  Bar graphs 231
  Category charts 52, 60, 184, 272
  Cause-and-effect charts and maps 222–223, 228–229, 234, 242
  Charts *See* Category charts, Comparison charts, and Data charts.
  Clusters 70–71, 82, 90, 106–107, 144, 152, 192–193, 204, 214, 252–253
  Comparison charts 79, 109, 207
  Concept webs *See* Clusters.
  Data charts 109, 112, 120, 184, 207
  Diagrams 162–163, 168–169, 201
  Graphs *See* Bar graphs.

Lists 38, 49, 122, 274
Main idea diagrams
162–163, 168–169, 174, 182
Observation logs 79
Problem-and-solution charts
and maps 100–101
Semantic maps/charts *See*
Clusters and Word maps.
Sequence chains, charts, and
diagrams 10–11, 16–17, 22, 30,
40–41, 46–47, 132–133, 201
Tables 109, 111–112, 117,
120 *See also* Category
charts and Data charts.
Word maps 81, 143, 173, 233, 263
Word webs *See* Clusters.
Inferences 156–157, 216–217
Judgments 34–35
Main idea and details
162–163, 168–169, 174, 182
Make comparisons *See*
Comparisons.
Make observations
64–65, 79, 94–95
Plan 125
Problem and solution 100–101
Relate to personal
experience 2–3, 6, 34–36, 39,
49, 126, 157, 159, 188, 248
Sequence 10–11, 16–17, 21, 22, 39,
46–47, 246–247
Signal words 16–17
Solve problems 19, 171
Steps in a process 40–41, 201
Strategies for learning
language 278
Summarize 30, 60, 90, 120,
152, 182, 201, 212, 242, 272
Text features
Bar graphs 231, 238
Diagrams 201, 209–210
Callouts 84–86
Headings 54–59, 114–119, 146–148,
150, 176–178, 180, 266–271
Maps 110, 141, 143, 146,
150, 237, 261, 266
Photos and captions 54–59, 83–89,
112–119, 175–181, 206–211, 269–270
Picture charts and category
labels 49, 52–58
Political maps 261–262, 266
Tables 109, 111–112, 117, 120, 207
Text structures *See*
Text Structures and
Literary Concepts.
Visualize 38, 66, 161

TEXT STRUCTURES AND
LITERARY CONCEPTS
Article 109, 141, 144–145, 198–199,
234–235, 258–259, 261, 264–265
Career sketch 40–41
Cartoon 98, 106–108, 228–229
Description 189
Essay 192–193
Expository text *See* **Nonfiction**.
Fantasy 70–71
Fiction 10–11, 16–17, 46–47, 70–71
Historical fiction 100–101
How-to article 40–41
Interview 231, 250, 274
Journal 153, 222–223
Letter or note 31
Narrative poetry 136, 196, 226
News article 138–139
Nonfiction 22–23, 40–41, 52–53,
82–83, 109, 138–139, 141, 144–145,
162–163, 192–193, 198–199, 201,
204–205, 234–235, 250, 252–253,
258–259, 261, 264–265
Order form 8
Personal narrative
112–113, 168–169, 174–175
Photo essay 22–23, 162–163,
192–193, 252–253
Poetry 4, 36, 74, 96, 136,
166, 188, 196, 226, 248
Postcard 189
Problem and solution 100–101
Rap 74
Realistic fiction 10–11,
16–17, 46–47
Repetition 14, 36, 44, 74,
104, 136, 248, 256
Respond to literature 11, 17, 30,
41, 47, 60, 71, 77, 90, 101, 107, 120,
133, 139, 152, 163, 169, 182, 193, 199,
212, 223, 229, 242, 253, 260, 272
Rhyme 4, 14, 44, 66, 74, 96, 104, 126,
136, 158, 166, 188, 196, 218, 226
Rhythm 4, 14, 36, 44, 66, 74,
96, 104, 126, 136, 158, 166,
188, 196, 218, 226, 248, 256
Science article 198, 201
Song 14, 44, 66, 104, 126,
158, 196, 218, 247
Travel article 144–145

LISTENING, SPEAKING,
VIEWING, AND
REPRESENTING
Listening 2–4, 8, 10, 12–14, 16–18,
22, 33, 34–36, 38, 40, 42– 44, 46–47,
52, 63, 64–66, 69, 70, 72–74, 76–77,
82, 93, 94–96, 99, 100, 102–104,
106–107, 109, 112, 123, 124–126,
128, 132, 134–136, 138–139, 141,
144, 155, 156–158, 160, 162, 164–166,
168–169, 174, 185, 186–188, 190,
192, 194–196, 198–199, 201, 204,
215, 216–218, 219, 222, 224–226,
228–229, 234, 245, 246–248, 250,
252, 254–256, 261, 264, 275
Non-verbal communication 4,
67, 69, 128, 160, 219, 248
Representing 4, 9–11, 35, 38,
40–41, 49, 60–65, 69–71, 76–77,
79, 93, 100–101, 123, 125, 128,
132–133, 138–139, 154, 157, 160–163,
168–169, 185, 192–193, 198–199, 201,
212–217, 219, 222–223, 228–229,
231, 245, 248, 252–253, 261, 275
Speaking 2–14, 16–17, 19, 33, 34–44,
46–47, 63, 64–74, 93, 94–104, 123,
124–136, 155, 156–166, 185, 186–196,
215, 216–226, 231, 245, 246–256, 275
Viewing 2–3, 34–35, 64–65,
69, 93, 94–95, 123, 124–125,
131, 156–157, 186–187, 216–217,
230, 245, 246–247, 275

WRITING
Audience 33, 63, 93, 123, 155,
185, 215, 245, 275, 314
Blog 273
Collect ideas 32, 62, 92, 122,
154, 184, 214, 244, 274, 314
Comparisons 183
Description 37, 61, 153, 183, 189,
213, 230, 243, 248–250, 260, 273
Details 154, 184, 244, 315
Directions 61
Draft 32, 62, 92, 122, 154,
184, 214, 244, 274, 316
Edit and proofread 33, 63, 93,
123, 155, 185, 215, 245, 275, 318
Effective sentences 18,
68, 280–282
E-mail 31
Evaluate your writing 33, 63, 93,
123, 155, 185, 215, 245, 275, 319
Expository writing 38, 91, 121, 213
Expressive writing 31, 153,
189, 243, 273
Fact sheet 121
Family description 183
Friendly letter *See*
Letters and notes.
Handwriting 306
How-to card 61
Interview 91, 231, 250, 274

Journal page 153
Labels 36, 66, 158
Letters and notes 31
List 38, 49, 122, 274
Memory story 243
Narrative writing 243
Opinions 183, 213, 273
Order form 8
Organization
  In logical order 92
  In sequential order 39, 61, 154, 244
  To make comparisons 184
Persuasive writing 213
Postcard 189
Prewrite 32, 62, 92, 122, 154,
  184, 214, 244, 274, 314
Proofread *See* **Edit** and **Proofread**.
Publish 33, 63, 93, 123, 155,
  185, 215, 245, 275, 319
Purpose
  To describe 37, 61, 153, 183, 189,
    213, 243, 248–250, 260, 272–273
  To entertain 243
  To express your thoughts and
    feelings 31, 153, 183, 213, 243, 273
  To inform or explain 31, 61,
    91, 121, 183, 213, 243, 273
  To learn 4–8, 18, 36–39, 48, 66–69,
    78, 91, 96–99, 108, 122, 126–131,
    140, 158–161, 170, 188–191,
    200, 218–221, 230, 248–251
  To persuade 213
Questions and answers 68–69,
  78, 92, 127–128, 170, 274
Revise
  Add details 33, 63, 93, 155,
    185, 215, 316
  Delete unrelated
    information 123, 245, 275
Sentences 5–7, 18, 32, 37, 39, 48,
  62, 67, 92, 97–99, 108, 122, 127–131,
  140, 159–161, 184, 191, 200, 214,
  218–221, 230, 244, 249, 251, 260, 274
Topic
  Choose a Topic 32, 62, 92,
    122, 184, 214, 244, 274, 314
Travel guide 213
Word choice 38, 189
Writing checklists 33, 63, 93,
  123, 155, 185, 215, 245, 275
Writing projects 31, 61, 91,
  121, 153, 183, 213, 243, 273
Writing process 314

RESEARCH SKILLS

Books 320–329
Charts 49, 109
Conduct research 79, 231, 320
Content area connections
  Language Arts and Literature
    10–11, 70–71, 132–133, 222–223
  Mathematics 19, 79, 171, 231
  Science 49, 79, 201
  Social Studies 40–41, 100–101,
    109, 141, 162–163, 192–193,
    250, 252–253, 261
Diagrams 49, 201
Gather information 49, 79,
  92, 94–95, 122, 315, 320
Graphs 231
Maps 141, 261, 328
Photographs 49, 79,
  109, 141, 171, 201
Take notes 92, 122, 184, 244, 274

Acknowledgments, continued from page ii

iii Gail Mooney/Masterfile. **iii** (bl) Tom Bean/Terra/Corbis. **iii** (b) Panoramic Images/Getty Images. **iii** (br) ©Adam Burton/Photolibrary/Getty Images. **xvi** (b) Rolf Kopfle/ KOPFL. **xvii** (t) Ron Watts/Corbis. **002** (fgd) Cartesia. **002** (fgd) NGS/HB/Liz Garza-Williams. **004** (c) NGS/HB/Liz Garza-Williams. **005** (tl) David Young-Wolff/PhotoEdit. **005** (cl) NGS/HB/Liz Garza-Williams. **005** (c) NGS/HB/Digital Studios. **005** (cl) NGS/HB/Liz Garza-Williams. **005** (c) NGS/HB/Liz Garza-Williams. **005** (cr) NGS/HB/Liz Garza-Williams. **005** (br) NGS/HB/Liz Garza-Williams. **005** (cr) NGS/HB/New Century Graphics. **006** (tl) NGS/HB/Liz Garza-Williams. **006** (c) NGS/HB/Liz Garza-Williams. **007** (tl) NGS/HB/Liz Garza-Williams. **007** (bl) NGS/HB/Liz Garza-Williams. **007** (br) NGS/HB/Liz Garza-Williams. **008** (c) NGS/HB/New Century Graphics. **009** ©Dusan Jankovic/ Shutterstock. **009** (c) NGS/HB/Liz Garza-Williams. **010** bkgd Creatas/Jupiterimages. **010** (fgd) NGS/HB. **010** bkgd Urban CGI/Alamy. **012** (tr) NGS/HB/Liz Garza-Williams. **014** (b) Ancil Nance/Getty Images. **014** (c) Ellen Denuto/ The Image Bank/Getty Images. **014** (bl) NGS/HB. **014** (br) NGS/HB. **014** (bl) NGS/HB/New Century Graphics. **015** (b) NGS/HB/Barbara Kelley. **016** bkgd YinYang/iStockphoto. com. **016** (cl) NGS/HB. **016** (c) NGS/HB. **016** (cr) NGS/HB/ Liz Garza-Williams. **017** (bc) NGS/HB/Digital Studios. **017** (tl) NGS/HB/Liz Garza-Williams. **017** (br) NGS/HB/Liz Garza-Williams. **017** (bl) Siede Preis/Photodisc/Getty Images. **017** (b) Siede Preis/Photodisc/Getty Images. **018** (tl) NGS/HB/Liz Garza-Williams. **019** (cl) Artville Produce. **020** (cl) Baerbel Schmidt/Stone/Getty Images. **020** (br) Inti St Clair/Digital Vision/Getty Images. **020** (tr) Elie Bernager/Stone/Getty Images. **021** (tl) David Young-Wolff/ Photographer's Choice/. **021** (cl) David Young-Wolff/ Stone/ Getty Images. **021** (bl) Hola Images/Getty Images. **021** (cr) John-Francis Bourke/The Image Bank/Getty Images. **021** (tr) NGS/HB/Luisa Henoo. **022** (r) Elie Bernager/Stone/ Getty Images. **022** bkgd NGS/HB/GGS. **024** (fgd) David Young-Wolff/ Stone/Getty Images. **025** (fgd) Inti St Clair/ Digital Vision/Getty Images. **025** bkgd NGS/HB/GGS. **026** (fgd) Baerbel Schmidt/Stone/Getty Images. **027** bkgd NGS/ HB/GGS. **027** (fgd) Michael Newman/PhotoEdit. **028** (t) Hola Images/Getty Images. **028** bkgd NGS/HB/GGS. **028** (c) Image Source/Jupiter Images. **029** (r) Amos Morgan/ Photodisc/Getty Images. **029** (tl) SW Productions/ Photodisc/Getty Images. **031** (b) Pat Doyle/Encyclopedia/ Corbis. **032** (b) PhotoDisc/Getty Images. **034** (c) G.K. & Vikki Hart/PhotoDisc/Getty Images. **034** (fgd) NGS/HB/ Ray Godfrey. **036** (c) NGS/HB/Lori Loestoeter. **037** (c) Artville Food Icons. **037** (cl) Artville Produce. **037** (b) Artville Produce. **037** (tl) Artville Produce. **037** (c) Artville Produce. **037** (t) NGS/HB/New Century Graphics. **037** (t) NGS/HB/New Century Graphics. **037** (tr) NGS/HB/New Century Graphics. **037** (cr) NGS/HB/New Century Graphics. **037** (bl) NGS/HB/New Century Graphics. **037** (br) NGS/HB/New Century Graphics. **037** (b) Stockbyte/ Getty Images. **038** (c) NGS/HB/Tom Casmer. **039** (tl) NGS/ HB/Liz Garza-Williams. **039** (c) NGS/HB/Liz Garza-Williams. **040** (r) NGS/Andy Adams. **040** (c) NGS/HB. **041** (fgd) NGS/Andy Adams. **042** (tr) Ian O'Leary/Stone/Getty Images. **042** (cr) NGS/Rachel Geswaldo. **043** (cr) NGS/ Rachel Geswaldo. **044** (c) NGS/HB/Lori Loestoeter. **044** (b) NGS/HB/New Century Graphics. **044** (br) Nick Koudis/ Photodisc/Getty Images. **044** (bl) John A. Rizzo/ Photodisc/Getty Images. **044** (b) Siede Preis/Photodisc/ Getty Images. **044** (br) Nick Koudis/Photodisc/Getty Images. **045** (b) NGS/HB/Barbara Kelley. **046** (fgd) Finn O'Hara/Getty Images. **046** (r) NGS/HB/GGS. **047** (b) NGS/ HB/Liz Garza-Williams. **047** (tl) NGS/HB/Liz Garza-Williams. **047** (br) NGS/HB/Liz Garza-Williams. **047** (bl) Jules Frazier/Photodisc/Getty Images. **047** (b) C Squared Studios/Photodisc/Getty Images. **048** (b) Artville Produce. **048** (cl) Artville fast food. **048** (tl) NGS/HB/Norm Bendell. **048** (cr) Siede Preis/Photodisc/Getty Images. **048** (br) C Squared Studios/Photodisc/Getty Images. **048** (bl) Stockbyte/Getty Images. **049** (t) NGS/Bud Endress. **049** John E. Kelly/Stone/Getty Images. **049** (t) ©Lew Robertson/Brand X Pictures/Getty Images. **049** ©Dennis Gottlieb/FoodPix/Getty Images. **049** (tc) ©PhotoDisc/ Getty Images. **049** (tc) ©Multi-bits/Photodisc/Getty Images. **049** (t) PhotoDisc/Getty Images. **050** (cr) Purestock/Getty Images. **050** (c) Hugh Threlfall/Alamy. **050** (cl) Tim Hill/Alamy. **050** (br) Chuck Savage/Cusp/ Corbis. **050** Mikael Andersson/Nordic Photos/Getty Images. **050** (tr) Jonathan Kantor/The Image Bank/Getty Images. **050** ©aleaimage/E+/Getty Images. **050** ©aleaimage/E+/Getty Images. **051** (tr) David Young-Wolff/ PhotoEdit. **051** (bl) Ariel Skelley/Taxi/Getty Images. **051** (c) Burazin/ Photographer's Choice/Getty Images. **051** (tr) Simone Metz/ StockFood Creative/Getty Images. **051** (cr) Siede Preis/Photodisc/Getty Images. **051** (cr) Lusoimages/ iStockphoto.com. **051** (cl) Image Source/Jupiterimages. **052** (bc) Tim Hill/Alamy. **052** (tr) Jonathan Kantor/The Image Bank/Getty Images. **052** Mikael Andersson/Nordic Photos/Getty Images. **053** (t) Hugh Threlfall/Alamy. **053** (bc) Purestock/Getty Images. **053** ©aleaimage/E+/Getty Images. **053** bkgd NGS/HB. **054** (cl) Tom Bean/Terra/ Corbis. **054** (l) NGS/HB/GGS. **054** (b) Image Source/ Jupiterimages. **054** (t) Image Source/Jupiter Images. **054** (t) Image Source/Jupiterimages. **054** (tl) Image Source/ Jupiter Images. **054** ©Jupiterimages. **055** (tr) Digital Vision/Alamy. **055** (t) lee hacker/Alamy. **055** (tl) Stockbyte/ Alamy. **055** (c) Wayne Hutchinson/Alamy. **055** (t) Maximilian Stock Ltd/photocuisine/Corbis. **055** (b) Rosemary Calvert/ Photographer's Choice/Getty Images. **055** (l) NGS/HB/GGS. **055** (cr) Exactostock / SuperStock. **055** (cr) Purestock/Getty Images. **056** (t) Stockbyte/Alamy. **056** (tl) Burazin/ Photographer's Choice/Getty Images. **056** (tr) Foodcollection /Getty Images. **056** (br) Christina Peters/StockFood Creative/Getty Images. **056** (t) Siede Preis/Photodisc/Getty Images. **056** (t) NGS/HB/GGS. **056** (t) Lusoimages/iStockphoto.com. **056** (cl) ©Vincenzo Lombardo/Photodisc/Getty Images. **057** (tl) MaRoDee Photography/Alamy. **057** (br) Simone Metz/ StockFood Creative/Getty Images. **057** (t) NGS/HB/GGS. **057** (tr) Jostein Hauge/iStockphoto. **057** (t) Kevin Russ/ iStockphoto. **057** (t) Image Source/Jupiter Images. **057** (t) Purestock/Jupiter Images. **057** (c) David Young-Wolff/ PhotoEdit. **058** (tl) Aleksandr Ugorenkov/Alamy. **058** (t) Geoffrey Kidd/Alamy. **058** (cr) Wilmar Photography/Alamy. **058** (cl) Lynda Richardson/Terra/Corbis. **058** (t) Eising/ Photodisc/Getty Images. **058** (t) Renee Comet/ StockFood Creative /Getty Images. **058** (t) Stockbyte/Getty Images. **058** (t) NGS/HB/GGS. **058** (tr) Jernej Borovin ek/ iStockphoto. **058** (c) Chuck Savage/Cusp/Corbis. **061** (c) NGS/HB/GGS. **063** (br) NGS/HB/Bud Endress. **064** (tl) Angela Maynard/PhotoDisc/Getty Images. **064** (c) Squared Studios/Photodisc/Getty Images. **064** (c) C. Borland/ PhotoDisc/Getty Images. **064** (bl) Bob Rowan/Progressive Image/Historical/Corbis. **064** (br) Gabe Palmer/ Cusp/ Corbis. **064** David Hiller/Photodisc/Getty Images. **064** (tr) Dick Luria/Taxi/Getty Images. **064** (br) Hugh Sitton/Stone/ Getty Images. **064** (c) Michael Krasowitz/Taxi/Getty Images. **064** ©Digital Vision/Alamy. **064** (fgd) Stephen Derr/Getty Images. **064** (c) Stephen Derr/Stone/Getty Images. **064** (tl) Jack Star/PhotoDisc/Getty Images. **064** (tl) Joshua Ets-Hokin/ Photodisc/Getty Images. **064** (fgd) NGS/HB/Digital Stock/New York City. **064** (cl) PhotoDisc/ Getty Images. **064** (c) Adam Crowley/ Photodisc/Getty Images. **064** (bl) Don Tremain/Photodisc/Getty Images. **064** (tc) Scott T. Baxter/Photodisc/Getty Images. **064** (bl) PhotoDisc/Getty Images. **064** (br) Adam Crowley/ Photodisc/Getty Images. **064** (cr) Adam Crowley/ Photodisc/Getty Images. **064** (tr) Arthur S. Aubry/ Photodisc/Getty Images. **064** (bl) Skip Nall/ Photodisc/ Getty Images. **064** (b) Arthur S. Aubry/Photodisc/Getty Images. **064** (tr) PhotoDisc/Getty Images. **064** (tl) David Buffington/Photodisc/Getty Images. **064** (bc) Arthur S. Aubry/Photodisc/Getty Images. **064** (cr) Hisham Ibrahim/ Photodisc/Getty Images. **064** (cl) Keith Brofsky/Photodisc/ Getty Images. **064** (t) PhotoDisc/Getty Images. **064** (tl) Don Tremain/Photodisc/Getty Images. **064** (cl) Keith Brofsky/ Photodisc/Getty Images. **064** (tl) PhotoDisc/Getty Images. **064** (c) "David Young-Wolff/PhotoEdit Inc." **064** (cr) Russell Illig/PhotoDisc/Getty Image. **064** Stockbyte/ Getty Images. **064** (tr) Stockbyte/Getty Images. **066** (bc) Ed Bock/Cusp/Corbis. **066** (cl) Andrea Pistolesi/ The Image Bank/Getty Images. **066** (tl) David Young-Wolff/Stone/ Getty Images. **066** (cl) ©Digital Vision/Alamy. **066** (b) NGS/HB. **066** (bl) Paul Conklin/PhotoEdit. **066** (br) Jeff Greenberg/PhotoEdit. **066** (br) Stockbyte/Getty Images. **067** (tl) JDC/LWA/Cusp/Corbis. **067** ©Angelo Cavalli/Tips Images/age fotostock. **067** (bc) Ancil Nance/Getty Images. **067** (cl) ©Thinkstock Images/Comstock Images/Getty Images. **067** (bl) David Toase/PhotoDisc/Getty Images. **067** (br) Michelle D. Bridwell/PhotoEdit. **068** (cr) "Jose Luis Pelaez Inc/Cusp/Corbis." **068** (cl) © Steve Chenn/ Corbis. **068** (tl) NGS/HB/Liz Garza-Williams. **068** (bl) Jonathan Nourok / PhotoEdit. **068** (br) "Bonnie Kamin/ PhotoEdit IncPhotoEdit." **068** (c) Dana White/PhotoEdit. **068** (bc) Michael Newman/PhotoEdit. **069** (cl) NGS/HB/ Robert Hynes. **069** (cr) NGS/HB/Robert Hynes. **070** (fgd) NGS/HB. **070** bkgd Mark Garlick / Science Source/Photo Researchers. **071** (b) NGS/HB/Micheal Slack. **072** (t) Ales Fevzer/ Documentary/Corbis. **072** (c) Rachel Geswaldo. **073** (b) NGS/Rachel Geswaldo. **074** (bl) David Frazier/ Spirit/Corbis. **074** Phillip Wallick/Corbis. **074** (cl) Kevin Laubacher/Taxi/Getty Images. **074** (b) NGS/HB/John Paul Endress. **074** (bl) NGS/HB—Digital Stock/transportation. **074** (tr) PhotoDisc/Getty Images. **074** (tc) PhotoDisc/Getty Images. **074** (bl) PhotoDisc/Getty Images. **074** (br) PhotoDisc/Getty Images. **074** (br) PhotoDisc/Getty Images. **074** (bc) Tony Freeman/PhotoEdit. **074** (l) Stockbyte/Getty Images. **075** (b) NGS/HB/Barbara Kelley. **076** (t) Superstudio/ The Image Bank/Getty Images. **076** (cl) NGS/ HB/John Paul Endress. **076** (br) Rudi Von Briel / PhotoEdit. **077** (fgd) Mark Weiss/Taxi/Getty Images. **078** (tl) Rudi Von Briel / PhotoEdit. **079** (tc) NGS/HB/Liz Garza-Williams. **079** (tr) NGS/HB/Liz Garza-Williams. **079** (t) NGS/HB/Liz Garza-Williams. **079** (r) NGS/HB/Liz Garza-Williams. **079** (c) NGS/HB/New Century Graphics. **079** (tl) NGS/HB/New Century Graphics. **080** (tr) BILL HATCHER/National Geographic Stock. **080** (cl) Grant Faint/The Image Bank / Getty Images. **080** (br) Royalty-Free/Corbis. **081** (cl) James L. Amos/ Documentary/Corbis. **081** (bl) Richard T. Nowitz/ Terra/Corbis. **081** (cr) "Michael Newman/PhotoEdit Inc." **081** (tl) Will Hart/PhotoEdit. **081** (cr) ©Robert Adrian Hillman/Shutterstock. **082** (r) BILL HATCHER/National Geographic Stock. **084** bkgd Grant Faint/The Image Bank / Getty Images. **084** (t) ©Adam Burton/Photolibrary/Getty Images. **085** (b) ©CLM/Shutterstock. **086** (br) Tom Bean/ Corbis. **086** (br) NGS/HB. **086** (tr) Robert Marien/Corbis. **087** (fgd) Robert Glusic/Corbis. **088** (cr) Albert J. Copley/ Stockbyte/Getty Images. **088** (bl) Steve Cole/Photodisc/ Getty Images. **088** (tr) MarcelClemens. **089** (b) James L. Amos/ Documentary/Corbis. **089** (t) Siede Preis/Photodisc/ Getty Images. **089** (tr) Siede Preis/Photodisc/Getty Images. **091** (b) PhotoDisc/Getty Images. **091** (t) NGS/HB/Liz Garza-Williams. **094** (tc) Corbis Images/PictureQuest. **094** (bl) Corbis Images/PictureQuest. **094** (cr) Corbis Images/ PictureQuest. **094** (cr) Image Ideas Inc./PictureQuest. **094** (br) Kent Knudson/PictureQuest. **094** (cl) Nick Koudis/ PictureQuest. **094** (c) PhotoLink. **094** (tl) S. Meltzer/ PhotoLink/Getty. **096** (cl) NGS/HB/Liz Garza-Williams. **096** (c) Ray McVay/PhotoDisc/Getty Images. **097** (cl) Alan Pappe/RubberBall Productions/PictureQuest. **097** (cr) Corbis Images/PictureQuest. **097** (tc) Michael McQueen/ Stone/Getty Images. **097** (bl) NGS/HB. **098** (br) Dag Sundberg/ The Image Bank /Getty Images. **098** (t) NGS/HB/ Norm Bendell. **099** NGS/HB/Norm Bendell. **100** (r) Robert Harding Picture Library Ltd/Alamy. **100** credit unknown. **102** (tr) David Young-Wolff/PhotoEdit. **102** (br) NGS/ Rachel Geswaldo. **104** (tr) Corbis Images/PictureQuest. **104** (c) Jake Rajs/ Stone/Getty Images. **104** (bc) NGS/HB/ John Paul Endress. **104** (tl) ©Jeremy Swinborne/ Shutterstock. **104** (br) C Squared Studios/Photodisc/Getty Images. **104** (tc) PhotoDisc/Getty Images. **104** (bc) Photodisc/Getty Images/Houghton Mifflin Harcourt. **104** (cr) Jules Frazier/Getty Images. **104** (bl) Ryan McVay/ Photodisc/Getty Images. **104** (cl) Siede Preis/Photodisc/ Getty Images. **104** (tr) PhotoLink/PhotoDisc/PictureQuest. **104** (c) Stockbyte/Getty Images. **106** (tr) ©Alan Schein Photography/Corbis/. **106** (tr) Gregor Schuster/ Flirt/ Corbis. **106** (br) Paul Colangelo/Terra/Corbis. **106** (cl) Stockbyte/Getty Images. **107** (t) NGS/HB/Norm Bendell. **108** (tl) NGS/HB/Norm Bendell. **109** (cr) Jeremy Horner/ Corbis. **109** (c) ©AND Inc/Shutterstock. **109** (cl) Harvey Lloyd/Taxi/Getty Images. **110** (tr) KENNETH GARRETT/ National Geographic Image Collection. **110** (c) KENNETH GARRETT/National Geographic Stock. **110** (br) NGS/HB/ National Geographic Maps. **111** (tr) Nic Cleave Photography / Alamy. **111** (bl) Danny Lehman/ Documentary Value/Corbis. **111** (tl) NGS/HB/National Geographic Maps. **111** (cr) Gabriela Medina/Superstock. **113** (c) KENNETH GARRETT/National Geographic Image Collection. **114** (tl) J Marshall - Tribaleye Images / Alamy. **114** (c) KENNETH GARRETT/National Geographic Stock. **114** (tr) NGS/HB/National Geographic Maps. **115** (c) Mural reconstruction by Heather Hurst. **116** (c) Jordi Camí/Age Fotostock. **116** (tl) J Marshall - Tribaleye Images / Alamy. **117** (t) ©Tom Schwabel/Flickr/Getty Images. **117** (cr) NGS/HB/National Geographic Maps. **118** (tr) NGS/HB/ National Geographic Maps. **118** (tl) J Marshall - Tribaleye Images / Alamy. **118** (c) Gabriela Medina/Superstock. **119** (t) Jorge Silva/Reuters. **122** (cr) David Young-Wolff/Stone/ Getty Images. **124** (bl) Ed Young/AgStock Images/Corbis. **124** (c) Getty Images/ Digital Stock Animals. **124** (tl) NGS/ HB. **124** NGS/HB/Liz Garza-Williams. **124** (br) Marty Honig/Photodisc/Getty Images. **124** (bl) PhotoDisc/Getty Images. **124** (tr) C Squared Studios/Photodisc/Getty Images. **124** (t) John Wang/Photodisc/Getty Images. **126** (cl) NGS/HB/Norm Bendell. **127** (bl) Chris Birck. **127** (bc) NGS/Chris Birck. **127** (c) Kevin Fleming/Corbis. **127** (tl) Courtesy of Brown Publishing Network. **127** (tc) Courtesy of Brown Publishing Network. **127** (tc) Courtesy of Brown Publishing Network. **127** (tr) Courtesy of Brown Publishing Network. **127** (br) Courtesy of Brown Publishing Network. **127** (bc) David Young-Wolff/Stone/Getty Images. **127** (c) Susan Van Etten/PhotoEdit. **128** (c) NGS/HB/Norm Bendell. **129** (tl) NGS/HB/Liz Garza-Williams. **129** (tc) NGS/HB/Liz Garza-Williams. **129** (cl) NGS/HB/Liz Garza-Williams. **129** (cl) NGS/HB/Liz Garza-Williams. **129** (cr) NGS/HB/Liz Garza-Williams. **129** (cr) NGS/HB/Liz Garza-Williams. **129** (bl) NGS/HB/Liz Garza-Williams— Royalty-Free. **129** (bl) NGS/HB/Liz Garza-Williams— Royalty-Free. **129** (br) NGS/HB/Liz Garza-Williams. **129** (br) NGS/HB/Liz Garza-Williams. **130** (br) Rob Gage/Taxi/ Getty Images. **130** (tl) David Young-Wolff/PhotoEdit. **131** (bl) Joseph Sohm; Visions of America/Encyclopedia/ CORBIS. **131** (tl) Michael Newman/PhotoEdit. **131** (br) "PhotoEdit Inc." **132** (r) Mario Tama/ Getty Images News / Getty Images. **132** (r) NGS/HB—publisher owned art. **134** (tr) John A. Rizzo/Photodisc/Getty Images. **134** (tr) NGS/ Rachel Geswaldo. **135** (cr) NGS/Rachel Geswaldo—work for hire art. **136** (tl) Digital Stock New York City. **136** (c) NGS/HB/Liz Garza-Williams. **136** (bc) C Squared Studios/ Photodisc/Getty Images. **138** (r) Peter M. Fisher/ Flirt/ Corbis. **138** (cl) Tim Ridley/Dorling Kindersley/Getty Images. **138** (cl) Brand X Pictures/Jupiterimages. **138** (tr) Don Farrall/Digital Vision/Getty Images. **138** (cl) NGS/HB/ Liz Garza-Williams. **138** (tc) NGS/HB/Liz Garza-Williams. **138** (cr) NGS/HB/Liz Garza-Williams. **139** (cl) NGS/HB/Liz Garza-Williams. **139** (tr) NGS/HB/Liz Garza-Williams. **140** (tl) Bonnie Kamin/PhotoEdit. **141** (bc) Colin Garratt; Milepost 92 _/ Historical/CORBIS. **141** (tr) Ryan McVay/ Photodisc/Getty Images. **141** (bc) NGS/HB—publisher owned art. **141** (tl) NGS/HB—publisher owned art. **141** (cl) NGS/HB—publisher owned art. **142** (cl) Bill Heinsohn/ Photographer's Choice /Getty Images. **142** (tr) John Kelly/ Stone /Getty Images. **142** Gail Mooney/Masterfile. **143** (tr) Ellen Isaacs/Alamy. **143** (cl) NGS/Michael Hortens. **143** (tl) Age fotostock/SuperStock. **143** (bl) Sal Maimone/ SuperStock. **143** (cr) ©Advertising Archive/Courtesy Everett Collection. **144** (r) John Kelly/ Stone /Getty Images. **146** (b) NGS/Michael Hortens—publisher owned art. **146** (tr) Sal Maimone/SuperStock. **147** (b) ©Huntington Library / SuperStock/1060-896. **147** (cr) Photolibrary/Index Stock. **147** (tr) ©Advertising Archive/Courtesy Everett Collection.

368

Common Core State Standards

Inside Fundamentals is designed to build foundational skills to help you succeed in middle school. The lessons meet the Common Core Anchor standards in all strands. Additional correlations are provided for grade-level Reading Foundational Skills and Language standards to show how those specific foundational skills are covered.

Unit 1   Glad to Meet You!

Language Development

SE Pages	Lesson	Code	Standards Text
2–3	Unit Launch	• CCRA.SL.2	Integrate and evaluate information presented in diverse media and formats, including visually, quantitatively, and orally.
4	Language: Exchange Greetings and Good-byes	• CCRA.SL.1	Prepare for and participate effectively in a range of conversations and collaborations with diverse partners, building on others' ideas and expressing their own clearly and persuasively.
		• CCRA.SL.6	Adapt speech to a variety of contexts and communicative tasks, demonstrating command of formal English when indicated or appropriate.
5	Grammar: Pronouns		Demonstrate command of the conventions of standard English grammar and usage when writing or speaking.
		• L.1.1d	Use personal, possessive, and indefinite pronouns (e.g., *I, me, my; they, them, their, anyone, everything*).
		• L.1.1j	Produce and expand complete simple and compound declarative, interrogative, imperative, and exclamatory sentences in response to prompts.
6	Grammar: Present Tense Verbs: *Am* and *Are*	• CCRA.SL.1	Prepare for and participate effectively in a range of conversations and collaborations with diverse partners, building on others' ideas and expressing their own clearly and persuasively.
		• CCRA.SL.6	Adapt speech to a variety of contexts and communicative tasks, demonstrating command of formal English when indicated or appropriate.
		• CCRA.L.2	Demonstrate command of the conventions of standard English capitalization, punctuation, and spelling when writing.
			Demonstrate command of the conventions of standard English grammar and usage when writing or speaking.
		• L.1.1c	Use singular and plural nouns with matching verbs in basic sentences (e.g., *He hops; We hop*).
		• L.1.1j	Produce and expand complete simple and compound declarative, interrogative, imperative, and exclamatory sentences in response to prompts.
		• L.3.1f	Ensure subject-verb and pronoun-antecedent agreement.
7	Grammar: Present Tense Verbs: *Is* and *Are*		Demonstrate command of the conventions of standard English grammar and usage when writing or speaking.
		• L.1.1c	Use singular and plural nouns with matching verbs in basic sentences (e.g., *He hops; We hop*).
		• L.1.1j	Produce and expand complete simple and compound declarative, interrogative, imperative, and exclamatory sentences in response to prompts.
		• L.3.1f	Ensure subject-verb and pronoun-antecedent agreement.
8	Vocabulary: Personal Information	• CCRA.SL.1	Prepare for and participate effectively in a range of conversations and collaborations with diverse partners, building on others' ideas and expressing their own clearly and persuasively.

Common Core State Standards, continued

Language Development, continued

SE Pages	Lesson	Code	Standards Text
8	**Language:** **Give Information**	• CCRA.L.6	Acquire and use accurately a range of general academic and domain-specific words and phrases sufficient for reading, writing, speaking, and listening at the college and career readiness level; demonstrate independence in gathering vocabulary knowledge when encountering an unknown term important to comprehension or expression.
9	**Vocabulary:** **Communication**	• CCRA.SL.1	Prepare for and participate effectively in a range of conversations and collaborations with diverse partners, building on others' ideas and expressing their own clearly and persuasively.
	Language: **Use the Telephone**	• CCRA.SL.6	Adapt speech to a variety of contexts and communicative tasks, demonstrating command of formal English when indicated or appropriate.
		• CCRA.L.6	Acquire and use accurately a range of general academic and domain-specific words and phrases sufficient for reading, writing, speaking, and listening at the college and career readiness level; demonstrate independence in gathering vocabulary knowledge when encountering an unknown term important to comprehension or expression.
10	**Listen and Read Along:** *Good News*	• CCRA.R.4	Interpret words and phrases as they are used in a text, including determining technical, connotative, and figurative meanings, and analyze how specific word choices shape meaning or tone.
		• CCRA.R.10	Read and comprehend complex literary and informational texts independently and proficiently.
		• L.1.5a	With guidance and support from adults, demonstrate understanding of word relationships and nuances in word meanings. Sort words into categories (e.g., colors, clothing) to gain a sense of the concepts the categories represent.
11	**Comprehension:** **Identify Sequence**	• CCRA.R.3	Analyze how and why individuals, events, or ideas develop and interact over the course of a text.
		• CCRA.R.5	Analyze the structure of texts, including how specific sentences, paragraphs, and larger portions of the text (e.g., a section, chapter, scene, or stanza) relate to each other and the whole.
		• CCRA.SL.1	Prepare for and participate effectively in a range of conversations and collaborations with diverse partners, building on others' ideas and expressing their own clearly and persuasively.

Language and Literacy

SE Pages	Lesson	Code	Standards Text
12–13	**High Frequency Words**		Know and apply grade-level phonics and word analysis skills in decoding words.
		RF.K.3c	Read common high-frequency words by sight (e.g., *the, of, to, you, she, my, is, are, do, does*).
		RF.1.3g RF.2.3f	Recognize and read grade-appropriate irregularly spelled words.
			Demonstrate command of the conventions of standard English capitalization, punctuation, and spelling when writing.
		• L.1.2.d	Use conventional spelling for words with common spelling patterns and for frequently occurring irregular words.
		• L.3.2e	Use conventional spelling for high-frequency and other studied words and for adding suffixes to base words (e.g., *sitting, smiled, cries, happiness*).
		• L.4.2d • L.5.2e	Spell grade-appropriate words correctly, consulting references as needed.

Language and Literacy, continued

SE Pages	Lesson	Code	Standards Text
14–15	**Reading and Spelling: Short *a*, Short *o***		Know and apply grade-level phonics and word analysis skills in decoding words.
		RF.K.3a	Demonstrate basic knowledge of one-to-one letter-sound correspondences by producing the primary or most frequent sound for each consonant.
		RF.K.3b	Associate the long and short sounds with the common spellings (graphemes) for the five major vowels.
		RF.1.3b	Decode regularly spelled one-syllable words.
		RF.2.3a	Distinguish long and short vowels when reading regularly spelled one-syllable words.
16–17	**Read on Your Own: "New at School"**	CCRA.R.3	Analyze how and why individuals, events, or ideas develop and interact over the course of a text.
		CCRA.R.5	Analyze the structure of texts, including how specific sentences, paragraphs, and larger portions of the text (e.g., a section, chapter, scene, or stanza) relate to each other and the whole.
		CCRA.R.10	Read and comprehend complex literary and informational texts independently and proficiently.
			Know and apply grade-level phonics and word analysis skills in decoding words.
		RF.K.3b	Associate the long and short sounds with the common spellings (graphemes) for the five major vowels.
		RF.K.3c	Read common high-frequency words by sight (e.g., *the, of, to, you, she, my, is, are, do, does*).
		RF.1.3b	Decode regularly spelled one-syllable words.
		RF.1.3g RF.2.3f	Recognize and read grade-appropriate irregularly spelled words.
		RF.2.3a	Distinguish long and short vowels when reading regularly spelled one-syllable words.
			Read with sufficient accuracy and fluency to support comprehension.
		RF.1.4a RF.2.4a	Read grade-level text with purpose and understanding.
		RF.1.4b RF.2.4b	Read grade-level text orally with accuracy, appropriate rate, and expression on successive readings.
		CCRA.SL.1	Prepare for and participate effectively in a range of conversations and collaborations with diverse partners, building on others' ideas and expressing their own clearly and persuasively.
18	**Grammar: Statements and Exclamations**		Demonstrate understanding of the organization and basic features of print.
		RF.1.1a	Recognize the distinguishing features of a sentence (e.g., first word, capitalization, ending punctuation).
		CCRA.L.2	Demonstrate command of the conventions of standard English capitalization, punctuation, and spelling when writing.

Common Core State Standards, continued

Language and Literacy, continued

SE Pages Lesson	Code	Standards Text
18 **Grammar: Statements and Exclamations,** continued	• L.1.1j	Demonstrate command of the conventions of standard English grammar and usage when writing or speaking. Produce and expand complete simple and compound declarative, interrogative, imperative, and exclamatory sentences in response to prompts.
	• L.1.2b	Demonstrate command of the conventions of standard English capitalization, punctuation, and spelling when writing. Use end punctuation for sentences.

Language and Content

SE Pages Lesson	Code	Standards Text
19 **Success in Mathematics: Learn About Math Problems**	• CCRA.R.4	Interpret words and phrases as they are used in a text, including determining technical, connotative, and figurative meanings, and analyze how specific word choices shape meaning or tone.
	• CCRA.R.10	Read and comprehend complex literary and informational texts independently and proficiently.
	• CCRA.SL.2	Integrate and evaluate information presented in diverse media and formats, including visually, quantitatively, and orally.
	• CCRA.L.6	Acquire and use accurately a range of general academic and domain-specific words and phrases sufficient for reading, writing, speaking, and listening at the college and career readiness level; demonstrate independence in gathering vocabulary knowledge when encountering an unknown term important to comprehension or expression.
20–21 **Build Background and Vocabulary**	• CCRA.R.7	Integrate and evaluate content presented in diverse media and formats, including visually and quantitatively, as well as in words.
	• CCRA.SL.1	Prepare for and participate effectively in a range of conversations and collaborations with diverse partners, building on others' ideas and expressing their own clearly and persuasively.
	• CCRA.L.6	Acquire and use accurately a range of general academic and domain-specific words and phrases sufficient for reading, writing, speaking, and listening at the college and career readiness level; demonstrate independence in gathering vocabulary knowledge when encountering an unknown term important to comprehension or expression.
	• L.1.4a • L.2.4a • L.3.4a • L.4.4a	Determine or clarify the meaning of unknown and multiple-meaning words and phrases based on grade-level reading and content, choosing flexibly from a range of strategies. Use sentence-level context as a clue to the meaning of a word or phrase. Use context (e.g., definitions, examples, or restatements in text) as a clue to the meaning of a word or phrase.
22–29 **Listen and Read Along: "Many People to Meet"**	• CCRA.R.2	Determine central ideas or themes of a text and analyze their development; summarize the key supporting details and ideas.
	• CCRA.R.3	Analyze how and why individuals, events, or ideas develop and interact over the course of a text.

Language and Content, continued

SE Pages	Lesson	Code	Standards Text
22–29	**Listen and Read Along: "Many People to Meet,"** continued	• CCRA.R.4	Interpret words and phrases as they are used in a text, including determining technical, connotative, and figurative meanings, and analyze how specific word choices shape meaning or tone.
		• CCRA.R.5	Analyze the structure of texts, including how specific sentences, paragraphs, and larger portions of the text (e.g., a section, chapter, scene, or stanza) relate to each other and the whole.
		• CCRA.R.7	Integrate and evaluate content presented in diverse media and formats, including visually and quantitatively, as well as in words.
		• CCRA.R.10	Read and comprehend complex literary and informational texts independently and proficiently.
30	**Check Your Understanding**	• CCRA.R.2	Determine central ideas or themes of a text and analyze their development; summarize the key supporting details and ideas.
		• CCRA.R.3	Analyze how and why individuals, events, or ideas develop and interact over the course of a text.
		• CCRA.W.2	Write informative/explanatory texts to examine and convey complex ideas and information clearly and accurately through the effective selection, organization, and analysis of content.
		• CCRA.SL.1	Prepare for and participate effectively in a range of conversations and collaborations with diverse partners, building on others' ideas and expressing their own clearly and persuasively.
	Review Vocabulary	• CCRA.R.4	Interpret words and phrases as they are used in a text, including determining technical, connotative, and figurative meanings, and analyze how specific word choices shape meaning or tone.
		• CCRA.SL.2	Integrate and evaluate information presented in diverse media and formats, including visually, quantitatively, and orally.
		• CCRA.SL.4	Present information, findings, and supporting evidence such that listeners can follow the line of reasoning and the organization, development, and style are appropriate to task, purpose, and audience.
		• CCRA.L.3	Apply knowledge of language to understand how language functions in different contexts, to make effective choices for meaning or style, and to comprehend more fully when reading or listening.
	Write About the People You Meet	• CCRA.W.4	Produce clear and coherent writing in which the development, organization, and style are appropriate to task, purpose, and audience.
		• CCRA.W.10	Write routinely over extended time frames (time for research, reflection, and revision) and shorter time frames (a single sitting or a day or two) for a range of tasks, purposes, and audiences.

Writing Project

SE Pages	Lesson	Code	Standards Text
31	**Model Study: E-mail**	• CCRA.R.5	Analyze the structure of texts, including how specific sentences, paragraphs, and larger portions of the text (e.g., a section, chapter, scene, or stanza) relate to each other and the whole.

Common Core State Standards, continued

Writing Project, continued

SE Pages	Lesson	Code	Standards Text
32	**Plan and Write**	• CCRA.W.3	Write narratives to develop real or imagined experiences or events using effective technique, well-chosen details and well-structured event sequences.
		• CCRA.W.4	Produce clear and coherent writing in which the development, organization, and style are appropriate to task, purpose, and audience.
		• CCRA.W.5	Develop and strengthen writing as needed by planning, revising, editing, rewriting, or trying a new approach.
		• CCRA.W.6	Use technology, including the Internet, to produce and publish writing and to interact and collaborate with others.
		• CCRA.W.10	Write routinely over extended time frames (time for research, reflection, and revision) and shorter time frames (a single sitting or a day or two) for a range of tasks, purposes, and audiences.
33	**Check Your Work**	• CCRA.W.4	Produce clear and coherent writing in which the development, organization, and style are appropriate to task, purpose, and audience.
		• CCRA.W.5	Develop and strengthen writing as needed by planning, revising, editing, rewriting, or trying a new approach.
			Demonstrate command of the conventions of standard English capitalization, punctuation, and spelling when writing.
		• L.1.2b	Use end punctuation for sentences.
		• L.2.2b	Use commas in greetings and closings of letters.
	Finish and Share	• CCRA.W.6	Use technology, including the Internet, to produce and publish writing and to interact and collaborate with others.
		• CCRA.SL.4	Present information, findings, and supporting evidence such that listeners can follow the line of reasoning and the organization, development, and style are appropriate to task, purpose, and audience.
		• CCRA.SL.6	Adapt speech to a variety of contexts and communicative tasks, demonstrating command of formal English when indicated or appropriate.

Unit 2   Set the Table

Language Development

SE Pages	Lesson	Code	Standards Text
34–35	**Unit Launch**	• CCRA.SL.2	Integrate and evaluate information presented in diverse media and formats, including visually, quantitatively, and orally.
36	**Language: Express Likes; Describe**	• CCRA.SL.1	Prepare for and participate effectively in a range of conversations and collaborations with diverse partners, building on others' ideas and expressing their own clearly and persuasively.
		• CCRA.SL.4	Present information, findings, and supporting evidence such that listeners can follow the line of reasoning and the organization, development, and style are appropriate to task, purpose, and audience.
37	**Vocabulary: Colors, Shapes, and Sizes**	• CCRA.L.6	Acquire and use accurately a range of general academic and domain-specific words and phrases sufficient for reading, writing, speaking, and listening at the college and career readiness level; demonstrate independence in gathering vocabulary knowledge when encountering an unknown term important to comprehension or expression.

Language Development, continued

SE Pages	Lesson	Code	Standards Text
37	**Vocabulary: Colors, Shapes, and Sizes,** continued		Demonstrate command of the conventions of standard English grammar and usage when writing or speaking.
		• L.1.1f	Use frequently occurring adjectives.
		• L.2.6	Use words and phrases acquired through conversations, reading and being read to, and responding to texts, including using adjectives and adverbs to describe (e.g., *When other kids are happy that makes me happy*).
38	**Vocabulary: Foods**	• CCRA.SL.2	Integrate and evaluate information presented in diverse media and formats, including visually, quantitatively, and orally.
		• CCRA.SL.3	Evaluate a speaker's point of view, reasoning, and use of evidence and rhetoric.
		• CCRA.L.6	Acquire and use accurately a range of general academic and domain-specific words and phrases sufficient for reading, writing, speaking, and listening at the college and career readiness level; demonstrate independence in gathering vocabulary knowledge when encountering an unknown term important to comprehension or expression.
	Language: Describe		Demonstrate command of the conventions of standard English grammar and usage when writing or speaking.
		• L.1.1f	Use frequently occurring adjectives.
		• L.2.6	Use words and phrases acquired through conversations, reading and being read to, and responding to texts, including using adjectives and adverbs to describe (e.g., *When other kids are happy that makes me happy*).
39	**Grammar: Action Verbs**	• CCRA.W.2	Write informative/explanatory texts to examine and convey complex ideas and information clearly and accurately through the effective selection, organization, and analysis of content.
			Demonstrate command of the conventions of standard English grammar and usage when writing or speaking.
		• L.1.1c	Use singular and plural nouns with matching verbs in basic sentences (e.g., *He hops; We hop*).
		• L.1.1e	Use verbs to convey a sense of past, present, and future (e.g., *Yesterday I walked home; Today I walk home; Tomorrow I will walk home*).
40	**Listen and Read Along:** *I Make Pictures Move!*	• CCRA.R.4	Interpret words and phrases as they are used in a text, including determining technical, connotative, and figurative meanings, and analyze how specific word choices shape meaning or tone.
		• CCRA.R.10	Read and comprehend complex literary and informational texts independently and proficiently.
			With guidance and support from adults, demonstrate understanding of word relationships and nuances in word meanings.
		• L.1.5a	Sort words into categories (e.g., colors, clothing) to gain a sense of the concepts the categories represent.
41	**Comprehension: Identify Steps in a Process**	• CCRA.R.3	Analyze how and why individuals, events, or ideas develop and interact over the course of a text.
		• CCRA.R.5	Analyze the structure of texts, including how specific sentences, paragraphs, and larger portions of the text (e.g., a section, chapter, scene, or stanza) relate to each other and the whole.

Common Core State Standards, continued

Language Development, continued

SE Pages	Lesson	Code	Standards Text
41	**Comprehension: Identify Steps in a Process,** continued	• CCRA.SL.1	Prepare for and participate effectively in a range of conversations and collaborations with diverse partners, building on others' ideas and expressing their own clearly and persuasively.
		• CCRA.SL.4	Present information, findings, and supporting evidence such that listeners can follow the line of reasoning and the organization, development, and style are appropriate to task, purpose, and audience.

Language and Literacy

SE Pages	Lesson	Code	Standards Text
42–43	**High Frequency Words**		Know and apply grade-level phonics and word analysis skills in decoding words.
		• RF.K.3c	Read common high-frequency words by sight (e.g., *the, of, to, you, she, my, is, are, do, does*).
		• RF.1.3g • RF.2.3f	Recognize and read grade-appropriate irregularly spelled words.
			Demonstrate command of the conventions of standard English capitalization, punctuation, and spelling when writing.
		• L.1.2d	Use conventional spelling for words with common spelling patterns and for frequently occurring irregular words.
		• L.3.2e	Use conventional spelling for high-frequency and other studied words and for adding suffixes to base words (e.g., *sitting, smiled, cries, happiness*).
		• L.4.2d • L.5.2e	Spell grade-appropriate words correctly, consulting references as needed.
44–45	**Reading and Spelling: Words with short *i*, short *u*, *ch*, and *tch***		Know and apply grade-level phonics and word analysis skills in decoding words.
		• RF.K.3a	Demonstrate basic knowledge of one-to-one letter-sound correspondences by producing the primary or most frequent sound for each consonant.
		• RF.K.3b	Associate the long and short sounds with the common spellings (graphemes) for the five major vowels.
		• RF.1.3a	Know the spelling-sound correspondences for common consonant digraphs.
		• RF.1.3b	Decode regularly spelled one-syllable words.
		• RF.2.3a	Distinguish long and short vowels when reading regularly spelled one-syllable words.
			Demonstrate command of the conventions of standard English capitalization, punctuation, and spelling when writing.
		• L.1.2d	Use conventional spelling for words with common spelling patterns and for frequently occurring irregular words.
		• L.3.2f	Use spelling patterns and generalizations (e.g., word families, position-based spellings, syllable patterns, ending rules, meaningful word parts) in writing words.

Language and Literacy, continued

SE Pages	Lesson	Code	Standards Text
46–47	Read On Your Own: "Something Good for Lunch"	• CCRA.R.3	Analyze how and why individuals, events, or ideas develop and interact over the course of a text.
		• CCRA.R.5	Analyze the structure of texts, including how specific sentences, paragraphs, and larger portions of the text (e.g., a section, chapter, scene, or stanza) relate to each other and the whole.
		• CCRA.R.10	Read and comprehend complex literary and informational texts independently and proficiently.
			Know and apply grade-level phonics and word analysis skills in decoding words.
		RF.K.3a	Demonstrate basic knowledge of one-to-one letter-sound correspondences by producing the primary sound or most frequent sounds for each consonant.
		RF.K.3b	Associate the long and short sounds with the common spellings (graphemes) for the five major vowels.
		RF.K.3c	Read common high-frequency words by sight (e.g., *the, of, to, you, she, my, is, are, do, does*).
		RF.1.3b	Decode regularly spelled one-syllable words.
		RF.1.3g RF.2.3f	Recognize and read grade-appropriate irregularly spelled words.
		RF.2.3a	Distinguish long and short vowels when reading regularly spelled one-syllable words.
			Read with sufficient accuracy and fluency to support comprehension.
		RF.1.4a RF.2.4a	Read grade-level text with purpose and understanding.
		RF.1.4b RF.2.4b	Read grade-level text orally with accuracy, appropriate rate, and expression on successive readings.
		• CCRA.SL.1	Prepare for and participate effectively in a range of conversations and collaborations with diverse partners, building on others' ideas and expressing their own clearly and persuasively.
48	Grammar: Negative Sentences		Demonstrate command of the conventions of standard English grammar and usage when writing or speaking.
		• L.1.1c	Use singular and plural nouns with matching verbs in basic sentences (e.g., *He hops; We hop*).
		• L.3.1f	Ensure subject-verb and pronoun-antecedent agreement.

Language and Content

SE Pages	Lesson	Code	Standards Text
49	Success in Science: Learn About Food Groups	• CCRA.R.7	Integrate and evaluate content presented in diverse media and formats, including visually and quantitatively, as well as in words.
		• CCRA.R.10	Read and comprehend complex literary and informational texts independently and proficiently.

Common Core State Standards, continued

Language and Content, continued

SE Pages	Lesson	Code	Standards Text
49	**Success in Science: Learn About Food Groups,** continued		With guidance and support from adults, demonstrate understanding of word relationships and nuances in word meanings.
		• L.1.5a	Sort words into categories (e.g., colors, clothing) to gain a sense of the concepts the categories represent.
		• L.1.5b	Define words by category and by one or more key attributes (e.g., a *duck* is a bird that swims; a *tiger* is a large cat with stripes).
50–51	**Build Background and Vocabulary**	• CCRA.R.7	Integrate and evaluate content presented in diverse media and formats, including visually and quantitatively, as well as in words.
		• CCRA.L.6	Acquire and use accurately a range of general academic and domain-specific words and phrases sufficient for reading, writing, speaking, and listening at the college and career readiness level; demonstrate independence in gathering vocabulary knowledge when encountering an unknown term important to comprehension or expression.
			Determine or clarify the meaning of unknown and multiple-meaning words and phrases based on grade-level reading and content, choosing flexibly from a range of strategies.
		• L.1.4a • L.2.4a • L.3.4a	Use sentence-level context as a clue to the meaning of a word or phrase.
		• L.4.4a	Use context (e.g., definitions, examples, or restatements in text) as a clue to the meaning of a word or phrase.
52–59	**Listen and Read Along: "U.S. Tour of Food"**	• CCRA.R.2	Determine central ideas or themes of a text and analyze their development; summarize the key supporting details and ideas.
		• CCRA.R.4	Interpret words and phrases as they are used in a text, including determining technical, connotative, and figurative meanings, and analyze how specific word choices shape meaning or tone.
		• CCRA.R.5	Analyze the structure of texts, including how specific sentences, paragraphs, and larger portions of the text (e.g., a section, chapter, scene, or stanza) relate to each other and the whole.
		• CCRA.R.7	Integrate and evaluate content presented in diverse media and formats, including visually and quantitatively, as well as in words.
		• CCRA.R.10	Read and comprehend complex literary and informational texts independently and proficiently.
		• CCRA.L.6	Acquire and use accurately a range of general academic and domain-specific words and phrases sufficient for reading, writing, speaking, and listening at the college and career readiness level; demonstrate independence in gathering vocabulary knowledge when encountering an unknown term important to comprehension or expression.
			With guidance and support from adults, demonstrate understanding of word relationships and nuances in word meanings.
		• L.1.5a	Sort words into categories (e.g., colors, clothing) to gain a sense of the concepts the categories represent.
		• L.1.5b	Define words by category and by one or more key attributes (e.g., a *duck* is a bird that swims; a *tiger* is a large cat with stripes).

Language and Content, continued

SE Pages	Lesson	Code	Standards Text
60	Check Your Understanding	• CCRA.R.2	Determine central ideas or themes of a text and analyze their development; summarize the key supporting details and ideas.
		• CCRA.SL.1	Prepare for and participate effectively in a range of conversations and collaborations with diverse partners, building on others' ideas and expressing their own clearly and persuasively.
		• CCRA.SL.2	Integrate and evaluate information presented in diverse media and formats, including visually, quantitatively, and orally.
			With guidance and support from adults, demonstrate understanding of word relationships and nuances in word meanings.
		• L.1.5a	Sort words into categories (e.g., colors, clothing) to gain a sense of the concepts the categories represent.
		• L.1.5b	Define words by category and by one or more key attributes (e.g., a *duck* is a bird that swims; a *tiger* is a large cat with stripes).
	Review Vocabulary	• CCRA.L.6	Acquire and use accurately a range of general academic and domain-specific words and phrases sufficient for reading, writing, speaking, and listening at the college and career readiness level; demonstrate independence in gathering vocabulary knowledge when encountering an unknown term important to comprehension or expression.
	Write About Food	• CCRA.W.3	Write narratives to develop real or imagined experiences or events using effective technique, well-chosen details and well-structured event sequences.
		• CCRA.W.4	Produce clear and coherent writing in which the development, organization, and style are appropriate to task, purpose, and audience.
		• CCRA.W.10	Write routinely over extended time frames (time for research, reflection, and revision) and shorter time frames (a single sitting or a day or two) for a range of tasks, purposes, and audiences.

Writing Project

SE Pages	Lesson	Code	Standards Text
61	Model Study: How-To-Card	• CCRA.R.5	Analyze the structure of texts, including how specific sentences, paragraphs, and larger portions of the text (e.g., a section, chapter, scene, or stanza) relate to each other and the whole.
62	Plan and Write	• CCRA.W.2	Write informative/explanatory texts to examine and convey complex ideas and information clearly and accurately through the effective selection, organization, and analysis of content.
		• CCRA.W.4	Produce clear and coherent writing in which the development, organization, and style are appropriate to task, purpose, and audience.
		• CCRA.W.5	Develop and strengthen writing as needed by planning, revising, editing, rewriting, or trying a new approach.
		• CCRA.W.10	Write routinely over extended time frames (time for research, reflection, and revision) and shorter time frames (a single sitting or a day or two) for a range of tasks, purposes, and audiences.
			Demonstrate command of the conventions of standard English grammar and usage when writing or speaking.
		• L.1.1f	Use frequently occurring adjectives.
		• L.2.6	Use words and phrases acquired through conversations, reading and being read to, and responding to texts, including using adjectives and adverbs to describe (e.g., *When other kids are happy that makes me happy*).

Common Core State Standards, continued

Writing Project, continued

SE Pages	Lesson	Code	Standards Text
63	Check Your Work	• CCRA.L.2	Demonstrate command of the conventions of standard English capitalization, punctuation, and spelling when writing.
			Demonstrate command of the conventions of standard English grammar and usage when writing or speaking.
		• L.1.1c	Use singular and plural nouns with matching verbs in basic sentences (e.g., *He hops; We hop*).
		• L.1.1f	Use frequently occurring adjectives.
		• L.3.1f	Ensure subject-verb and pronoun-antecedent agreement.
		• L.2.6	Use words and phrases acquired through conversations, reading and being read to, and responding to texts, including using adjectives and adverbs to describe (e.g., *When other kids are happy that makes me happy*).
		• CCRA.W.4	Produce clear and coherent writing in which the development, organization, and style are appropriate to task, purpose, and audience.
		• CCRA.W.10	Write routinely over extended time frames (time for research, reflection, and revision) and shorter time frames (a single sitting or a day or two) for a range of tasks, purposes, and audiences.
	Finish and Share	• CCRA.SL.4	Present information, findings, and supporting evidence such that listeners can follow the line of reasoning and the organization, development, and style are appropriate to task, purpose, and audience.
		• CCRA.W.5	Develop and strengthen writing as needed by planning, revising, editing, rewriting, or trying a new approach.

Unit 3   On the Job

Language Development

SE Pages	Lesson	Code	Standards Text
64–65	Unit Launch	• CCRA.SL.2	Integrate and evaluate information presented in diverse media and formats, including visually, quantitatively, and orally.
66	Language: Give Information	• CCRA.SL.1	Prepare for and participate effectively in a range of conversations and collaborations with diverse partners, building on others' ideas and expressing their own clearly and persuasively.
		• CCRA.SL.4	Present information, findings, and supporting evidence such that listeners can follow the line of reasoning and the organization, development, and style are appropriate to task, purpose, and audience.
67	Grammar: Present Tense Verbs	• CCRA.SL.1	Prepare for and participate effectively in a range of conversations and collaborations with diverse partners, building on others' ideas and expressing their own clearly and persuasively.
			Demonstrate command of the conventions of standard English grammar and usage when writing or speaking.
		• L.1.1c	Use singular and plural nouns with matching verbs in basic sentences (e.g., *He hops; We hop*).
		• L.1.1j	Produce and expand complete simple and compound declarative, interrogative, imperative, and exclamatory sentences in response to prompts.
		• L.3.1e	Form and use the simple (e.g., *I walked; I walk; I will walk*) verb tenses.
		• L.3.1f	Ensure subject-verb and pronoun-antecedent agreement.

Language Development, continued

SE Pages	Lesson	Code	Standards Text
68	**Grammar:** **Yes-or-No Questions**	• CCRA.L.1	Demonstrate command of the conventions of standard English grammar and usage when writing or speaking.
		• L.1.1j	Demonstrate command of the conventions of standard English grammar and usage when writing or speaking. Produce and expand complete simple and compound declarative, interrogative, imperative, and exclamatory sentences in response to prompts.
		• L.3.1f	Ensure subject-verb and pronoun-antecedent agreement.
		• L.1.2b	Demonstrate command of the conventions of standard English capitalization, punctuation, and spelling when writing. Use end punctuation for sentences.
69	**Vocabulary:** **Tools and Careers**	• CCRA.SL.1	Prepare for and participate effectively in a range of conversations and collaborations with diverse partners, building on others' ideas and expressing their own clearly and persuasively.
	Language: **Ask and Answer Questions**	• CCRA.SL.2	Integrate and evaluate information presented in diverse media and formats, including visually, quantitatively, and orally.
		• CCRA.SL.6	Adapt speech to a variety of contexts and communicative tasks, demonstrating command of formal English when indicated or appropriate.
		• CCRA.L.6	Acquire and use accurately a range of general academic and domain-specific words and phrases sufficient for reading, writing, speaking, and listening at the college and career readiness level; demonstrate independence in gathering vocabulary knowledge when encountering an unknown term important to comprehension or expression.
		• L.1.1j	Demonstrate command of the conventions of standard English grammar and usage when writing or speaking. Produce and expand complete simple and compound declarative, interrogative, imperative, and exclamatory sentences in response to prompts.
		• L.3.1f	Ensure subject-verb and pronoun-antecedent agreement.
70	**Listen and Read Along:** *What Is It?*	• CCRA.R.4	Interpret words and phrases as they are used in a text, including determining technical, connotative, and figurative meanings, and analyze how specific word choices shape meaning or tone.
		• CCRA.R.10	Read and comprehend complex literary and informational texts independently and proficiently.
		• L.1.5a	With guidance and support from adults, demonstrate understanding of word relationships and nuances in word meanings. Sort words into categories (e.g., colors, clothing) to gain a sense of the concepts the categories represent.
71	**Comprehension:** **Identify Details**	• CCRA.R.2	Determine central ideas or themes of a text and analyze their development; summarize the key supporting details and ideas.
		• CCRA.SL.1	Prepare for and participate effectively in a range of conversations and collaborations with diverse partners, building on others' ideas and expressing their own clearly and persuasively.
		• CCRA.SL.4	Present information, findings, and supporting evidence such that listeners can follow the line of reasoning and the organization, development, and style are appropriate to task, purpose, and audience.

Common Core State Standards, continued

Language and Literacy

SE Pages	Lesson	Code	Standards Text
72–73	**High Frequency Words**		Know and apply grade-level phonics and word analysis skills in decoding words.
		RF.K.3c	Read common high-frequency words by sight (e.g., *the, of, to, you, she, my, is, are, do, does*).
		RF.1.3g	Recognize and read grade-appropriate irregularly spelled words.
		RF.2.3f	
			Demonstrate command of the conventions of standard English capitalization, punctuation, and spelling when writing.
		● L.1.2d	Use conventional spelling for words with common spelling patterns and for frequently occurring irregular words.
		● L.3.2e	Use conventional spelling for high-frequency and other studied words and for adding suffixes to base words (e.g., *sitting, smiled, cries, happiness*).
		● L.4.2d	Spell grade-appropriate words correctly, consulting references as needed.
		● L.5.2e	
74–75	**Reading and Spelling: Short *e*, *sh*, *ck*, and Double Consonants**		Know and apply grade-level phonics and word analysis skills in decoding words.
		RF.K.3a	Demonstrate basic knowledge of one-to-one letter-sound correspondences by producing the primary sound or many of the most frequent sounds for each consonant.
		RF.K.3b	Associate the long and short sounds with the common spellings (graphemes) for the five major vowels.
		RF.1.3a	Know the spelling-sound correspondences for common consonant digraphs.
		RF.1.3b	Decode regularly spelled one-syllable words.
		RF.2.3a	Distinguish long and short vowels when reading regularly spelled one-syllable words.
			Demonstrate command of the conventions of standard English capitalization, punctuation, and spelling when writing.
		● L.1.2d	Use conventional spelling for words with common spelling patterns and for frequently occurring irregular words.
		● L.3.2f	Use spelling patterns and generalizations (e.g., word families, position-based spellings, syllable patterns, ending rules, meaningful word parts) in writing words.
		● L.4.2d	Spell grade-appropriate words correctly, consulting references as needed.
		● L.5.2e	
76–77	**Read On Your Own: "Let Ben Take It"**	● CCRA.R.1	Read closely to determine what the text says explicitly and to make logical inferences from it; cite specific textual evidence when writing or speaking to support conclusions drawn from the text.
		● CCRA.R.10	Read and comprehend complex literary and informational texts independently and proficiently.

Language and Literacy, continued

SE Pages	Lesson	Code	Standards Text
76–77	**Read On Your Own: "Let Ben Take It,"** continued		Know and apply grade-level phonics and word analysis skills in decoding words.
		RF.K.3a	Demonstrate basic knowledge of one-to-one letter-sound correspondences by producing the primary sound or many of the most frequent sounds for each consonant.
		RF.K.3b	Associate the long and short sounds with the common spellings (graphemes) for the five major vowels.
		RF.K.3c	Read common high-frequency words by sight (e.g., *the, of, to, you, she, my, is, are, do, does*).
		RF.1.3a	Know the spelling-sound correspondences for common consonant digraphs.
		RF.1.3b	Decode regularly spelled one-syllable words.
		RF.2.3a	Distinguish long and short vowels when reading regularly spelled one-syllable words.
		RF.1.3g RF.2.3f	Recognize and read grade-appropriate irregularly spelled words.
			Read with sufficient accuracy and fluency to support comprehension.
		RF.1.4a RF.2.4a	Read grade-level text with purpose and understanding.
		RF.1.4b RF.2.4b	Read grade-level text orally with accuracy, appropriate rate, and expression on successive readings.
78	**Grammar: Questions with *Who?*, *What?*, *Where?*, and *When?***		Demonstrate understanding of the organization and basic features of print.
		RF.1.1a	Recognize the distinguishing features of a sentence (e.g., first word, capitalization, ending punctuation).
		CCRA.SL.1	Prepare for and participate effectively in a range of conversations and collaborations with diverse partners, building on others' ideas and expressing their own clearly and persuasively.
			Demonstrate command of the conventions of standard English grammar and usage when writing or speaking.
		L.1.1j	Produce and expand complete simple and compound declarative, interrogative, imperative, and exclamatory sentences in response to prompts.
		L.4.1a	Use relative pronouns (who, whose, whom, which, that) and relative adverbs (where, when, why).
			Demonstrate command of the conventions of standard English capitalization, punctuation, and spelling when writing.
		L.1.2b	Use end punctuation for sentences.

Common Core State Standards, continued

Language and Content

SE Pages	Lesson	Code	Standards Text
79	Success in Science and Mathematics: Learn About Measurement	• CCRA.R.4	Interpret words and phrases as they are used in a text, including determining technical, connotative, and figurative meanings, and analyze how specific word choices shape meaning or tone.
		• CCRA.R.5	Analyze the structure of texts, including how specific sentences, paragraphs, and larger portions of the text (e.g., a section, chapter, scene, or stanza) relate to each other and the whole.
		• CCRA.R.7	Integrate and evaluate content presented in diverse media and formats, including visually and quantitatively, as well as in words.
		• CCRA.R.10	Read and comprehend complex literary and informational texts independently and proficiently.
		• CCRA.W.7	Conduct short as well as more sustained research projects based on focused questions, demonstrating understanding of the subject under investigation.
		• CCRA.W.9	Draw evidence from literary or informational texts to support analysis, reflection, and research.
		• CCRA.L.6	Acquire and use accurately a range of general academic and domain-specific words and phrases sufficient for reading, writing, speaking, and listening at the college and career readiness level; demonstrate independence in gathering vocabulary knowledge when encountering an unknown term important to comprehension or expression.
80–81	Build Background and Vocabulary	• CCRA.R.7	Integrate and evaluate content presented in diverse media and formats, including visually and quantitatively, as well as in words.
		• CCRA.SL.1	Prepare for and participate effectively in a range of conversations and collaborations with diverse partners, building on others' ideas and expressing their own clearly and persuasively.
		• CCRA.L.6	Acquire and use accurately a range of general academic and domain-specific words and phrases sufficient for reading, writing, speaking, and listening at the college and career readiness level; demonstrate independence in gathering vocabulary knowledge when encountering an unknown term important to comprehension or expression.
			Determine or clarify the meaning of unknown and multiple-meaning words and phrases based on grade-level reading and content, choosing flexibly from a range of strategies.
		• L.1.4a • L.2.4a • L.3.4a	Use sentence-level context as a clue to the meaning of a word or phrase.
		• L.4.4a	Use context (e.g., definitions, examples, or restatements in text) as a clue to the meaning of a word or phrase.
82–89	Listen and Read Along: "Geologists: Rock Scientists"	• CCRA.R.1	Read closely to determine what the text says explicitly and to make logical inferences from it; cite specific textual evidence when writing or speaking to support conclusions drawn from the text.
		• CCRA.R.2	Determine central ideas or themes of a text and analyze their development; summarize the key supporting details and ideas.

Language and Content, continued

SE Pages	Lesson	Code	Standards Text
82–89	**Listen and Read Along:** **"Geologists: Rock Scientists,"** continued	• CCRA.R.4	Interpret words and phrases as they are used in a text, including determining technical, connotative, and figurative meanings, and analyze how specific word choices shape meaning or tone.
		• CCRA.L.6	Acquire and use accurately a range of general academic and domain-specific words and phrases sufficient for reading, writing, speaking, and listening at the college and career readiness level; demonstrate independence in gathering vocabulary knowledge when encountering an unknown term important to comprehension or expression.
90	**Check Your Understanding**	• CCRA.R.2	Determine central ideas or themes of a text and analyze their development; summarize the key supporting details and ideas.
		• CCRA.SL.1	Prepare for and participate effectively in a range of conversations and collaborations with diverse partners, building on others' ideas and expressing their own clearly and persuasively.
		• CCRA.SL.2	Integrate and evaluate information presented in diverse media and formats, including visually, quantitatively, and orally.
	Review Vocabulary	• CCRA.L.6	Acquire and use accurately a range of general academic and domain-specific words and phrases sufficient for reading, writing, speaking, and listening at the college and career readiness level; demonstrate independence in gathering vocabulary knowledge when encountering an unknown term important to comprehension or expression.
	Write About Jobs	• CCRA.W.2	Write informative/explanatory texts to examine and convey complex ideas and information clearly and accurately through the effective selection, organization, and analysis of content.
		• CCRA.W.4	Produce clear and coherent writing in which the development, organization, and style are appropriate to task, purpose, and audience.
		• CCRA.W.10	Write routinely over extended time frames (time for research, reflection, and revision) and shorter time frames (a single sitting or a day or two) for a range of tasks, purposes, and audiences.

Writing Project

91	**Model Study: Interview**	• CCRA.R.5	Analyze the structure of texts, including how specific sentences, paragraphs, and larger portions of the text (e.g., a section, chapter, scene, or stanza) relate to each other and the whole.
92	**Plan and Write**	• CCRA.W.2	Write informative/explanatory texts to examine and convey complex ideas and information clearly and accurately through the effective selection, organization, and analysis of content.
		• CCRA.W.4	Produce clear and coherent writing in which the development, organization, and style are appropriate to task, purpose, and audience.
		• CCRA.W.5	Develop and strengthen writing as needed by planning, revising, editing, rewriting, or trying a new approach.
		• CCRA.W.8	Gather relevant information from multiple print and digital sources, assess the credibility and accuracy of each source, and integrate the information while avoiding plagiarism.

Common Core State Standards, continued

Writing Project, continued

SE Pages	Lesson	Code	Standards Text
92	Plan and Write, continued	• CCRA.W.10	Write routinely over extended time frames (time for research, reflection, and revision) and shorter time frames (a single sitting or a day or two) for a range of tasks, purposes, and audiences.
		• CCRA.SL.1	Prepare for and participate effectively in a range of conversations and collaborations with diverse partners, building on others' ideas and expressing their own clearly and persuasively.
		• CCRA.L.2	Demonstrate command of the conventions of standard English capitalization, punctuation, and spelling when writing.
93	Check Your Work		Demonstrate command of the conventions of standard English grammar and usage when writing or speaking.
		• L.1.1j	Produce and expand complete simple and compound declarative, interrogative, imperative, and exclamatory sentences in response to prompts.
			Demonstrate command of the conventions of standard English capitalization, punctuation, and spelling when writing.
		• L.1.2b	Use end punctuation for sentences.
	Finish and Share	• CCRA.W.4	Produce clear and coherent writing in which the development, organization, and style are appropriate to task, purpose, and audience.
		• CCRA.W.5	Develop and strengthen writing as needed by planning, revising, editing, rewriting, or trying a new approach.
		• CCRA.SL.4	Present information, findings, and supporting evidence such that listeners can follow the line of reasoning and the organization, development, and style are appropriate to task, purpose, and audience.

Unit 4   Numbers Count

Language Development

SE Pages	Lesson	Code	Standards Text
94–95	Unit Launch	• CCRA.SL.2	Integrate and evaluate information presented in diverse media and formats, including visually, quantitatively, and orally.
96	Language: Ask Question	• CCRA.SL.1	Prepare for and participate effectively in a range of conversations and collaborations with diverse partners, building on others' ideas and expressing their own clearly and persuasively.
		• CCRA.SL.6	Adapt speech to a variety of contexts and communicative tasks, demonstrating command of formal English when indicated or appropriate.
		• CCRA.L.1	Demonstrate command of the conventions of standard English grammar and usage when writing or speaking.
97	Vocabulary: Cardinal Numbers	• CCRA.L.6	Acquire and use accurately a range of general academic and domain-specific words and phrases sufficient for reading, writing, speaking, and listening at the college and career readiness level; demonstrate independence in gathering vocabulary knowledge when encountering an unknown term important to comprehension or expression.
	Language: Give Information	• CCRA.SL.1	Prepare for and participate effectively in a range of conversations and collaborations with diverse partners, building on others' ideas and expressing their own clearly and persuasively.

Language Development, continued

SE Pages	Lesson	Code	Standards Text
97	**Language: Give Information,** continued	• CCRA.SL.4	Present information, findings, and supporting evidence such that listeners can follow the line of reasoning and the organization, development, and style are appropriate to task, purpose, and audience.
		• L.1.1j	Demonstrate command of the conventions of standard English grammar and usage when writing or speaking. Produce and expand complete simple and compound declarative, interrogative, imperative, and exclamatory sentences in response to prompts.
		• L.1.5c	With guidance and support from adults, demonstrate understanding of word relationships and nuances in word meanings. Identify real-life connections between words and their use (e.g., note places at home that are *cozy*).
		• L.2.5a	Identify real-life connections between words and their use (e.g., describe foods that are *spicy* or *juicy*).
		• L.3.5b	Identify real-life connections between words and their use (e.g., describe people who are *friendly* or *helpful*).
98	**Grammar: Negative Sentences**	• CCRA.SL.6	Adapt speech to a variety of contexts and communicative tasks, demonstrating command of formal English when indicated or appropriate.
		• L.1.1c	Demonstrate command of the conventions of standard English grammar and usage when writing or speaking. Use singular and plural nouns with matching verbs in basic sentences (e.g., *He hops; We hop*).
		• L.3.1f	Ensure subject-verb and pronoun-antecedent agreement.
		• L.5.1c	Use verb tense to convey various times, sequences, states, and conditions.
99	**Vocabulary: Ordinal Numbers**	• CCRA.L.6	Acquire and use accurately a range of general academic and domain-specific words and phrases sufficient for reading, writing, speaking, and listening at the college and career readiness level; demonstrate independence in gathering vocabulary knowledge when encountering an unknown term important to comprehension or expression.
	Language: Express Needs	• CCRA.SL.2	Integrate and evaluate information presented in diverse media and formats, including visually, quantitatively, and orally.
		• CCRA.SL.3	Evaluate a speaker's point of view, reasoning, and use of evidence and rhetoric.
100	**Listen and Read Along:** *A Year Without Rain*	• CCRA.R.4	Interpret words and phrases as they are used in a text, including determining technical, connotative, and figurative meanings, and analyze how specific word choices shape meaning or tone.
		• CCRA.R.10	Read and comprehend complex literary and informational texts independently and proficiently.
101	**Comprehension: Identify Problem and Solution**	• CCRA.R.2	Determine central ideas or themes of a text and analyze their development; summarize the key supporting details and ideas.
		• CCRA.R.3	Analyze how and why individuals, events, or ideas develop and interact over the course of a text.

Common Core State Standards, continued

Language Development, continued

SE Pages	Lesson	Code	Standards Text
101	Comprehension: Identify Problem and Solution, continued	• CCRA.W.9	Draw evidence from literary or informational texts to support analysis, reflection, and research.
		• CCRA.SL.4	Present information, findings, and supporting evidence such that listeners can follow the line of reasoning and the organization, development, and style are appropriate to task, purpose, and audience.

Language and Literacy

SE Pages	Lesson	Code	Standards Text
102–103	High Frequency Words		Know and apply grade-level phonics and word analysis skills in decoding words.
		• RF.K.3c	Read common high-frequency words by sight (e.g., *the, of, to, you, she, my, is, are, do, does*).
		• RF.1.3g	Recognize and read grade-appropriate irregularly spelled words.
		• RF.2.3f	
			Demonstrate command of the conventions of standard English capitalization, punctuation, and spelling when writing.
		• L.1.2d	Use conventional spelling for words with common spelling patterns and for frequently occurring irregular words.
		• L.3.2e	Use conventional spelling for high-frequency and other studied words and for adding suffixes to base words (e.g., *sitting, smiled, cries, happiness*).
		• L.4.2d	Spell grade-appropriate words correctly, consulting references as needed.
		• L.5.2e	
104–105	Reading and Spelling: Blends and Digraphs		Know and apply grade-level phonics and word analysis skills in decoding words.
		• RF.K.3a	Demonstrate basic knowledge of one-to-one letter-sound correspondences by producing the primary sound or many of the most most frequent sounds for each consonant.
		• RF.1.3a	Know the spelling-sound correspondences for common consonant digraphs.
		• RF.1.3b	Decode regularly spelled one-syllable words.
		• CCRA.SL.2	Integrate and evaluate information presented in diverse media and formats, including visually, quantitatively, and orally.
			Demonstrate command of the conventions of standard English capitalization, punctuation, and spelling when writing.
		• L.1.2d	Use conventional spelling for words with common spelling patterns and for frequently occurring irregular words.
		• L.4.2d	Spell grade-appropriate words correctly, consulting references as needed.
		• L.5.2e	
106–107	Read On Your Own: "Rush!"	• CCRA.R.3	Analyze how and why individuals, events, or ideas develop and interact over the course of a text.
		• CCRA.R.10	Read and comprehend complex literary and informational texts independently and proficiently.

Language and Literacy, continued

SE Pages	Lesson	Code	Standards Text
106–107	Read On Your Own: "Rush!," continued		Know and apply grade-level phonics and word analysis skills in decoding words.
		• RF.K.3a	Demonstrate basic knowledge of one-to-one letter-sound correspondences by producing the primary sound or many of the most frequent sounds for each consonant.
		• RF.1.3a	Know the spelling-sound correspondences for common consonant digraphs.
		• RF.1.3b	Decode regularly spelled one-syllable words.
		• RF.1.3g	Recognize and read grade-appropriate irregularly spelled words.
		• RF.2.3f	
			Read with sufficient accuracy and fluency to support comprehension.
		• RF.1.4a	Read grade-level text with purpose and understanding.
		• RF.2.4a	
		• RF.1.4b	Read grade-level text orally with accuracy, appropriate rate, and expression on successive readings.
		• RF.2.4b	
		• RF.1.4c	Use context to confirm or self-correct word recognition and understanding, rereading as necessary.
		• RF.2.4c	
		• CCRA.SL.1	Prepare for and participate effectively in a range of conversations and collaborations with diverse partners, building on others' ideas and expressing their own clearly and persuasively.
		• CCRA.SL.4	Present information, findings, and supporting evidence such that listeners can follow the line of reasoning and the organization, development, and style are appropriate to task, purpose, and audience.
108	Grammar: Contractions with *not*	• CCRA.L.2	Demonstrate command of the conventions of standard English capitalization, punctuation, and spelling when writing.
			Demonstrate command of the conventions of standard English grammar and usage when writing or speaking.
		• L.1.1j	Produce and expand complete simple and compound declarative, interrogative, imperative, and exclamatory sentences in response to prompts.
			Demonstrate command of the conventions of standard English capitalization, punctuation, and spelling when writing.
		• L.2.2c	Use an apostrophe to form contractions and frequently occurring possessives.
		• L.4.2d	Spell grade-appropriate words correctly, consulting references as needed.
		• L.5.2e	

Language and Content

SE Pages	Lesson	Code	Standards Text
109	Success in Social Science: Learn About Geography	• CCRA.R.1	Read closely to determine what the text says explicitly and to make logical inferences from it; cite specific textual evidence when writing or speaking to support conclusions drawn from the text.
		• CCRA.R.7	Integrate and evaluate content presented in diverse media and formats, including visually and quantitatively, as well as in words.

Common Core State Standards, continued

Language and Content, continued

SE Pages	Lesson	Code	Standards Text
109	**Success in Social Science: Learn About Geography,** continued	• CCRA.R.10	Read and comprehend complex literary and informational texts independently and proficiently.
		• CCRA.L.6	Acquire and use accurately a range of general academic and domain-specific words and phrases sufficient for reading, writing, speaking, and listening at the college and career readiness level; demonstrate independence in gathering vocabulary knowledge when encountering an unknown term important to comprehension or expression.
110–111	**Build Background and Vocabulary**	• CCRA.R.7	Integrate and evaluate content presented in diverse media and formats, including visually and quantitatively, as well as in words.
		• CCRA.SL.1	Prepare for and participate effectively in a range of conversations and collaborations with diverse partners, building on others' ideas and expressing their own clearly and persuasively.
		• CCRA.SL.2	Integrate and evaluate information presented in diverse media and formats, including visually, quantitatively, and orally.
		• CCRA.L.6	Acquire and use accurately a range of general academic and domain-specific words and phrases sufficient for reading, writing, speaking, and listening at the college and career readiness level; demonstrate independence in gathering vocabulary knowledge when encountering an unknown term important to comprehension or expression.
			Determine or clarify the meaning of unknown and multiple-meaning words and phrases based on grade-level reading and content, choosing flexibly from a range of strategies.
		◦ L.1.4a ◦ L.2.4a ◦ L.3.4a	Use sentence-level context as a clue to the meaning of a word or phrase.
		◦ L.4.4a	Use context (e.g., definitions, examples, or restatements in text) as a clue to the meaning of a word or phrase.
112–119	**Listen and Read Along: "The Mighty Maya"**	• CCRA.R.1	Read closely to determine what the text says explicitly and to make logical inferences from it; cite specific textual evidence when writing or speaking to support conclusions drawn from the text.
		• CCRA.R.4	Interpret words and phrases as they are used in a text, including determining technical, connotative, and figurative meanings, and analyze how specific word choices shape meaning or tone.
		• CCRA.R.6	Assess how point of view or purpose shapes the content and style of a text.
		• CCRA.R.7	Integrate and evaluate content presented in diverse media and formats, including visually and quantitatively, as well as in words.
		• CCRA.R.10	Read and comprehend complex literary and informational texts independently and proficiently.
		• CCRA.L.6	Acquire and use accurately a range of general academic and domain-specific words and phrases sufficient for reading, writing, speaking, and listening at the college and career readiness level; demonstrate independence in gathering vocabulary knowledge when encountering an unknown term important to comprehension or expression.

Language and Content, continued

SE Pages	Lesson	Code	Standards Text
120	**Check Your Understanding**	● CCRA.R.2	Determine central ideas or themes of a text and analyze their development; summarize the key supporting details and ideas.
		● CCRA.SL.1	Prepare for and participate effectively in a range of conversations and collaborations with diverse partners, building on others' ideas and expressing their own clearly and persuasively.
	Review Vocabulary	● CCRA.L.6	Acquire and use accurately a range of general academic and domain-specific words and phrases sufficient for reading, writing, speaking, and listening at the college and career readiness level; demonstrate independence in gathering vocabulary knowledge when encountering an unknown term important to comprehension or expression.
	Write About Populations	● CCRA.W.2	Write informative/explanatory texts to examine and convey complex ideas and information clearly and accurately through the effective selection, organization, and analysis of content.
		● CCRA.W.4	Produce clear and coherent writing in which the development, organization, and style are appropriate to task, purpose, and audience.
		● CCRA.W.10	Write routinely over extended time frames (time for research, reflection, and revision) and shorter time frames (a single sitting or a day or two) for a range of tasks, purposes, and audiences.

Writing Project

SE Pages	Lesson	Code	Standards Text
121	**Model Study: Fact Sheet**	● CCRA.R.5	Analyze the structure of texts, including how specific sentences, paragraphs, and larger portions of the text (e.g., a section, chapter, scene, or stanza) relate to each other and the whole.
122	**Plan and Write**	● CCRA.W.2	Write informative/explanatory texts to examine and convey complex ideas and information clearly and accurately through the effective selection, organization, and analysis of content.
		● CCRA.W.4	Produce clear and coherent writing in which the development, organization, and style are appropriate to task, purpose, and audience.
		● CCRA.W.5	Develop and strengthen writing as needed by planning, revising, editing, rewriting, or trying a new approach.
		● CCRA.W.7	Conduct short as well as more sustained research projects based on focused questions, demonstrating understanding of the subject under investigation.
		● CCRA.W.8	Gather relevant information from multiple print and digital sources, assess the credibility and accuracy of each source, and integrate the information while avoiding plagiarism.
		● CCRA.W.9	Draw evidence from literary or informational texts to support analysis, reflection, and research.
		● CCRA.W.10	Write routinely over extended time frames (time for research, reflection, and revision) and shorter time frames (a single sitting or a day or two) for a range of tasks, purposes, and audiences.
123	**Check Your Work**		Demonstrate command of the conventions of standard English grammar and usage when writing or speaking.
		● L.1.1j	Produce and expand complete simple and compound declarative, interrogative, imperative, and exclamatory sentences in response to prompts.

Common Core State Standards, continued

Writing Project, continued

SE Pages	Lesson	Code	Standards Text
123	**Check Your Work,** continued		Demonstrate command of the conventions of standard English capitalization, punctuation, and spelling when writing.
		• L.1.2b	Use end punctuation for sentences.
		• L.2.2a	Capitalize holidays, product names, and geographic names.
		• L.4.2a	Use correct capitalization.
	Finish and Share	• CCRA.W.4	Produce clear and coherent writing in which the development, organization, and style are appropriate to task, purpose, and audience.
		• CCRA.W.5	Develop and strengthen writing as needed by planning, revising, editing, rewriting, or trying a new approach.
		• CCRA.W.10	Write routinely over extended time frames (time for research, reflection, and revision) and shorter time frames (a single sitting or a day or two) for a range of tasks, purposes, and audiences.
		• CCRA.SL.4	Present information, findings, and supporting evidence such that listeners can follow the line of reasoning and the organization, development, and style are appropriate to task, purpose, and audience.
		• CCRA.SL.5	Make strategic use of digital media and visual displays of data to express information and enhance understanding of presentations.

Unit 5   City Sights

Language Development

SE Pages	Lesson	Code	Standards Text
124–125	**Unit Launch**	• CCRA.SL.2	Integrate and evaluate information presented in diverse media and formats, including visually, quantitatively, and orally.
126	**Language: Ask for and Give Information**	• CCRA.SL.1	Prepare for and participate effectively in a range of conversations and collaborations with diverse partners, building on others' ideas and expressing their own clearly and persuasively.
		• CCRA.SL.4	Present information, findings, and supporting evidence such that listeners can follow the line of reasoning and the organization, development, and style are appropriate to task, purpose, and audience.
		• CCRA.SL.6	Adapt speech to a variety of contexts and communicative tasks, demonstrating command of formal English when indicated or appropriate.
127–128	**Vocabulary: Neighborhood**	• CCRA.SL.1	Prepare for and participate effectively in a range of conversations and collaborations with diverse partners, building on others' ideas and expressing their own clearly and persuasively.
		• CCRA.SL.2	Integrate and evaluate information presented in diverse media and formats, including visually, quantitatively, and orally.
		• CCRA.SL.6	Adapt speech to a variety of contexts and communicative tasks, demonstrating command of formal English when indicated or appropriate.
		• CCRA.L.6	Acquire and use accurately a range of general academic and domain-specific words and phrases sufficient for reading, writing, speaking, and listening at the college and career readiness level; demonstrate independence in gathering vocabulary knowledge when encountering an unknown term important to comprehension or expression.

Language Development, continued

SE Pages	Lesson	Code	Standards Text
127–128	Vocabulary: Neighborhood, continued		Demonstrate command of the conventions of standard English grammar and usage when writing or speaking.
		• L.1.1i	Use frequently occurring prepositions (e.g., *during, beyond, toward*).
		• L.1.1j	Produce and expand complete simple and compound declarative, interrogative, imperative, and exclamatory sentences in response to prompts.
			With guidance and support from adults, demonstrate understanding of word relationships and nuances in word meanings.
		• L.1.5a	Sort words into categories (e.g., colors, clothing) to gain a sense of the concepts the categories represent.
129–130	Grammar: Regular Past Tense Verbs	• CCRA.SL.6	Adapt speech to a variety of contexts and communicative tasks, demonstrating command of formal English when indicated or appropriate.
			Demonstrate command of the conventions of standard English grammar and usage when writing or speaking.
		• L.1.1e	Use verbs to convey a sense of past, present, and future (e.g., *Yesterday I walked home; Today I walk home; Tomorrow I will walk home*).
		• L.3.1e	Form and use the simple (e.g., *I walked; I walk; I will walk*) verb tenses.
131	Grammar: Statements with *There Is* and *There Are*	• CCRA.SL.6	Adapt speech to a variety of contexts and communicative tasks, demonstrating command of formal English when indicated or appropriate.
			Demonstrate command of the conventions of standard English grammar and usage when writing or speaking.
		• L.3.1d	Form and use regular and irregular verbs.
		• L.3.1f	Ensure subject-verb and pronoun-antecedent agreement.
132	Listen and Read Along: *More Than a Meal*	• CCRA.R.4	Interpret words and phrases as they are used in a text, including determining technical, connotative, and figurative meanings, and analyze how specific word choices shape meaning or tone.
		• CCRA.R.10	Read and comprehend complex literary and informational texts independently and proficiently.
			With guidance and support from adults, demonstrate understanding of word relationships and nuances in word meanings.
		• L.1.5a	Sort words into categories (e.g., colors, clothing) to gain a sense of the concepts the categories represent.
133	Comprehension: Identify Details	• CCRA.R.3	Analyze how and why individuals, events, or ideas develop and interact over the course of a text.
		• CCRA.SL.1	Prepare for and participate effectively in a range of conversations and collaborations with diverse partners, building on others' ideas and expressing their own clearly and persuasively.
		• CCRA.SL.4	Present information, findings, and supporting evidence such that listeners can follow the line of reasoning and the organization, development, and style are appropriate to task, purpose, and audience.

Common Core State Standards, continued

Language and Literacy

SE Pages	Lesson	Code	Standards Text
134–135	High Frequency Words		Know and apply grade-level phonics and word analysis skills in decoding words.
		• RF.K.3c	Read common high-frequency words by sight (e.g., *the, of, to, you, she, my, is, are, do, does*).
		• RF.1.3g • RF.2.3f	Recognize and read grade-appropriate irregularly spelled words.
			Demonstrate command of the conventions of standard English capitalization, punctuation, and spelling when writing.
		• L.1.2.d	Use conventional spelling for words with common spelling patterns and for frequently occurring irregular words.
		• L.3.2e	Use conventional spelling for high-frequency and other studied words and for adding suffixes to base words (e.g., *sitting, smiled, cries, happiness*).
		• L.3.2f	Use spelling patterns and generalizations (e.g., word families, position-based spellings, syllable patterns, ending rules, meaningful word parts) in writing words.
		• L.4.2d • L.5.2e	Spell grade-appropriate words correctly, consulting references as needed.
136–137	Reading and Spelling: Word Patterns and Multisyllabic Words		Know and apply grade-level phonics and word analysis skills in decoding words.
		• RF.K.3a	Demonstrate basic knowledge of one-to-one letter-sound correspondences by producing the primary sound or many of the most frequent sounds for each consonant.
		• RF.K.3b	Associate the long and short sounds with the common spellings (graphemes) for the five major vowels.
		• RF.K.3c	Read common high-frequency words by sight (e.g., *the, of, to, you, she, my, is, are, do, does*).
		• RF.K.3d	Distinguish between similarly spelled words by identifying the sounds of the letters that differ.
		• RF.1.3b	Decode regularly spelled one-syllable words.
		• RF.2.3a	Distinguish long and short vowels when reading regularly spelled one-syllable words.
			Demonstrate command of the conventions of standard English capitalization, punctuation, and spelling when writing.
		• L.1.2d	Use conventional spelling for words with common spelling patterns and for frequently occurring irregular words.
		• L.3.2f	Use spelling patterns and generalizations (e.g., word families, position-based spellings, syllable patterns, ending rules, meaningful word parts) in writing words.
138–139	Read On Your Own: "Meet Jo"	• CCRA.R.3	Analyze how and why individuals, events, or ideas develop and interact over the course of a text.
		• CCRA.R.7	Integrate and evaluate content presented in diverse media and formats, including visually and quantitatively, as well as in words.

Language and Literacy, continued

SE Pages	Lesson	Code	Standards Text
138–139	**Read On Your Own:** "Meet Jo," continued	• CCRA.R.10	Read and comprehend complex literary and informational texts independently and proficiently.
			Know and apply grade-level phonics and word analysis skills in decoding words.
		• RF.K.3a	Demonstrate basic knowledge of one-to-one letter-sound correspondences by producing the primary sound or many of the most frequent sounds for each consonant.
		• RF.K.3b	Associate the long and short sounds with the common spellings (graphemes) for the five major vowels.
		• RF.K.3d	Distinguish between similarly spelled words by identifying the sounds of the letters that differ.
		• RF.1.3b	Decode regularly spelled one-syllable words.
		• RF.2.3a	Distinguish long and short vowels when reading regularly spelled one-syllable words.
			Read with sufficient accuracy and fluency to support comprehension.
		• RF.1.4a • RF.2.4a	Read grade-level text with purpose and understanding.
		• RF.1.4b • RF.2.4b	Read grade-level text orally with accuracy, appropriate rate, and expression on successive readings.
		• RF.1.4c • RF.2.4c	Use context to confirm or self-correct word recognition and understanding, rereading as necessary.
		• CCRA.SL.4	Present information, findings, and supporting evidence such that listeners can follow the line of reasoning and the organization, development, and style are appropriate to task, purpose, and audience.
140	**Grammar: Pronoun-Verb Contractions**		Demonstrate command of the conventions of standard English grammar and usage when writing or speaking.
		• L.1.1c	Use singular and plural nouns with matching verbs in basic sentences (e.g., *He hops; We hop*).
		• L.1.1d	Use personal, possessive, and indefinite pronouns (e.g., *I, me, my; they, them, their, anyone, everything*).
		• L.3.1f	Ensure subject-verb and pronoun-antecedent agreement.
			Demonstrate command of the conventions of standard English capitalization, punctuation, and spelling when writing.
		• L.1.2d	Use conventional spelling for words with common spelling patterns and for frequently occurring irregular words.
		• L.2.2c	Use an apostrophe to form contractions and frequently occurring possessives.
		• L.3.2f	Use spelling patterns and generalizations (e.g., word families, position-based spellings, syllable patterns, ending rules, meaningful word parts) in writing words.

Common Core State Standards, continued

Language and Content

SE Pages	Lesson	Code	Standards Text
141	Success in Social Science: Learn About Cities	• CCRA.R.1	Read closely to determine what the text says explicitly and to make logical inferences from it; cite specific textual evidence when writing or speaking to support conclusions drawn from the text.
		• CCRA.R.7	Integrate and evaluate content presented in diverse media and formats, including visually and quantitatively, as well as in words.
		• CCRA.R.10	Read and comprehend complex literary and informational texts independently and proficiently.
		• CCRA.L.6	Acquire and use accurately a range of general academic and domain-specific words and phrases sufficient for reading, writing, speaking, and listening at the college and career readiness level; demonstrate independence in gathering vocabulary knowledge when encountering an unknown term important to comprehension or expression.
142–143	Build Background and Vocabulary	• CCRA.R.7	Integrate and evaluate content presented in diverse media and formats, including visually and quantitatively, as well as in words.
		• CCRA.SL.1	Prepare for and participate effectively in a range of conversations and collaborations with diverse partners, building on others' ideas and expressing their own clearly and persuasively.
		• CCRA.L.6	Acquire and use accurately a range of general academic and domain-specific words and phrases sufficient for reading, writing, speaking, and listening at the college and career readiness level; demonstrate independence in gathering vocabulary knowledge when encountering an unknown term important to comprehension or expression.
			Determine or clarify the meaning of unknown and multiple-meaning words and phrases based on grade-level reading and content, choosing flexibly from a range of strategies.
		• L.1.4a • L.2.4a • L.3.4a	Use sentence-level context as a clue to the meaning of a word or phrase.
		• L.4.4a	Use context (e.g., definitions, examples, or restatements in text) as a clue to the meaning of a word or phrase.
144–151	Listen and Read Along: "San Francisco"	• CCRA.R.2	Determine central ideas or themes of a text and analyze their development; summarize the key supporting details and ideas.
		• CCRA.R.4	Interpret words and phrases as they are used in a text, including determining technical, connotative, and figurative meanings, and analyze how specific word choices shape meaning or tone.
		• CCRA.R.7	Integrate and evaluate content presented in diverse media and formats, including visually and quantitatively, as well as in words.
		• CCRA.R.10	Read and comprehend complex literary and informational texts independently and proficiently.
		• CCRA.L.6	Acquire and use accurately a range of general academic and domain-specific words and phrases sufficient for reading, writing, speaking, and listening at the college and career readiness level; demonstrate independence in gathering vocabulary knowledge when encountering an unknown term important to comprehension or expression.

Language and Content, continued

SE Pages	Lesson	Code	Standards Text
152	Check Your Understanding	• CCRA.R.2	Determine central ideas or themes of a text and analyze their development; summarize the key supporting details and ideas.
		• CCRA.R.4	Interpret words and phrases as they are used in a text, including determining technical, connotative, and figurative meanings, and analyze how specific word choices shape meaning or tone.
		• CCRA.SL.1	Prepare for and participate effectively in a range of conversations and collaborations with diverse partners, building on others' ideas and expressing their own clearly and persuasively.
	Review Vocabulary	• CCRA.L.6	Acquire and use accurately a range of general academic and domain-specific words and phrases sufficient for reading, writing, speaking, and listening at the college and career readiness level; demonstrate independence in gathering vocabulary knowledge when encountering an unknown term important to comprehension or expression.
	Write About Neighborhoods	• CCRA.W.2	Write informative/explanatory texts to examine and convey complex ideas and information clearly and accurately through the effective selection, organization, and analysis of content.
		• CCRA.W.4	Produce clear and coherent writing in which the development, organization, and style are appropriate to task, purpose, and audience.
		• CCRA.W.10	Write routinely over extended time frames (time for research, reflection, and revision) and shorter time frames (a single sitting or a day or two) for a range of tasks, purposes, and audiences.

Writing Project

SE Pages	Lesson	Code	Standards Text
153	Model Study: Journal	• CCRA.R.5	Analyze the structure of texts, including how specific sentences, paragraphs, and larger portions of the text (e.g., a section, chapter, scene, or stanza) relate to each other and the whole.
154	Plan and Write	• CCRA.W.3	Write narratives to develop real or imagined experiences or events using effective technique, well-chosen details and well-structured event sequences.
		• CCRA.W.4	Produce clear and coherent writing in which the development, organization, and style are appropriate to task, purpose, and audience.
		• CCRA.W.5	Develop and strengthen writing as needed by planning, revising, editing, rewriting, or trying a new approach.
		• CCRA.W.10	Write routinely over extended time frames (time for research, reflection, and revision) and shorter time frames (a single sitting or a day or two) for a range of tasks, purposes, and audiences.
		• CCRA.L.6	Acquire and use accurately a range of general academic and domain-specific words and phrases sufficient for reading, writing, speaking, and listening at the college and career readiness level; demonstrate independence in gathering vocabulary knowledge when encountering an unknown term important to comprehension or expression.
155	Check Your Work		Demonstrate command of the conventions of standard English grammar and usage when writing or speaking.
		• L.1.1e	Use verbs to convey a sense of past, present, and future (e.g., *Yesterday I walked home; Today I walk home; Tomorrow I will walk home*).

Common Core State Standards, continued

Writing Project, continued

SE Pages	Lesson	Code	Standards Text
155	**Check Your Work,** continued		Demonstrate command of the conventions of standard English capitalization, punctuation, and spelling when writing.
		• L.1.2b	Use end punctuation for sentences.
		• L.4.2a	Use correct capitalization.
	Finish and Share	• CCRA.W.4	Produce clear and coherent writing in which the development, organization, and style are appropriate to task, purpose, and audience.
		• CCRA.W.5	Develop and strengthen writing as needed by planning, revising, editing, rewriting, or trying a new approach.
		• CCRA.W.10	Write routinely over extended time frames (time for research, reflection, and revision) and shorter time frames (a single sitting or a day or two) for a range of tasks, purposes, and audiences.
		• CCRA.SL.4	Present information, findings, and supporting evidence such that listeners can follow the line of reasoning and the organization, development, and style are appropriate to task, purpose, and audience.

Unit 6   Welcome Home!

Language Development

SE Pages	Lesson	Code	Standards Text
156–157	**Unit Launch**	• CCRA.SL.2	Integrate and evaluate information presented in diverse media and formats, including visually, quantitatively, and orally.
158	**Language: Give Information**	• CCRA.SL.2	Integrate and evaluate information presented in diverse media and formats, including visually, quantitatively, and orally.
		• CCRA.SL.4	Present information, findings, and supporting evidence such that listeners can follow the line of reasoning and the organization, development, and style are appropriate to task, purpose, and audience.
159	**Grammar: Present Tense Verbs: Have and Has**		Demonstrate command of the conventions of standard English grammar and usage when writing or speaking.
		• L.1.1d	Use personal, possessive, and indefinite pronouns (e.g., *I, me, my; they, them, their, anyone, everything*).
		• L.3.1d	Form and use regular and irregular verbs.
		• L.3.1f	Ensure subject-verb and pronoun-antecedent agreement.
160	**Vocabulary: Rooms in a House**	• CCRA.L.6	Acquire and use accurately a range of general academic and domain-specific words and phrases sufficient for reading, writing, speaking, and listening at the college and career readiness level; demonstrate independence in gathering vocabulary knowledge when encountering an unknown term important to comprehension or expression.
	Language: Give Information	• CCRA.SL.1	Prepare for and participate effectively in a range of conversations and collaborations with diverse partners, building on others' ideas and expressing their own clearly and persuasively.
		• CCRA.SL.2	Integrate and evaluate information presented in diverse media and formats, including visually, quantitatively, and orally.
		• CCRA.SL.3	Evaluate a speaker's point of view, reasoning, and use of evidence and rhetoric.

Language Development, continued

SE Pages	Lesson	Code	Standards Text
161	**Vocabulary: Household Objects**	• CCRA.L.6	Acquire and use accurately a range of general academic and domain-specific words and phrases sufficient for reading, writing, speaking, and listening at the college and career readiness level; demonstrate independence in gathering vocabulary knowledge when encountering an unknown term important to comprehension or expression.
	Language: Ask and Answer Questions	• CCRA.SL.1	Prepare for and participate effectively in a range of conversations and collaborations with diverse partners, building on others' ideas and expressing their own clearly and persuasively.
		• CCRA.SL.2	Integrate and evaluate information presented in diverse media and formats, including visually, quantitatively, and orally.
			Demonstrate command of the conventions of standard English grammar and usage when writing or speaking.
		• L.1.1j	Produce and expand complete simple and compound declarative, interrogative, imperative, and exclamatory sentences in response to prompts.
162	**Listen and Read Along:** *Families*	• CCRA.R.4	Interpret words and phrases as they are used in a text, including determining technical, connotative, and figurative meanings, and analyze how specific word choices shape meaning or tone.
		• CCRA.R.10	Read and comprehend complex literary and informational texts independently and proficiently.
		• CCRA.L.5	Demonstrate understanding of figurative language, word relationships, and nuances in word meanings.
			With guidance and support from adults, demonstrate understanding of word relationships and nuances in word meanings.
		• L.1.5a	Sort words into categories (e.g., colors, clothing) to gain a sense of the concepts the categories represent.
163	**Comprehension: Identify Details that Support a Main Idea**	• CCRA.R.2	Determine central ideas or themes of a text and analyze their development; summarize the key supporting details and ideas.
		• CCRA.SL.4	Present information, findings, and supporting evidence such that listeners can follow the line of reasoning and the organization, development, and style are appropriate to task, purpose, and audience.

Language and Literacy

SE Pages	Lesson	Code	Standards Text
164–165	**High Frequency Words**		Know and apply grade-level phonics and word analysis skills in decoding words.
		RF.K.3c	Read common high-frequency words by sight (e.g., *the, of, to, you, she, my, is, are, do, does*).
		RF.1.3g	Recognize and read grade-appropriate irregularly spelled words.
		RF.2.3f	
			Demonstrate command of the conventions of standard English capitalization, punctuation, and spelling when writing.
		• L.1.2.d	Use conventional spelling for words with common spelling patterns and for frequently occurring irregular words.
		• L.3.2e	Use conventional spelling for high-frequency and other studied words and for adding suffixes to base words (e.g., *sitting, smiled, cries, happiness*).
		• L.4.2d	Spell grade-appropriate words correctly, consulting references as needed.
		• L.5.2e	

Common Core State Standards, continued

Language and Literacy, continued

SE Pages	Lesson	Code	Standards Text
166–167	**Reading and Spelling: Long Vowels: *a, i, o, u***		Know and apply grade-level phonics and word analysis skills in decoding words.
		RF.K.3a	Demonstrate basic knowledge of one-to-one letter-sound correspondences by producing the primary sound or many of the most frequent sounds for each consonant.
		RF.K.3b	Associate the long and short sounds with the common spellings (graphemes) for the five major vowels.
		RF.1.3b	Decode regularly spelled one-syllable words.
		RF.1.3c	Know final -e and common vowel team conventions for representing long vowel sounds.
		RF.2.3a	Distinguish long and short vowels when reading regularly spelled one-syllable words.
			Demonstrate command of the conventions of standard English grammar and usage when writing or speaking.
		L.3.1b	Form and use regular and irregular plural nouns.
			Demonstrate command of the conventions of standard English capitalization, punctuation, and spelling when writing.
		L.1.2d	Use conventional spelling for words with common spelling patterns and for frequently occurring irregular words.
		L.3.2f	Use spelling patterns and generalizations (e.g., word families, position-based spellings, syllable patterns, ending rules, meaningful word parts) in writing words.
168–169	**Read On Your Own: "When We Came to Wisconsin"**	CCRA.R.10	Read and comprehend complex literary and informational texts independently and proficiently.
			Know and apply grade-level phonics and word analysis skills in decoding words.
		RF.K.3b	Associate the long and short sounds with the common spellings (graphemes) for the five major vowels.
		RF.K.3c	Read common high-frequency words by sight (e.g., *the, of, to, you, she, my, is, are, do, does*).
		RF.1.3b	Decode regularly spelled one-syllable words.
		RF.1.3c	Know final -e and common vowel team conventions for representing long vowel sounds.
		RF.1.3g RF.2.3f	Recognize and read grade-appropriate irregularly spelled words.
		RF.2.3a	Distinguish long and short vowels when reading regularly spelled one-syllable words.

Language and Literacy, continued

SE Pages	Lesson	Code	Standards Text
168–169	**Read On Your Own: "When We Came to Wisconsin,"** continued	RF.1.4a RF.2.4a RF.1.4b RF.2.4b	Read with sufficient accuracy and fluency to support comprehension. Read grade-level text with purpose and understanding. Read grade-level text orally with accuracy, appropriate rate, and expression on successive readings.
		CCRA.SL.4	Present information, findings, and supporting evidence such that listeners can follow the line of reasoning and the organization, development, and style are appropriate to task, purpose, and audience.
170	**Grammar: Plural Nouns**	CCRA.SL.1	Prepare for and participate effectively in a range of conversations and collaborations with diverse partners, building on others' ideas and expressing their own clearly and persuasively.
		L.1.1c L.2.1b L.3.1b	Demonstrate command of the conventions of standard English grammar and usage when writing or speaking. Use singular and plural nouns with matching verbs in basic sentences (e.g., *He hops; We hop*). Form and use frequently occurring irregular plural nouns (e.g., *feet, children, teeth, mice, fish*). Form and use regular and irregular plural nouns.

Language and Content

SE Pages	Lesson	Code	Standards Text
171	**Success in Mathematics: Learn About Fractions, Decimals, and Percents**	CCRA.R.4	Interpret words and phrases as they are used in a text, including determining technical, connotative, and figurative meanings, and analyze how specific word choices shape meaning or tone.
		CCRA.R.10	Read and comprehend complex literary and informational texts independently and proficiently.
		CCRA.SL.2	Integrate and evaluate information presented in diverse media and formats, including visually, quantitatively, and orally.
		CCRA.L.6	Acquire and use accurately a range of general academic and domain-specific words and phrases sufficient for reading, writing, speaking, and listening at the college and career readiness level; demonstrate independence in gathering vocabulary knowledge when encountering an unknown term important to comprehension or expression.
172–173	**Build Background and Vocabulary**	CCRA.R.7	Integrate and evaluate content presented in diverse media and formats, including visually and quantitatively, as well as in words.
		CCRA.SL.1	Prepare for and participate effectively in a range of conversations and collaborations with diverse partners, building on others' ideas and expressing their own clearly and persuasively.
		CCRA.L.6	Acquire and use accurately a range of general academic and domain-specific words and phrases sufficient for reading, writing, speaking, and listening at the college and career readiness level; demonstrate independence in gathering vocabulary knowledge when encountering an unknown term important to comprehension or expression.

Common Core State Standards, continued

Language and Content, continued

SE Pages	Lesson	Code	Standards Text
172–173	**Build Background and Vocabulary,** continued		Determine or clarify the meaning of unknown and multiple-meaning words and phrases based on grade-level reading and content, choosing flexibly from a range of strategies.
		• L.1.4a • L.2.4a • L.3.4a	Use sentence-level context as a clue to the meaning of a word or phrase.
		• L.4.4a	Use context (e.g., definitions, examples, or restatements in text) as a clue to the meaning of a word or phrase.
174–181	**Listen and Read Along: "The Family Reunion"**	• CCRA.R.2	Determine central ideas or themes of a text and analyze their development; summarize the key supporting details and ideas.
		• CCRA.R.4	Interpret words and phrases as they are used in a text, including determining technical, connotative, and figurative meanings, and analyze how specific word choices shape meaning or tone.
182	**Check Your Understanding**	• CCRA.R.2	Determine central ideas or themes of a text and analyze their development; summarize the key supporting details and ideas.
		• CCRA.SL.4	Present information, findings, and supporting evidence such that listeners can follow the line of reasoning and the organization, development, and style are appropriate to task, purpose, and audience.
	Review Vocabulary	• CCRA.L.6	Acquire and use accurately a range of general academic and domain-specific words and phrases sufficient for reading, writing, speaking, and listening at the college and career readiness level; demonstrate independence in gathering vocabulary knowledge when encountering an unknown term important to comprehension or expression.
	Write About Family	• CCRA.W.3	Write narratives to develop real or imagined experiences or events using effective technique, well-chosen details and well-structured event sequences.
		• CCRA.W.10	Write routinely over extended time frames (time for research, reflection, and revision) and shorter time frames (a single sitting or a day or two) for a range of tasks, purposes, and audiences.

Writing Project

SE Pages	Lesson	Code	Standards Text
183	**Model Study: Description**	• CCRA.R.5	Analyze the structure of texts, including how specific sentences, paragraphs, and larger portions of the text (e.g., a section, chapter, scene, or stanza) relate to each other and the whole.
184	**Plan and Write**	• CCRA.W.2	Write informative/explanatory texts to examine and convey complex ideas and information clearly and accurately through the effective selection, organization, and analysis of content.
		• CCRA.W.4	Produce clear and coherent writing in which the development, organization, and style are appropriate to task, purpose, and audience.
		• CCRA.W.5	Develop and strengthen writing as needed by planning, revising, editing, rewriting, or trying a new approach.
		• CCRA.W.10	Write routinely over extended time frames (time for research, reflection, and revision) and shorter time frames (a single sitting or a day or two) for a range of tasks, purposes, and audiences.

Writing Project, continued

SE Pages	Lesson	Code	Standards Text
185	**Check Your Work**	• CCRA.L.1	Demonstrate command of the conventions of standard English grammar and usage when writing or speaking.
		• CCRA.L.2	Demonstrate command of the conventions of standard English capitalization, punctuation, and spelling when writing.
	Finish and Share	• CCRA.W.2	Write informative/explanatory texts to examine and convey complex ideas and information clearly and accurately through the effective selection, organization, and analysis of content.
		• CCRA.W.4	Produce clear and coherent writing in which the development, organization, and style are appropriate to task, purpose, and audience.
		• CCRA.W.5	Develop and strengthen writing as needed by planning, revising, editing, rewriting, or trying a new approach.
		• CCRA.SL.4	Present information, findings, and supporting evidence such that listeners can follow the line of reasoning and the organization, development, and style are appropriate to task, purpose, and audience.

Unit 7   Pack Your Bags

Language Development

SE Pages	Lesson	Code	Standards Text
186–187	**Unit Launch**	• CCRA.SL.2	Integrate and evaluate information presented in diverse media and formats, including visually, quantitatively, and orally.
188	**Language: Give and Carry Out Commands**	• CCRA.SL.1	Prepare for and participate effectively in a range of conversations and collaborations with diverse partners, building on others' ideas and expressing their own clearly and persuasively.
		• CCRA.SL.6	Adapt speech to a variety of contexts and communicative tasks, demonstrating command of formal English when indicated or appropriate.
189	**Vocabulary: Landforms and Transportation**	• CCRA.L.6	Acquire and use accurately a range of general academic and domain-specific words and phrases sufficient for reading, writing, speaking, and listening at the college and career readiness level; demonstrate independence in gathering vocabulary knowledge when encountering an unknown term important to comprehension or expression.
	Language: Describe Places	• CCRA.W.10	Write routinely over extended time frames (time for research, reflection, and revision) and shorter time frames (a single sitting or a day or two) for a range of tasks, purposes, and audiences.
		• CCRA.SL.1	Prepare for and participate effectively in a range of conversations and collaborations with diverse partners, building on others' ideas and expressing their own clearly and persuasively.
			Demonstrate command of the conventions of standard English grammar and usage when writing or speaking.
		• L.1.1f	Use frequently occurring adjectives.
190	**Vocabulary: Weather and Clothing**	• CCRA.L.6	Acquire and use accurately a range of general academic and domain-specific words and phrases sufficient for reading, writing, speaking, and listening at the college and career readiness level; demonstrate independence in gathering vocabulary knowledge when encountering an unknown term important to comprehension or expression.

Common Core State Standards, continued

Language Development, continued

SE Pages	Lesson	Code	Standards Text
190	Language: Give Information	● CCRA.SL.2	Integrate and evaluate information presented in diverse media and formats, including visually, quantitatively, and orally.
		● CCRA.SL.3	Evaluate a speaker's point of view, reasoning, and use of evidence and rhetoric.
		● L.1.1f	Demonstrate command of the conventions of standard English grammar and usage when writing or speaking. Use frequently occurring adjectives.
191	Grammar: Verbs: *Can*	● L.3.1d	Demonstrate command of the conventions of standard English grammar and usage when writing or speaking. Form and use regular and irregular verbs.
192	Listen and Read Along: *Explore!*	● CCRA.R.4	Interpret words and phrases as they are used in a text, including determining technical, connotative, and figurative meanings, and analyze how specific word choices shape meaning or tone.
		● CCRA.R.10	Read and comprehend complex literary and informational texts independently and proficiently.
		● L.1.5a	With guidance and support from adults, demonstrate understanding of word relationships and nuances in word meanings. Sort words into categories (e.g., colors, clothing) to gain a sense of the concepts the categories represent.
193	Comprehension: Classify Information	● CCRA.R.2	Determine central ideas or themes of a text and analyze their development; summarize the key supporting details and ideas.
		● CCRA.SL.4	Present information, findings, and supporting evidence such that listeners can follow the line of reasoning and the organization, development, and style are appropriate to task, purpose, and audience.
		● CCRA.L.5	Demonstrate understanding of figurative language, word relationships, and nuances in word meanings.
		● L.1.5b	With guidance and support from adults, demonstrate understanding of word relationships and nuances in word meanings. Define words by category and by one or more key attributes (e.g., a *duck* is a bird that swims; a *tiger* is a large cat with stripes).

Language and Literacy

SE Pages	Lesson	Code	Standards Text
194–195	High Frequency Words		Know and apply grade-level phonics and word analysis skills in decoding words.
		● RF.K.3c	Read common high-frequency words by sight (e.g., *the, of, to, you, she, my, is, are, do, does*).
		● RF.1.3g ● RF.2.3f	Recognize and read grade-appropriate irregularly spelled words.

Language and Literacy, continued

SE Pages	Lesson	Code	Standards Text
194–195	**High Frequency Words,** continued		Demonstrate command of the conventions of standard English capitalization, punctuation, and spelling when writing.
		• L.1.2.d	Use conventional spelling for words with common spelling patterns and for frequently occurring irregular words.
		• L.3.2e	Use conventional spelling for high-frequency and other studied words and for adding suffixes to base words (e.g., *sitting, smiled, cries, happiness*).
		• L.3.2f	Use spelling patterns and generalizations (e.g., word families, position-based spellings, syllable patterns, ending rules, meaningful word parts) in writing words.
		• L.4.2d	Spell grade-appropriate words correctly, consulting references as needed.
		• L.5.2e	
196–197	**Reading and Spelling: Long Vowels: *ai, ay; ee, ea; oa, ow***		Know and apply grade-level phonics and word analysis skills in decoding words.
		RF.K.3a	Demonstrate basic knowledge of one-to-one letter-sound correspondences by producing the primary sound or many of the most frequent sounds for each consonant.
		RF.K.3b	Associate the long and short sounds with the common spellings (graphemes) for the five major vowels.
		RF.1.3b	Decode regularly spelled one-syllable words.
		RF.1.3e	Decode two-syllable words following basic patterns by breaking the words into syllables.
		RF.2.3a	Distinguish long and short vowels when reading regularly spelled one-syllable words.
		RF.2.3b	Know spelling-sound correspondences for additional common vowel teams.
		RF.2.3c	Decode regularly spelled two-syllable words with long vowels.
			Demonstrate command of the conventions of standard English capitalization, punctuation, and spelling when writing.
		• L.1.2d	Use conventional spelling for words with common spelling patterns and for frequently occurring irregular words.
		• L.3.2f	Use spelling patterns and generalizations (e.g., word families, position-based spellings, syllable patterns, ending rules, meaningful word parts) in writing words.
198–199	**Read On Your Own: "Explore a Wetland"**	• CCRA.R.4	Interpret words and phrases as they are used in a text, including determining technical, connotative, and figurative meanings, and analyze how specific word choices shape meaning or tone.
		• CCRA.R.10	Read and comprehend complex literary and informational texts independently and proficiently.

Common Core State Standards, continued

Language and Literacy, continued

SE Pages	Lesson	Code	Standards Text
198–199	**Read On Your Own: "Explore a Wetland,"** continued		Know and apply grade-level phonics and word analysis skills in decoding words.
		RF.K.3b	Associate the long and short sounds with the common spellings (graphemes) for the five major vowels.
		RF.K.3c	Read common high-frequency words by sight (e.g., *the, of, to, you, she, my, is, are, do, does).*
		RF.1.3b	Decode regularly spelled one-syllable words.
		RF.2.3a	Distinguish long and short vowels when reading regularly spelled one-syllable words.
		RF.2.3b	Know spelling-sound correspondences for additional common vowel teams.
		RF.2.3c	Decode regularly spelled two-syllable words with long vowels.
			Read with sufficient accuracy and fluency to support comprehension.
		RF.1.4a RF.2.4a	Read grade-level text with purpose and understanding.
		RF.1.4b RF.2.4b	Read grade-level text orally with accuracy, appropriate rate, and expression on successive readings.
		CCRA.SL.4	Present information, findings, and supporting evidence such that listeners can follow the line of reasoning and the organization, development, and style are appropriate to task, purpose, and audience.
200	**Grammar: Capitalization: Proper Nouns**		Demonstrate command of the conventions of standard English grammar and usage when writing or speaking.
		L.1.1b	Use common, proper, and possessive nouns.
			Demonstrate command of the conventions of standard English capitalization, punctuation, and spelling when writing.
		L.1.2a	Capitalize dates and names of people.
		L.2.2a	Capitalize holidays, product names, and geographic names.

Language and Content

SE Pages	Lesson	Code	Standards Text
201	**Success In Science: Learn About Cycles**	CCRA.R.2	Determine central ideas or themes of a text and analyze their development; summarize the key supporting details and ideas.
		CCRA.R.4	Interpret words and phrases as they are used in a text, including determining technical, connotative, and figurative meanings, and analyze how specific word choices shape meaning or tone.
		CCRA.R.7	Integrate and evaluate content presented in diverse media and formats, including visually and quantitatively, as well as in words.
		CCRA.R.10	Read and comprehend complex literary and informational texts independently and proficiently.
		CCRA.L.6	Acquire and use accurately a range of general academic and domain-specific words and phrases sufficient for reading, writing, speaking, and listening at the college and career readiness level; demonstrate independence in gathering vocabulary knowledge when encountering an unknown term important to comprehension or expression.

Language and Content, continued

SE Pages	Lesson	Code	Standards Text
202–203	**Build Background and Vocabulary**	• CCRA.R.7	Integrate and evaluate content presented in diverse media and formats, including visually and quantitatively, as well as in words.
		• CCRA.SL.1	Prepare for and participate effectively in a range of conversations and collaborations with diverse partners, building on others' ideas and expressing their own clearly and persuasively.
		• CCRA.L.6	Acquire and use accurately a range of general academic and domain-specific words and phrases sufficient for reading, writing, speaking, and listening at the college and career readiness level; demonstrate independence in gathering vocabulary knowledge when encountering an unknown term important to comprehension or expression.
			Determine or clarify the meaning of unknown and multiple-meaning words and phrases based on grade-level reading and content, choosing flexibly from a range of strategies.
		• L.1.4a • L.2.4a • L.3.4a	Use sentence-level context as a clue to the meaning of a word or phrase.
		• L.4.4a	Use context (e.g., definitions, examples, or restatements in text) as a clue to the meaning of a word or phrase.
204–211	**Listen and Read Along: "The Water Planet"**	• CCRA.R.1	Read closely to determine what the text says explicitly and to make logical inferences from it; cite specific textual evidence when writing or speaking to support conclusions drawn from the text.
		• CCRA.R.2	Determine central ideas or themes of a text and analyze their development; summarize the key supporting details and ideas.
		• CCRA.R.4	Interpret words and phrases as they are used in a text, including determining technical, connotative, and figurative meanings, and analyze how specific word choices shape meaning or tone.
		• CCRA.R.7	Integrate and evaluate content presented in diverse media and formats, including visually and quantitatively, as well as in words.
		• CCRA.R.10	Read and comprehend complex literary and informational texts independently and proficiently.
		• CCRA.L.6	Acquire and use accurately a range of general academic and domain-specific words and phrases sufficient for reading, writing, speaking, and listening at the college and career readiness level; demonstrate independence in gathering vocabulary knowledge when encountering an unknown term important to comprehension or expression.
212	**Check Your Understanding**	• CCRA.R.2	Determine central ideas or themes of a text and analyze their development; summarize the key supporting details and ideas.
			With guidance and support from adults, demonstrate understanding of word relationships and nuances in word meanings.
		• L.1.5a	Sort words into categories (e.g., colors, clothing) to gain a sense of the concepts the categories represent.
	Review Vocabulary	• CCRA.L.6	Acquire and use accurately a range of general academic and domain-specific words and phrases sufficient for reading, writing, speaking, and listening at the college and career readiness level; demonstrate independence in gathering vocabulary knowledge when encountering an unknown term important to comprehension or expression.

Common Core State Standards, continued

Language and Content, continued

SE Pages	Lesson	Code	Standards Text
212	Write About the Ocean	• CCRA.W.3	Write narratives to develop real or imagined experiences or events using effective technique, well-chosen details and well-structured event sequences.
		• CCRA.W.4	Produce clear and coherent writing in which the development, organization, and style are appropriate to task, purpose, and audience.
		• CCRA.W.10	Write routinely over extended time frames (time for research, reflection, and revision) and shorter time frames (a single sitting or a day or two) for a range of tasks, purposes, and audiences.

Writing Project

SE Pages	Lesson	Code	Standards Text
213	Model Study: Travel Guide	• CCRA.R.5	Analyze the structure of texts, including how specific sentences, paragraphs, and larger portions of the text (e.g., a section, chapter, scene, or stanza) relate to each other and the whole.
214	Plan and Write	• CCRA.W.1	Write arguments to support claims in an analysis of substantive topics or texts using valid reasoning and relevant and sufficient evidence.
		• CCRA.W.4	Produce clear and coherent writing in which the development, organization, and style are appropriate to task, purpose, and audience.
		• CCRA.W.5	Develop and strengthen writing as needed by planning, revising, editing, rewriting, or trying a new approach.
		• CCRA.W.7	Conduct short as well as more sustained research projects based on focused questions, demonstrating understanding of the subject under investigation.
		• CCRA.W.8	Gather relevant information from multiple print and digital sources, assess the credibility and accuracy of each source, and integrate the information while avoiding plagiarism.
		• CCRA.W.9	Draw evidence from literary or informational texts to support analysis, reflection, and research.
		• CCRA.W.10	Write routinely over extended time frames (time for research, reflection, and revision) and shorter time frames (a single sitting or a day or two) for a range of tasks, purposes, and audiences.
215	Check Your Work		Demonstrate command of the conventions of standard English grammar and usage when writing or speaking.
		• L.1.1c	Use singular and plural nouns with matching verbs in basic sentences (e.g., *He hops; We hop*).
		• L.2.1b	Form and use frequently occurring irregular plural nouns (e.g., *feet, children, teeth, mice, fish*).
		• L.2.1f	Produce, expand, and rearrange complete simple and compound sentences (e.g., *The boy watched the movie; The little boy watched the movie; The action movie was watched by the little boy*).
		• L.3.1b	Form and use regular and irregular plural nouns.
			Demonstrate command of the conventions of standard English capitalization, punctuation, and spelling when writing.
		• L.2.2a	Capitalize holidays, product names, and geographic names.

Writing Project, continued

SE Pages	Lesson	Code	Standards Text
215	**Check Your Work,** continued		Use knowledge of language and its conventions when writing, speaking, reading, or listening.
		• L.5.3a	Expand, combine, and reduce sentences for meaning, reader/listener interest, and style.
	Finish and Share	• CCRA.W.1	Write arguments to support claims in an analysis of substantive topics or texts using valid reasoning and relevant and sufficient evidence.
		• CCRA.W.4	Produce clear and coherent writing in which the development, organization, and style are appropriate to task, purpose, and audience.
		• CCRA.W.5	Develop and strengthen writing as needed by planning, revising, editing, rewriting, or trying a new approach.
		• CCRA.W.10	Write routinely over extended time frames (time for research, reflection, and revision) and shorter time frames (a single sitting or a day or two) for a range of tasks, purposes, and audiences.
		• CCRA.SL.4	Present information, findings, and supporting evidence such that listeners can follow the line of reasoning and the organization, development, and style are appropriate to task, purpose, and audience.

Unit 8   Friend to Friend

Language Development

SE Pages	Lesson	Code	Standards Text
216–217	**Unit Launch**	• CCRA.SL.2	Integrate and evaluate information presented in diverse media and formats, including visually, quantitatively, and orally.
218	**Language: Describe Actions**	• CCRA.SL.4	Present information, findings, and supporting evidence such that listeners can follow the line of reasoning and the organization, development, and style are appropriate to task, purpose, and audience.
219	**Vocabulary: Feelings**	• CCRA.L.6	Acquire and use accurately a range of general academic and domain-specific words and phrases sufficient for reading, writing, speaking, and listening at the college and career readiness level; demonstrate independence in gathering vocabulary knowledge when encountering an unknown term important to comprehension or expression.
	Language: Express Feelings	• CCRA.SL.1	Prepare for and participate effectively in a range of conversations and collaborations with diverse partners, building on others' ideas and expressing their own clearly and persuasively.
		• CCRA.SL.3	Evaluate a speaker's point of view, reasoning, and use of evidence and rhetoric.
220	**Grammar: Irregular Past Tense Verbs: Was and Were**	• CCRA.SL.1	Prepare for and participate effectively in a range of conversations and collaborations with diverse partners, building on others' ideas and expressing their own clearly and persuasively.
		• CCRA.L.1	Demonstrate command of the conventions of standard English grammar and usage when writing or speaking.

Common Core State Standards, continued

Language Development, continued

SE Pages	Lesson	Code	Standards Text
220	**Grammar: Irregular Past Tense Verbs: *Was* and *Were,*** continued		Demonstrate command of the conventions of standard English grammar and usage when writing or speaking.
		• L.1.1e	Use verbs to convey a sense of past, present, and future (e.g., *Yesterday I walked home; Today I walk home; Tomorrow I will walk home*).
		• L.2.1d	Form and use the past tense of frequently occurring irregular verbs (e.g., *sat, hid, told*).
		• L.3.1d	Form and use regular and irregular verbs.
		• L.3.1e	Form and use the simple (e.g., *I walked; I walk; I will walk*) verb tenses.
221	**Grammar: Negative Sentences and Contractions with *Not***		Demonstrate command of the conventions of standard English capitalization, punctuation, and spelling when writing.
		• L.2.2c	Use an apostrophe to form contractions and frequently occurring possessives.
222	**Listen and Read Along: *Friends Are Like That***	• CCRA.R.4	Interpret words and phrases as they are used in a text, including determining technical, connotative, and figurative meanings, and analyze how specific word choices shape meaning or tone.
		• CCRA.R.10	Read and comprehend complex literary and informational texts independently and proficiently.
			With guidance and support from adults, demonstrate understanding of word relationships and nuances in word meanings.
		• L.1.5a	Sort words into categories (e.g., colors, clothing) to gain a sense of the concepts the categories represent.
223	**Comprehension: Identify Cause and Effect**	• CCRA.R.3	Analyze how and why individuals, events, or ideas develop and interact over the course of a text.
		• CCRA.SL.1	Prepare for and participate effectively in a range of conversations and collaborations with diverse partners, building on others' ideas and expressing their own clearly and persuasively.

Language and Literacy

SE Pages	Lesson	Code	Standards Text
224–225	**High Frequency Words**		Know and apply grade-level phonics and word analysis skills in decoding words.
		• RF.K.3c	Read common high-frequency words by sight (e.g., *the, of, to, you, she, my, is, are, do, does*).
		• RF.1.3g	Recognize and read grade-appropriate irregularly spelled words.
		• RF.2.3f	
			Demonstrate command of the conventions of standard English capitalization, punctuation, and spelling when writing.
		• L.1.2d	Use conventional spelling for words with common spelling patterns and for frequently occurring irregular words.
		• L.3.2e	Use conventional spelling for high-frequency and other studied words and for adding suffixes to base words (e.g., *sitting, smiled, cries, happiness*).
		• L.3.2f	Use spelling patterns and generalizations (e.g., word families, position-based spellings, syllable patterns, ending rules, meaningful word parts) in writing words.
		• L.4.2d	Spell grade-appropriate words correctly, consulting references as needed.
		• L.5.2e	

Language and Literacy, continued

SE Pages	Lesson	Code	Standards Text
226–227	**Reading and Spelling: Verb Ending: -ed**		Know and apply grade-level phonics and word analysis skills in decoding words.
		RF.K.3a	Demonstrate basic knowledge of one-to-one letter-sound correspondences by producing the primary sound or many of the most frequent sounds for each consonant.
		RF.1.3b	Decode regularly spelled one-syllable words.
		RF.1.3e	Decode two-syllable words following basic patterns by breaking the words into syllables.
		RF.1.3f	Read words with inflectional endings.
			Demonstrate command of the conventions of standard English grammar and usage when writing or speaking.
		L.3.1e	Form and use the simple (e.g., *I walked; I walk; I will walk*) verb tenses.
			Demonstrate command of the conventions of standard English capitalization, punctuation, and spelling when writing.
		L.1.2d	Use conventional spelling for words with common spelling patterns and for frequently occurring irregular words.
		L.3.2e	Use conventional spelling for high-frequency and other studied words and for adding suffixes to base words (e.g., *sitting, smiled, cries, happiness*).
		L.3.2f	Use spelling patterns and generalizations (e.g., word families, position-based spellings, syllable patterns, ending rules, meaningful word parts) in writing words.
			Determine or clarify the meaning of unknown and multiple-meaning words and phrases based on grade 1 reading and content, choosing flexibly from a range of strategies.
		L.1.4c	Identify frequently occurring root words (e.g., *look*) and their inflectional forms (e.g., *looks, looked, looking*).
228–229	**Read On Your Own: "Eva's Lesson"**	CCRA.R.1	Read closely to determine what the text says explicitly and to make logical inferences from it; cite specific textual evidence when writing or speaking to support conclusions drawn from the text.
		CCRA.R.10	Read and comprehend complex literary and informational texts independently and proficiently.
			Know and apply grade-level phonics and word analysis skills in decoding words.
		RF.K.3c	Read common high-frequency words by sight (e.g., *the, of, to, you, she, my, is, are, do, does*).
		RF.1.3b	Decode regularly spelled one-syllable words.
		RF.1.3f	Read words with inflectional endings.
		RF.1.3g	Recognize and read grade-appropriate irregularly spelled words.
		RF.2.3f	

Common Core State Standards, continued

Language and Literacy, continued

SE Pages	Lesson	Code	Standards Text
228–229	**Read On Your Own: "Eva's Lesson,"** continued		Read with sufficient accuracy and fluency to support comprehension.
		• RF.1.4a • RF.2.4a	Read grade-level text with purpose and understanding.
		• RF.1.4b • RF.2.4b	Read grade-level text orally with accuracy, appropriate rate, and expression on successive readings.
		• CCRA.SL.1	Prepare for and participate effectively in a range of conversations and collaborations with diverse partners, building on others' ideas and expressing their own clearly and persuasively.
			Determine or clarify the meaning of unknown and multiple-meaning words and phrases based on grade 1 reading and content, choosing flexibly from a range of strategies.
		• L.1.4c	Identify frequently occurring root words (e.g., *look*) and their inflectional forms (e.g., *looks, looked, looking*).
230	**Grammar: Possessive Nouns**		Demonstrate command of the conventions of standard English grammar and usage when writing or speaking.
		• L.1.1b	Use common, proper, and possessive nouns.
			Demonstrate command of the conventions of standard English capitalization, punctuation, and spelling when writing.
		• L.2.2c	Use an apostrophe to form contractions and frequently occurring possessives.
		• L.3.2d	Form and use possessives.

Language and Content

SE Pages	Lesson	Code	Standards Text
231	**Success in Mathematics: Learn About Bar Graphs**	• CCRA.R.7	Integrate and evaluate content presented in diverse media and formats, including visually and quantitatively, as well as in words.
232–233	**Build Background and Vocabulary**	• CCRA.R.7	Integrate and evaluate content presented in diverse media and formats, including visually and quantitatively, as well as in words.
		• CCRA.SL.1	Prepare for and participate effectively in a range of conversations and collaborations with diverse partners, building on others' ideas and expressing their own clearly and persuasively.
		• CCRA.L.6	Acquire and use accurately a range of general academic and domain-specific words and phrases sufficient for reading, writing, speaking, and listening at the college and career readiness level; demonstrate independence in gathering vocabulary knowledge when encountering an unknown term important to comprehension or expression.
			Determine or clarify the meaning of unknown and multiple-meaning words and phrases based on grade-level reading and content, choosing flexibly from a range of strategies.
		• L.1.4a • L.2.4a • L.3.4a	Use sentence-level context as a clue to the meaning of a word or phrase.
		• L.4.4a	Use context (e.g., definitions, examples, or restatements in text) as a clue to the meaning of a word or phrase.

Language and Content, continued

SE Pages	Lesson	Code	Standards Text
234–241	Listen and Read Along: "Hand in Hand"	• CCRA.R.3	Analyze how and why individuals, events, or ideas develop and interact over the course of a text.
		• CCRA.R.4	Interpret words and phrases as they are used in a text, including determining technical, connotative, and figurative meanings, and analyze how specific word choices shape meaning or tone.
		• CCRA.R.7	Integrate and evaluate content presented in diverse media and formats, including visually and quantitatively, as well as in words.
		• CCRA.R.10	Read and comprehend complex literary and informational texts independently and proficiently.
		• CCRA.L.6	Acquire and use accurately a range of general academic and domain-specific words and phrases sufficient for reading, writing, speaking, and listening at the college and career readiness level; demonstrate independence in gathering vocabulary knowledge when encountering an unknown term important to comprehension or expression.
242	Check Your Understanding	• CCRA.R.3	Analyze how and why individuals, events, or ideas develop and interact over the course of a text.
		• CCRA.SL.1	Prepare for and participate effectively in a range of conversations and collaborations with diverse partners, building on others' ideas and expressing their own clearly and persuasively.
	Review Vocabulary	• CCRA.L.6	Acquire and use accurately a range of general academic and domain-specific words and phrases sufficient for reading, writing, speaking, and listening at the college and career readiness level; demonstrate independence in gathering vocabulary knowledge when encountering an unknown term important to comprehension or expression.
	Write About Friendship	• CCRA.W.3	Write narratives to develop real or imagined experiences or events using effective technique, well-chosen details and well-structured event sequences.
		• CCRA.W.4	Produce clear and coherent writing in which the development, organization, and style are appropriate to task, purpose, and audience.
		• CCRA.W.10	Write routinely over extended time frames (time for research, reflection, and revision) and shorter time frames (a single sitting or a day or two) for a range of tasks, purposes, and audiences.

Writing Project

SE Pages	Lesson	Code	Standards Text
243	Model Study: Memory Story	• CCRA.R.5	Analyze the structure of texts, including how specific sentences, paragraphs, and larger portions of the text (e.g., a section, chapter, scene, or stanza) relate to each other and the whole.
244	Plan and Write	• CCRA.W.3	Write narratives to develop real or imagined experiences or events using effective technique, well-chosen details and well-structured event sequences.
		• CCRA.W.4	Produce clear and coherent writing in which the development, organization, and style are appropriate to task, purpose, and audience.
		• CCRA.W.5	Develop and strengthen writing as needed by planning, revising, editing, rewriting, or trying a new approach.
		• CCRA.W.10	Write routinely over extended time frames (time for research, reflection, and revision) and shorter time frames (a single sitting or a day or two) for a range of tasks, purposes, and audiences.

Common Core State Standards, continued

Writing Project, continued

SE Pages	Lesson	Code	Standards Text
244	**Plan and Write,** continued	• CCRA.L.1	Demonstrate command of the conventions of standard English grammar and usage when writing or speaking.
		• CCRA.L.6	Acquire and use accurately a range of general academic and domain-specific words and phrases sufficient for reading, writing, speaking, and listening at the college and career readiness level; demonstrate independence in gathering vocabulary knowledge when encountering an unknown term important to comprehension or expression.
245	**Check Your Work**		Demonstrate command of the conventions of standard English capitalization, punctuation, and spelling when writing.
		• L.1.2a	Capitalize dates and names of people.
		• L.1.2b	Use end punctuation for sentences.
			Use knowledge of language and its conventions when writing, speaking, reading, or listening.
		• L.5.3a	Expand, combine, and reduce sentences for meaning, reader/listener interest, and style.
	Finish and Share	• CCRA.W.4	Produce clear and coherent writing in which the development, organization, and style are appropriate to task, purpose, and audience.
		• CCRA.W.5	Develop and strengthen writing as needed by planning, revising, editing, rewriting, or trying a new approach.
		• CCRA.SL.6	Adapt speech to a variety of contexts and communicative tasks, demonstrating command of formal English when indicated or appropriate.

Unit 9   Let's Celebrate!

Language Development

SE Pages	Lesson	Code	Standards Text
246–247	**Unit Launch**	• CCRA.SL.2	Integrate and evaluate information presented in diverse media and formats, including visually, quantitatively, and orally.
248	**Language: Ask and Answer Questions**	• CCRA.SL.1	Prepare for and participate effectively in a range of conversations and collaborations with diverse partners, building on others' ideas and expressing their own clearly and persuasively.
249	**Grammar: Present Progressive Verbs**		Demonstrate command of the conventions of standard English grammar and usage when writing or speaking.
		• L.1.1j	Produce and expand complete simple and compound declarative, interrogative, imperative, and exclamatory sentences in response to prompts.
		• L.2.1e	Use adjectives and adverbs, and choose between them depending on what is to be modified.
		• L.4.1b	Form and use the progressive (e.g., *I was walking; I am walking; I will be walking*) verb tenses.
250	**Vocabulary: Country Words**	• CCRA.L.6	Acquire and use accurately a range of general academic and domain-specific words and phrases sufficient for reading, writing, speaking, and listening at the college and career readiness level; demonstrate independence in gathering vocabulary knowledge when encountering an unknown term important to comprehension or expression.

Language Development, continued

SE Pages	Lesson	Code	Standards Text
250	**Language: Describe People**	• CCRA.SL.2	Integrate and evaluate information presented in diverse media and formats, including visually, quantitatively, and orally.
		• CCRA.SL.3	Evaluate a speaker's point of view, reasoning, and use of evidence and rhetoric.
		• CCRA.SL.6	Adapt speech to a variety of contexts and communicative tasks, demonstrating command of formal English when indicated or appropriate.
251	**Grammar: Phrases with *Like To* and *Want To***		Demonstrate command of the conventions of standard English grammar and usage when writing or speaking.
		• L.1.1d	Use personal, possessive, and indefinite pronouns (e.g., *I, me, my; they, them, their, anyone, everything*).
		• L.1.1j	Produce and expand complete simple and compound declarative, interrogative, imperative, and exclamatory sentences in response to prompts.
		• L.3.1d	Form and use regular and irregular verbs.
		• L.3.1f	Ensure subject-verb and pronoun-antecedent agreement.
252	**Listen and Read Along: *Let's Dance!***	• CCRA.R.4	Interpret words and phrases as they are used in a text, including determining technical, connotative, and figurative meanings, and analyze how specific word choices shape meaning or tone.
		• CCRA.R.10	Read and comprehend complex literary and informational texts independently and proficiently.
			With guidance and support from adults, demonstrate understanding of word relationships and nuances in word meanings.
		• L.1.5a	Sort words into categories (e.g., colors, clothing) to gain a sense of the concepts the categories represent.
253	**Comprehension: Classify Information**	• CCRA.R.2	Determine central ideas or themes of a text and analyze their development; summarize the key supporting details and ideas.
			With guidance and support from adults, demonstrate understanding of word relationships and nuances in word meanings.
		• L.1.5a	Sort words into categories (e.g., colors, clothing) to gain a sense of the concepts the categories represent.
			Demonstrate command of the conventions of standard English grammar and usage when writing or speaking.
		• L.4.1a	Use relative pronouns (who, whose, whom, which, that) and relative adverbs (where, when, why).

Language and Literacy

SE Pages	Lesson	Code	Standards Text
254–255	**High Frequency Words**		Know and apply grade-level phonics and word analysis skills in decoding words.
		RF.K.3c	Read common high-frequency words by sight (e.g., *the, of, to, you, she, my, is, are, do, does*).
		RF.1.3g	Recognize and read grade-appropriate irregularly spelled words.
		RF.2.3f	

Common Core State Standards, continued

SE Pages	Lesson	Code	Standards Text
254–255	**High Frequency Words,** continued		Demonstrate command of the conventions of standard English capitalization, punctuation, and spelling when writing.
		• L.1.2.d	Use conventional spelling for words with common spelling patterns and for frequently occurring irregular words.
		• L.3.2e	Use conventional spelling for high-frequency and other studied words and for adding suffixes to base words (e.g., *sitting, smiled, cries, happiness*).
		• L.3.2f	Use spelling patterns and generalizations (e.g., word families, position-based spellings, syllable patterns, ending rules, meaningful word parts) in writing words.
		• L.4.2d • L.5.2e	Spell grade-appropriate words correctly, consulting references as needed.
256–257	**Reading and Spelling: Verb Ending: -ing**		Know and apply grade-level phonics and word analysis skills in decoding words.
		• RF.K.3a	Demonstrate basic knowledge of one-to-one letter-sound correspondences by producing the primary sound or many of the most frequent sounds for each consonant.
		• RF.1.3b	Decode regularly spelled one-syllable words.
		• RF.1.3e	Decode two-syllable words following basic patterns by breaking the words into syllables.
		• RF.1.3f	Read words with inflectional endings.
			Demonstrate command of the conventions of standard English grammar and usage when writing or speaking.
		• L.4.1b	Form and use the progressive (e.g., *I was walking; I am walking; I will be walking*) verb tenses.
			Demonstrate command of the conventions of standard English capitalization, punctuation, and spelling when writing.
		• L.1.2d	Use conventional spelling for words with common spelling patterns and for frequently occurring irregular words.
		• L.3.2e	Use conventional spelling for high-frequency and other studied words and for adding suffixes to base words (e.g., *sitting, smiled, cries, happiness*).
		• L.3.2f	Use spelling patterns and generalizations (e.g., word families, position-based spellings, syllable patterns, ending rules, meaningful word parts) in writing words.
			Determine or clarify the meaning of unknown and multiple-meaning words and phrases based on grade 1 reading and content, choosing flexibly from a range of strategies.
		• L.1.4c	Identify frequently occurring root words (e.g., *look*) and their inflectional forms (e.g., *looks, looked, looking*).
258–259	**Read On Your Own: "Dance To Celebrate!"**	• CCRA.R.10	Read and comprehend complex literary and informational texts independently and proficiently.

Language and Literacy, continued

SE Pages	Lesson	Code	Standards Text
258–259	**Read On Your Own: "Dance To Celebrate!"**, continued		Know and apply grade-level phonics and word analysis skills in decoding words.
		RF.K.3c	Read common high-frequency words by sight (e.g., *the, of, to, you, she, my, is, are, do, does*).
		RF.1.3b	Decode regularly spelled one-syllable words.
		RF.1.3f	Read words with inflectional endings.
		RF.2.3d	Decode words with common prefixes and suffixes.
		RF.1.3g RF.2.3f	Recognize and read grade-appropriate irregularly spelled words.
			Read with sufficient accuracy and fluency to support comprehension.
		RF.1.4a RF.2.4a	Read grade-level text with purpose and understanding.
		RF.1.4b RF.2.4b	Read grade-level text orally with accuracy, appropriate rate, and expression on successive readings.
		RF.1.4c RF.2.4c	Use context to confirm or self-correct word recognition and understanding, rereading as necessary.
			Determine or clarify the meaning of unknown and multiple-meaning words and phrases based on grade 1 reading and content, choosing flexibly from a range of strategies.
		• L.1.4c	Identify frequently occurring root words (e.g., *look*) and their inflectional forms (e.g., *looks, looked, looking*).
260	**Check Your Understanding**	• CCRA.R.2	Determine central ideas or themes of a text and analyze their development; summarize the key supporting details and ideas.
	Review Vocabulary	• CCRA.L.6	Acquire and use accurately a range of general academic and domain-specific words and phrases sufficient for reading, writing, speaking, and listening at the college and career readiness level; demonstrate independence in gathering vocabulary knowledge when encountering an unknown term important to comprehension or expression.
	Write About Celebrations	• CCRA.W.10	Write routinely over extended time frames (time for research, reflection, and revision) and shorter time frames (a single sitting or a day or two) for a range of tasks, purposes, and audiences.

Language and Content

SE Pages	Lesson	Code	Standards Text
261	**Success in Social Studies: Learn About Maps**	• CCRA.R.2	Determine central ideas or themes of a text and analyze their development; summarize the key supporting details and ideas.
		• CCRA.R.7	Integrate and evaluate content presented in diverse media and formats, including visually and quantitatively, as well as in words.
		• CCRA.L.6	Acquire and use accurately a range of general academic and domain-specific words and phrases sufficient for reading, writing, speaking, and listening at the college and career readiness level; demonstrate independence in gathering vocabulary knowledge when encountering an unknown term important to comprehension or expression.

Common Core State Standards, continued

Language and Content, continued

SE Pages	Lesson	Code	Standards Text
262–263	Build Background and Vocabulary	• CCRA.R.7	Integrate and evaluate content presented in diverse media and formats, including visually and quantitatively, as well as in words.
		• CCRA.SL.1	Prepare for and participate effectively in a range of conversations and collaborations with diverse partners, building on others' ideas and expressing their own clearly and persuasively.
		• CCRA.L.6	Acquire and use accurately a range of general academic and domain-specific words and phrases sufficient for reading, writing, speaking, and listening at the college and career readiness level; demonstrate independence in gathering vocabulary knowledge when encountering an unknown term important to comprehension or expression.
			Determine or clarify the meaning of unknown and multiple-meaning words and phrases based on grade-level reading and content, choosing flexibly from a range of strategies.
		• L.1.4a • L.2.4a • L.3.4a	Use sentence-level context as a clue to the meaning of a word or phrase.
		• L.4.4a	Use context (e.g., definitions, examples, or restatements in text) as a clue to the meaning of a word or phrase.
264–271	Listen and Read Along: "Kite Festival"	• CCRA.R.1	Read closely to determine what the text says explicitly and to make logical inferences from it; cite specific textual evidence when writing or speaking to support conclusions drawn from the text.
		• CCRA.R.2	Determine central ideas or themes of a text and analyze their development; summarize the key supporting details and ideas.
		• CCRA.R.3	Analyze how and why individuals, events, or ideas develop and interact over the course of a text.
		• CCRA.R.4	Interpret words and phrases as they are used in a text, including determining technical, connotative, and figurative meanings, and analyze how specific word choices shape meaning or tone.
		• CCRA.R.10	Read and comprehend complex literary and informational texts independently and proficiently.
			Determine or clarify the meaning of unknown and multiple-meaning words and phrases based on grade-level reading and content, choosing flexibly from a range of strategies.
		• L.1.4a • L.2.4a • L.3.4a	Use sentence-level context as a clue to the meaning of a word or phrase.
		• L.4.4a	Use context (e.g., definitions, examples, or restatements in text) as a clue to the meaning of a word or phrase.
272	Check Your Understanding	• CCRA.R.2	Determine central ideas or themes of a text and analyze their development; summarize the key supporting details and ideas.
		• CCRA.SL.4	Present information, findings, and supporting evidence such that listeners can follow the line of reasoning and the organization, development, and style are appropriate to task, purpose, and audience.

Language and Content, continued

SE Pages	Lesson	Code	Standards Text
272	Review Vocabulary	• CCRA.L.6	Acquire and use accurately a range of general academic and domain-specific words and phrases sufficient for reading, writing, speaking, and listening at the college and career readiness level; demonstrate independence in gathering vocabulary knowledge when encountering an unknown term important to comprehension or expression.
	Write About Celebrations	• CCRA.W.2	Write informative/explanatory texts to examine and convey complex ideas and information clearly and accurately through the effective selection, organization, and analysis of content.
		• CCRA.W.9	Draw evidence from literary or informational texts to support analysis, reflection, and research.
		• CCRA.W.10	Write routinely over extended time frames (time for research, reflection, and revision) and shorter time frames (a single sitting or a day or two) for a range of tasks, purposes, and audiences.

Writing Project

SE Pages	Lesson	Code	Standards Text
273	Model Study: Blog	• CCRA.R.5	Analyze the structure of texts, including how specific sentences, paragraphs, and larger portions of the text (e.g., a section, chapter, scene, or stanza) relate to each other and the whole.
		• CCRA.R.7	Integrate and evaluate content presented in diverse media and formats, including visually and quantitatively, as well as in words.
274	Plan and Write	• CCRA.W.2	Write informative/explanatory texts to examine and convey complex ideas and information clearly and accurately through the effective selection, organization, and analysis of content.
		• CCRA.W.4	Produce clear and coherent writing in which the development, organization, and style are appropriate to task, purpose, and audience.
		• CCRA.W.5	Develop and strengthen writing as needed by planning, revising, editing, rewriting, or trying a new approach.
		• CCRA.W.7	Conduct short as well as more sustained research projects based on focused questions, demonstrating understanding of the subject under investigation.
		• CCRA.W.10	Write routinely over extended time frames (time for research, reflection, and revision) and shorter time frames (a single sitting or a day or two) for a range of tasks, purposes, and audiences.
		• CCRA.SL.1	Prepare for and participate effectively in a range of conversations and collaborations with diverse partners, building on others' ideas and expressing their own clearly and persuasively.
		• CCRA.SL.2	Integrate and evaluate information presented in diverse media and formats, including visually, quantitatively, and orally.
		• CCRA.SL.3	Evaluate a speaker's point of view, reasoning, and use of evidence and rhetoric.
		• CCRA.SL.6	Adapt speech to a variety of contexts and communicative tasks, demonstrating command of formal English when indicated or appropriate.

Common Core State Standards, continued

Writing Project, continued

SE Pages	Lesson	Code	Standards Text
275	**Check Your Work**		Demonstrate command of the conventions of standard English capitalization, punctuation, and spelling when writing.
		• L.1.2a	Capitalize dates and names of people.
		• L.1.2b	Use end punctuation for sentences.
		• L.2.2a	Capitalize holidays, product names, and geographic names.
			Use knowledge of language and its conventions when writing, speaking, reading, or listening.
		• L.5.3a	Expand, combine, and reduce sentences for meaning, reader/listener interest, and style.
	Finish and Share	• CCRA.W.4	Produce clear and coherent writing in which the development, organization, and style are appropriate to task, purpose, and audience.
		• CCRA.W.5	Develop and strengthen writing as needed by planning, revising, editing, rewriting, or trying a new approach.
		• CCRA.SL.5	Make strategic use of digital media and visual displays of data to express information and enhance understanding of presentations.
		• CCRA.SL.6	Adapt speech to a variety of contexts and communicative tasks, demonstrating command of formal English when indicated or appropriate.

Handbook

Strategies for Learning Language

SE Pages	Lesson	Code	Standards Text
278–279	**Strategies for Learning Language**	• CCRA.SL.1	Prepare for and participate effectively in a range of conversations and collaborations with diverse partners, building on others' ideas and expressing their own clearly and persuasively.
		• CCRA.SL.6	Adapt speech to a variety of contexts and communicative tasks, demonstrating command of formal English when indicated or appropriate.
		• CCRA.L.3	Apply knowledge of language to understand how language functions in different contexts, to make effective choices for meaning or style, and to comprehend more fully when reading or listening.

Grammar

SE Pages	Lesson	Code	Standards Text
280–282	**Sentences**	• CCRA.L.1	Demonstrate command of the conventions of standard English grammar and usage when writing or speaking.
			Demonstrate command of the conventions of standard English capitalization, punctuation, and spelling when writing.
		• L.2.2c	Use an apostrophe to form contractions and frequently occurring possessives.
283–285	**Punctuation Marks**	• CCRA.L.3	Apply knowledge of language to understand how language functions in different contexts, to make effective choices for meaning or style, and to comprehend more fully when reading or listening.

Grammar, cotinued

SE Pages	Lesson	Code	Standards Text
283–285	**Punctuation Marks,** continued		Demonstrate command of the conventions of standard English capitalization, punctuation, and spelling when writing.
		• L.1.2b	Use end punctuation for sentences.
		• L.1.2c	Use commas in dates and to separate single words in a series.
		• L.2.2b	Use commas in greetings and closings of letters.
		• L.3.2b	Use commas in addresses.
		• L.3.2c	Use commas and quotation marks in dialogue.
		• L.4.2b	Use commas and quotation marks to mark direct speech and quotations from a text.
		• L.5.2a	Use punctuation to separate items in a series.
		• L.5.2d	Use underlining, quotation marks, or italics to indicate titles of works.
286–288	**Capital Letters**		Demonstrate command of the conventions of standard English capitalization, punctuation, and spelling when writing.
		• L.1.2a	Capitalize dates and names of people.
		• L.2.2a	Capitalize holidays, product names, and geographic names.
		• L.3.2a	Capitalize appropriate words in titles.
		• L.4.2a	Use correct capitalization.
289–293	**Nouns**		Demonstrate command of the conventions of standard English grammar and usage when writing or speaking.
		• L.1.1b	Use common, proper, and possessive nouns.
		• L.2.1b	Form and use frequently occurring irregular plural nouns (e.g., *feet, children, teeth, mice, fish*).
		• L.3.1a	Explain the function of nouns, pronouns, verbs, adjectives, and adverbs in general and their functions in particular sentences.
		• L.3.1b	Form and use regular and irregular plural nouns.
		• L.3.1c	Use abstract nouns (e.g., *childhood*).
294–295	**Pronouns**		Demonstrate command of the conventions of standard English grammar and usage when writing or speaking.
		• L.1.1d	Use personal, possessive, and indefinite pronouns (e.g., *I, me, my; they, them, their, anyone, everything*).
		• L.3.1a	Explain the function of nouns, pronouns, verbs, adjectives, and adverbs in general and their functions in particular sentences.
296–300	**Adjectives**	• CCRA.L.1	Demonstrate command of the conventions of standard English grammar and usage when writing or speaking.

Common Core State Standards, continued

Grammar, continued

SE Pages	Lesson	Code	Standards Text
296–300	**Adjectives,** continued		Demonstrate command of the conventions of standard English grammar and usage when writing or speaking.
		• L.1.1f	Use frequently occurring adjectives.
		• L.3.1a	Explain the function of nouns, pronouns, verbs, adjectives, and adverbs in general and their functions in particular sentences.
301–305	**Verbs**		Demonstrate command of the conventions of standard English grammar and usage when writing or speaking.
		• L.1.1e	Use verbs to convey a sense of past, present, and future (e.g., *Yesterday I walked home; Today I walk home; Tomorrow I will walk home*).
		• L.2.1d	Form and use the past tense of frequently occurring irregular verbs (e.g., *sat, hid, told*).
		• L.3.1a	Explain the function of nouns, pronouns, verbs, adjectives, and adverbs in general and their functions in particular sentences.
		• L.3.1d	Form and use regular and irregular verbs.
		• L.3.1e	Form and use the simple (e.g., *I walked; I walk; I will walk*) verb tenses.
		• L.4.1b	Form and use the progressive (e.g., *I was walking; I am walking; I will be walking*) verb tenses.

Handwriting

SE Pages	Lesson	Code	Standards Text
306–313	**Writing Letters, Words, and Sentences**		Demonstrate command of the conventions of standard English grammar and usage when writing or speaking.
		• L.1.1a	Print all upper- and lowercase letters.

The Writing Process

SE Pages	Lesson	Code	Standards Text
314–315	**Prewrite** **Collect Ideas, Choose a Topic, and Plan Your Writing**	• CCRA.W.5	Develop and strengthen writing as needed by planning, revising, editing, rewriting, or trying a new approach.
	Gather Details and Get Organized	• CCRA.W.7	Conduct short as well as more sustained research projects based on focused questions, demonstrating understanding of the subject under investigation.
		• CCRA.W.8	Gather relevant information from multiple print and digital sources, assess the credibility and accuracy of each source, and integrate the information while avoiding plagiarism.
316–318	**Draft and Revise** **Edit and Proofread**	• CCRA.W.5	Develop and strengthen writing as needed by planning, revising, editing, rewriting, or trying a new approach.
319	**Publish**	• CCRA.W.6	Use technology, including the Internet, to produce and publish writing and to interact and collaborate with others.

Using Information Resources

SE Pages	Lesson	Code	Standards Text
320–321	**How to Find Information**	• CCRA.R.7	Integrate and evaluate content presented in diverse media and formats, including visually and quantitatively, as well as in words.
		• CCRA.W.8	Gather relevant information from multiple print and digital sources, assess the credibility and accuracy of each source, and integrate the information while avoiding plagiarism.
322–325	**Dictionary and Thesaurus**	• CCRA.L.4	Determine or clarify the meaning of unknown and multiple-meaning words and phrases by using context clues, analyzing meaningful word parts, and consulting general and specialized reference materials, as appropriate.
326–327	**Parts of a Book**	• CCRA.R.5	Analyze the structure of texts, including how specific sentences, paragraphs, and larger portions of the text (e.g., a section, chapter, scene, or stanza) relate to each other and the whole.
328–329	**Atlas: Maps**	• CCRA.R.7	Integrate and evaluate content presented in diverse media and formats, including visually and quantitatively, as well as in words.
330–333	**Internet**	• CCRA.W.8	Gather relevant information from multiple print and digital sources, assess the credibility and accuracy of each source, and integrate the information while avoiding plagiarism.